Sport and Nationalism in Ireland

Gaelic games, soccer
and Irish identity since 1884

Mike Cronin

FOUR COURTS PRESS

Set in 10 on 13 point Janson Text for
FOUR COURTS PRESS LTD
Fumbally Lane, Dublin 8, Ireland
e-mail: info@four-courts-press.ie
and in North America
FOUR COURTS PRESS
c/o ISBS, 5804 N.E. Hassalo Street, Portland, OR 97213.

A catalogue record for this title
is available from the British Library.

ISBN 1-85182-408-1 hbk
ISBN 1-85182-456-1 pbk

Printed in Great Britain
by MPG Books, Bodmin, Cornwall.

To Julie, for everything

Contents

Preface

Having spent many hours of my life watching sport in its different forms, the opportunity of making such viewing part of my working life was too good to miss. The original idea for this project emerged from my previous work that examined the life and times of the Blueshirts in Ireland. One constant theme during my meetings with former Blueshirts that kept emerging was the vibrancy of their social and sporting life during the 1930s. In attempting to place this theme in an historical context it became clear that very little work had ever been conducted which took sport in Ireland, and the many functions which it has and does perform in society, very seriously. In the writing of this book I have attempted in some small way to place sport in a far more central position within the history of Ireland. Sport has played a hugely important political role in Ireland since the late nineteenth century, it has had a central function in constructing different ideas of what it is to be Irish and, as we reach the end of the twentieth century, sport in Ireland, as elsewhere, is big business.

In conducting the research that has gone into this work I have received much help and assistance. Without such help the book would have never been possible. The Football Association of Ireland and the Gaelic Athletic Association have both provided information at different times during the last few years, allowing me to look at much-needed material from minute books and suchlike. The staffs of the National Library and National Archive in Dublin, the Linen Hall Library in Belfast, the Sports Information Library in Sheffield, the Centre for Sports Science and History in Birmingham, and the University Libraries of Sheffield Hallam and De Montfort have all furnished me with mountains of material for which I am thankful. Within the academic world there are simply too many people who have spoken to me over the years and shaped my thinking with regard to sport, nationalism or Irish history to mention them all. In one broad sweep I thank the many diverse individuals who make up the memberships of the British Society of Sports History, the North American Society for Sport History and the Irish History Seminar at Oxford University. I have been fortunate to work in two excellent departments during the course of this research, and thus the staffs in the History Departments at Sheffield Hallam and De Montfort deserve special praise.

On a more personal level I have a very real sense of debt to the following: Alan Bairner, Fergus Campbell, Peter Craig, Roy Foster, Neal Garnham,

Roger Griffin, Pierre Lanfranchi, Donal Lowry, David Mayall, Tony Mason, John Regan, John Sugden, Matt Taylor and Wray Vamplew. All these people, with their different expertise, made me see my work in a far clearer way and provided endless entertainment and support in the process. Friends and family always deserve special praise for living with such projects, but this time they have all been especially important. I also have to acknowledge the help of the various people I have met over the years who have listened with an open mind to my thoughts on Irish sport, but have not seen eye to eye with some of my ideas. Those who have been (and surely will be) critical of what I have said about Irish sport, have informed my thinking in such a fundamental way. These people are usually those who love their sport and belong to it. Without them my appreciation of the whole subject would have been much lessened, and I apologise if some of the work here still upsets them (Gerry Moran, you know I'm talking about you!). Richard Holt read the final drafts of the book, and made many incisive comments that improved the work hugely. For this, his constant encouragement and friendship, I am profoundly grateful.

All the staff at Four Courts Press, as always, have been a pleasure to work with. Whenever and wherever I spoke to them, they were always encouraging and gave me all the help and time that I could have asked for.

During the research that went into this book, I found endless excuses to sit in bars, in soccer stadiums and at various GAA grounds around Ireland. I have to say a special thanks to all the men and women, who talked to me, told me what their game meant to them, bought me a pint and got me tickets for games (especially those in Croke Park). Without them, it wouldn't have been so much fun, and I hope, that there is something of your enthusiasm captured in the pages here.

Finally, I especially say a totally inadequate thank you to Julie Anderson. She came into my life in the middle of this project and gave me a sense of purpose and self-belief that I had lost, and a love I had never known. As she understands what drives someone who wishes to try and comprehend a subject, to believe in it and to write about it, she will share in my pleasure of seeing this book finished.

Leicester 1998

Terminology

The history, politics and geography of the island of Ireland conspire to make the use of the word Ireland difficult and multifaceted in any work such as this. I have attempted to keep the whole process as simple as possible. When referring to the pre-1921 period I have used the term Ireland to signify the whole of the nation as it existed under the provisions of the Act of Union. In the post 1921 period I have used the terms Irish Free State (1921–49) and Irish Republic (1949–present) to signify the twenty-six southern counties, and the name Northern Ireland in relation to the six northern counties.

When the word Ireland is used elsewhere it is taken as a geographical and not political term, that is, short hand to identify the thirty-two counties as a single land mass.

Prologue

Summer 1998, the Soccer World Cup Finals are being held in France.

I sit in a dark, very stuffy and overly warm room in the middle of Italy. Live on television is the France versus Italy quarter-final match in the World Cup. Everyone in the room is passionately cheering for Italy. Every Italian attack is met with screams of excitement, every French excursion into the Italian half brings on an anxious hush. When the referee makes a decision that goes against the Italians, the people in the room scream and gesticulate at the television. It appears from the reaction of the people around me, all failing to sit still in their armchairs, that the referee is regularly committing crimes against humanity. The game slips into extra time, and the atmosphere becomes ever more tense. There is no golden goal and so the game will have to be decided by a penalty shoot out. The French are the first to miss a penalty. The room erupts as the Italian supporters begin to sense that possibly, victory may be theirs. Unfortunately for the Italians it was not to be. Despite the cheering, wishing and hoping of my fellow viewers the Italians miss two penalties. They are beaten and they are out of the World Cup. For the people in the room there is now only the sad reality of defeat, a national pride severely dented and the temporary solidarity offered by the national football team is gone.

This scene was probably repeated across the globe many times during the World Cup. In pubs, clubs and in family sitting rooms the viewers would see their team depart the stage as all but one of the national groups represented in the World Cup had to taste defeat at some time. The hopes of the nation evaporated in an instant because a ball hit the back of a net. What was incredible about the France and Italy game which I watched was my fellow viewers, the Italian supporters. They showed all the usual signs of the partisan national football supporter. The opposition were worthless, the referee dreadful and their own team faultless. Eleven men in blue were representing the Italian nation, and belonged, for that night at least, to all the people in the room. The people in the room were not even Italian, indeed I was the only European there. All the Italian 'supporters' were Americans who were spending their holidays in Italy. All but one of them had never even seen a game of soccer before, they did not understand the rules and could not appreciate the game. They all, however, claimed Italian origins, although it seemed that the most recent departure from the Italian shore had been someone's grandfather before the First World War.

Visiting Italy obviously gave all these Americans some sense of having returned 'home'. They could drink Italian wine, try the local food, engage in national customs and even try out the mother tongue. However, the one single thing that would give them an Italian identity that they could genuinely and collectively experience, that they could scream for and celebrate, was brought to them by eleven men on television, playing a game that they had never seen before. For all my research into the question of sport, its links with nationalism and national identity, the darkened television room stands out as the perfect example of what this book is about.

1 / Introduction

We might have won the game, but I just didn't care,
you went and let it go, just like I wasn't there.
I saw you comin' in, I wasn't marked at all,
I had it in the net, if you had passed the ball.

I was standin' on the edge of the parallelogram,
roarin' me head off, 'Pass it in sham!'
Don't hesitate or stall, will you open your eyes,
for Christ's sake pass me the ball.[1]

Sport is the cause of much joy and an equal amount of pain for those who take part as well as those who watch. The introductory quote from the Saw Doctors perfectly encapsulates the pain which a teenager can feel when let down by a selfish team mate. The game of Gaelic football in this instance may only be at the junior and local level, but the pain of defeat is as intense and real as the pain inflicted by the ravages of teenage love. For the spectator of any game, the defeat of their team, especially in key matches or tournaments, will lead to a dull ache, a contemplation of what might have been. The reverse of these emotions is equally powerful. To execute the perfect pass, to score the majestic goal or to scream as your team wins brings untold amounts of joy. This pleasure can be remembered long into the future, to be relived, discussed, poured over and replayed until the feeling of ecstasy returns. Obviously it has to remembered that for every person who is fascinated and moved by the experience of playing or watching sport, there are many others who are disinterested and are unaffected by the turns and twists of the soccer season or the All-Ireland final.

The aim of this book is to explore how sport, with all the accompanying tears and joy, has played a role in defining notions of Irish nationalism and national identity since the late nineteenth century. This book is not aiming to offer a history of the Gaelic Athletic Association (GAA) nor of Irish soccer. It is not an Irish equivalent of Richard Holt's *Sport and the British*,[2] although I would suggest that such a project does need undertaking with respect to Ireland. The aim of this book is to use specific examples and themes within the long histories of Gaelic games and soccer as a way of demonstrating how closely sport has been linked to the many different ideas of Irish nationalism that have existed since the late nineteenth century. A large part of the motivation behind the research that went into this book was the apparent lack of work within Irish historical writing that attempts to understand the force of nationalism across the island through broad social and cultural structures, especially through that of sport. As such, much of the book should be viewed as an historiographical investigation rather than one that is explicitly historical. The history of nationalism in Ireland has been written with only two forces in mind. The first, which dominates in the majority of texts, champions the view that nationalism in Ireland is the product of a political struggle. This struggle has been ongoing since the nineteenth century and exists as part of a chronological history that sees nationalism defined by, and involved in, a battle for Irish political independence from Britain.[3] Within such history writing, nationalism is understood at a variety of levels – all of which are political. Nationalism will exist in political organisations such as the Fenian movement or the Provisional Irish Republican Army, it will be expressed by the insurgents of 1916, or it will be defined by the government of the Irish State after independence in 1922. Although a multi-layered, highly complex and ever-changing nationalism, it is a version of Irish nationalism which has always been understood at the political level. The second major force that has been identified by Irish historians as central to any understanding or definition of Irish nationalism is that of literature.[4] In seeking to understand the intellectual force behind the national movements which emerged in the mid-to-late nineteenth century in Ireland, academics have focused on the literary revival and the various writers which emerged from that tradition. Within such work writers such as Yeats and Joyce, and more recently Friel and Heaney, are seen as defining what nationalism was or is.

While having no reservations as to the value of such work or the manner in which it has been executed, I have always had doubts as to how representative such historical understanding of Irish nationalism actually is. At the political level it is clearly possible to identify what level of support there was for the Easter Rising of 1916, or to specifically state how many voters backed de Valera's Fianna Fáil in 1932 who fought an election under the message 'On to the Republic'. However, as the work of David Fitzpatrick demonstrated in relation to membership of the IRA during the revolutionary period, not everyone confirms their belief in a political message or an ideology of nationalism by becoming active in a movement which champions such views.[5] As historians we have used political movements and moments as a way of understanding Irish nationalism, as there is a clear ideology which accompanies such. The ideology is tangible, it is written, it is easy to find. We can examine the writings and pronouncements of Patrick Pearse or Eamon de Valera for example, and state quite definitely how they defined Irish nationalism and the nature of the national identity.[6] What historians have failed to do is bridge the gap between ideology and popular sentiment and examine whether the ideals of Irish nationalism as expounded by politicians and political movements are actually shared by the Irish population at large. If those ideas are indeed shared, then how do they function across the country and how are they transmitted from group to group or person to person?

The study of literary nationalism is equally problematic. Literary nationalism is relatively easy to trace and identify, as there is clearly a body of nationalist writing (although it may be far more difficult for academics to reach a consensus as to what such writing means or represents).[7] Equally it is relatively straightforward to find the areas of focus which existed over the years for the leading figures in literary nationalism such as the Abbey Theatre or literary journals such as *The Bell*. In such arenas the exponents of literary nationalism could exchange views and develop their ideas. In a more extreme manner than the force of political nationalism I have to question how such a literary nationalism actually works. That it existed is beyond doubt, but how does it spread? How do the works of Yeats, for example, influence and change the population's notion of who and what they are? While such a key and prolific figure as Yeats would have massive effect on the intellectual and chattering classes of Dublin, did he, or the staging of one of his plays at the Abbey, really help an Irish man or woman in the far reaches of county Kerry know what it was to be Irish?

My challenge to the general way in which historians have dealt with the question of nationalism in Ireland is that the whole process has been based on the elite of society. The political and especially the literary definitions of nationalism that have been advanced over the years are products of examinations of high culture. While the over concentration on the elite is an understandable by-product of the long troubles in Ireland, both north and south, it has meant that many wider views of the history of nationalism have been overlooked. Irish historians have simply had too much to deal with. There has been no closure or ending in Irish history, no neat and tidy dates at which we can draw a line. As a result of the ongoing conflict in Northern Ireland, historians, even if they are writing about issues long past, have had to put forward their ideas in the context of the present, and thus the elite have dominated. The nature of conflict, the sensitivity surrounding the past and a welter of other issues have also made it difficult for historians to access the archive material which is the stock of their trade. As Tom Garvin noted in relation to the Irish Republic's 1988 Archive Act,

> the relatively recent decision by the Irish government to release a seventy-year backlog of official records has caused an information revo-

lution in the study of Irish politics. It will take many years for the small community of Irish historians, political scientists and journalists to absorb even a large fraction of this new information.[8]

What this book attempts to do is to widen the focus for our understanding of Irish nationalism. While the focus has been quite rightly widened from the elites of high culture in the last few years with regard to the role of women in Irish nationalism, it has not taken place in broader historical areas.[9] Any examination of recently published and much-celebrated research surveys of Irish history such as those by Roy Foster, Joseph Lee or Dermot Keogh will show that sport and its effect on Irish society and identity receives no mention apart from the identification of the GAA as a political organisation.[10]

This book seeks to broaden previous perspectives and examine the links between sport, nationalism and national identity in Ireland. Sports and pastimes have historically been an important part of Irish life. The various fairs that took place across Ireland in the pre-famine years became a central focus of sporting life. Although the famine of the mid nineteenth century led to an understandable dislocation of life across Ireland and the disappearance of many of the fairs, sport, in its various forms, survived.[11] The development of modern codified sport in Britain during the second half of the nineteenth century[12] had a clear effect across the island of Ireland. In many of the larger towns and cities soccer, rugby and hockey clubs, as well as many others, emerged. These new clubs formed leagues and conducted cup competitions. They were also organized into formal associations: the Irish Football Association was formed in 1880, the Irish Rugby Football Union in 1879 and the Irish Amateur Athletic Association in 1885. The process of codification and organisation was mirrored in 1884 by a specifically Irish sporting body with the foundation of the Gaelic Athletic Association. Since the late nineteenth century, sport in Ireland, despite the upheavals of the revolutionary period and the troubles of the modern north, has flourished. The numbers of competitors in the wealth of different sports in Ireland have always been high, and many of the sportsmen and women of Ireland have excelled at the international level. Alongside the tradition of actually taking part, those who follow sport across Ireland form an enthusiastic and well-informed spectator base. In recent years the numbers of supporters who travelled to watch the Irish Republic's soccer team, who make the pilgrimage to Croke Park, or who screamed their support at television screens as Michelle Smith won yet another gold at the Atlanta Olympic Games in 1996, are a clear indication of how popular sport is across Ireland.

As sport is so popular and has such a long history in Ireland it is the ideal vehicle to use to establish an understanding and appreciation of how Irish nationalism has been formed and has functioned over the last century or so. While the political and literary versions of nationalism are elitist, the nationalism that is propagated by sport is not. While literature is high culture and the preserve of the few, sport is low culture and the passion of the many. In using sport as the vehicle then, a more general idea of what Irish nationalism is, how it has changed and how it works, will emerge. Sport in Ireland has been intensely political as evidenced by the Gaelic Athletic Association, has been touched by the troubles both past and present as with Bloody Sunday at Croke Park and the departure of Derry City from senior soccer in Northern Ireland, yet has also remained a source of debate, enthusiasm and glorious celebration, personified by the Republic's journey to the World Cup finals. While the men or women of Ireland may have read the literature of high culture and taken some part of their national identity from that experience, literature is not a communal experience. Sport is a communal experience. The crowd at a sporting event is brought together for a period of time with a single focus in mind. They are accompanied by a radio or television audience sitting in their homes or in public houses, who will later be joined by the newspaper-reading masses who will devour the details of the days events. All three groups will then commune in their workplaces, their homes or their schools and dissect every last glorious or inglorious moment of the previous day's events. Whether following the fortunes of an individual athlete, watching the team of the county or the national squad, all those who have followed that particular event have been brought together. An identity and a commonality of experience emerge. In this, sport functions in a way that elite politics or literature cannot. While the message of the politician or writer may slowly be spread across the nation, distilled and retold, the experience of sport is available to all. Ideas of identity and of nationalism are formed quickly and are widespread. The play at the Abbey Theatre may have been written as a way of exploring the Irish national psyche, but it cannot be quickly transferred across the nation to become a common expression. The team playing in green, or the men playing at Croke Park are transferred across the nation, more readily now in the days of the mass media, but even before then, because that team was representing the nation and the men at Croke Park were playing the national game.

This book will use sport as a way of understanding what Irish nationalism is and what it has been. Neither nationalism in Ireland generally, nor that which has been expressed through sport, is a single entity. While a generic concept of nationalism can be defined as a single type, the actual practice of nationalism has always been diverse. One of the most basic problems for a book such as this is how to deal with the presence of two clearly identifiable forms of nationalism in the island of Ireland. The first, Irish nationalism, desires, at the most general and traditional level, an Ireland that is unified and

Catholic, while the second is a nationalism which is linked with Britain through the forces of unionism and loyalism and desires that Northern Ireland remains part of the United Kingdom. While both varieties of nationalism are equally valid and have long historic, political and cultural roots, a decision was made to concentrate specifically on the first variety, that is, Irish nationalism. There has been some work carried out which examines the links between the nationalism of unionism and loyalism in the sporting arena and on general issues of unionist identity.[13] This will be referred to in the text, but the whole question of the nationalism of unionism and loyalism will be seen only as an area of potential and actual conflict against which Irish nationalism, at times, seeks to define itself. The whole question of what a British identity actually is, whether from an Ulster, English, Scots or Welsh perspective, has fired much recent debate in the academic world, and the works of Linda Colley, Keith Robbins and even Jeremy Paxman illustrate many of the themes present in this highly complex debate.[14]

In concentrating specifically on Irish nationalism, I have also made the decision to look only at the sports of Gaelic games and soccer. These are used, as they are the two most popular team sports across Ireland. At the domestic level for Gaelic games and at the international level for soccer, they attract huge amounts of support. Both sports are popular at the amateur, club and school level. The media, in its various forms, gives the largest amount of space to Gaelic games and soccer of any of the sports which take place in Ireland. I also felt that these sports have been the most representative of nationalism and national identity across the years. The GAA was founded with nationalism at the forefront of its agenda, an agenda that has changed little since 1884. As a sporting body the GAA is organized across the thirty-two counties of Ireland and as such fails to recognize the fact that Northern Ireland is legally part of another nation. Gaelic games are also fascinating in the context of nationalism and national identity as they are only played at domestic level. In this the GAA is self-defining. While Gaelic games are played by the world-wide Irish diaspora, and there have been attempts to organize regular international test series with Australia and other nations, they are ultimately a parochial sport in a globalized world. Soccer provided the perfect comparisons to sit alongside Gaelic games. At the national level soccer recognizes the border as it was established in 1921, and it remains organized in Northern Ireland under the auspices of the Irish Football Association (IFA) and in the Republic by the Football Association of Ireland (FAI). Domestically the two associations run separate national leagues and cup competitions, and internationally are recognized by soccer's world governing body FIFA as separate national teams: Northern Ireland and the Republic of Ireland. Soccer is the most popular sport in the world, and the World Cup Finals the biggest global event for a single sport. In this it is the total opposite of Gaelic games. While the book attempts to understand how notions of nationalism have affected domestic soccer in Ireland, it also concentrates on the impact of top-level international competition. Put simply, while Gaelic games seek to define Irish nationalism in an insular thirty-two county context, soccer defines Irish nationalism in the context of the global.

Despite the concentration here on Gaelic games and soccer, other sports in Ireland are worthy of attention. While they are omitted here, it should be remembered how many different sports have had an impact in defining different notions of Irish nationalism and have been affected by the nature of Irish national identity. Two quick examples serve to make the point. In 1992, at the Barcelona Olympics, Wayne McCullough won boxing silver for Ireland, while Michael Carruth went one better and took gold. While Olympic medals are usually a source of great celebration for the nation, the Irish boxing medals only brought division in parts of Ireland. Wayne McCullough was a Protestant from the lower end of Belfast's Shankill Road. In boxing the International Olympic Committee recognizes only the Irish Amateur Boxing Association (IABA). The IABA organizes on a thirty-two county basis. If McCullough wanted to go to the Olympics he had to fight under the Irish tricolour, a fact that was problematic to many of his fellow Protestants and unionists. On the return of the Irish team from Barcelona both McCullough and Carruth were feted in Dublin as heroes. In contrast, Belfast City Council held only a low-key reception for McCullough, as his victory had been under a foreign flag, and they refused to invite Carruth. As a serving member of the Republic of Ireland's army, Carruth was spurned by the unionist Belfast City Council because he was serving in the army of a nation whose constitution laid territorial claim to Northern Ireland.[15] The McCullough–Carruth case demonstrates quite clearly how notions of nationality are confused and contested in Ireland, not only by bodies such as Belfast City Council domestically, but also by external organisations such as the International Olympic Committee. The second example of the impact of sport on the forces of Irish nationalism and the issues of national identity is Rugby Union. Rugby Union, despite being considered by many as a quintessentially English game with its origins in the Public Schools, has always been popular in Ireland. It is organized, and always has been, on a thirty-two county basis. The Irish Rugby Football Union's Headquarters are in Dublin, the team plays in green, and until recently the national anthem for the team was the Irish Republic's *A Soldier's Song*. Irish rugby has always had a large following in Northern Ireland; indeed Ulster is one of the game's powerhouses. It attracts players and support from both sides of the sectarian divide and from either side of the border. Rugby is a problematic case for anyone studying the nature of sport and nationalism in Ireland. On the surface it throws up many contradictions and poses too many questions. What I would suggest briefly is that rugby has its base in three main areas: parts of Ulster, county Limerick and around Dublin. It is a highly localized game that relies heavily on parochial traditions and the nature of its 'middle and upper class' support base and a tradition of Anglo-centric schooling that provides a constant supply of new players. It is a sport that has never been affected in any great way by the ravages of the past or present troubles and one which, although forging an all-Ireland identity, does not make a huge impact on any undersatnding of Irish nationalism or national identity.[16]

The final piece of explanation and qualification that I would add in the context of this book relates to the whole issue of gender. A quick and simple criticism of the approach taken throughout this book would be to ask 'Where are the women?' While agreeing that many sports, especially those which dominate in the popular imagination and within the media are predominantly male, I would argue against such a simple construction in relation to the discussion here. The majority of Gaelic games' players in Ireland are male. There are, however, large numbers of women who have played camogie[17] over the years and have, in the last two decades, begun to play ladies' Gaelic football. These games do not receive the same media attention as their male equivalents. They are, however, popular and regularly played. Women's Gaelic games are played under the broad auspices of the GAA. The women who play Gaelic games are knowledgeable about their sports and can obviously, when a spectator, appreciate a game from the stand or on television as well as any male. I would argue that Gaelic games are dominantly male and the discourse that has surrounded them over the years is located within notions of dominant masculinity. However, women have always played a key role in the sport and thus the GAA and its games have an equally profound effect on the nationalism and national identity of women as it does on men. Soccer should be regarded as equally gender-free with respect of sport and the nature of nationalism. Again, while I accept that the dominant discourse surrounding soccer has always been male (especially in the light of the spectator violence that has often accompanied it), I would argue that my attention here is concerned mainly with the celebratory and carnivalesque support for the Irish Republic's soccer team at the 1990 and 1994 World Cup Finals. A cursory glance at pictures of the Irish terraces in Italy or America or newspaper coverage of the celebrations within Ireland shows that both genders were captivated by Irish success on the world stage. For these reasons the book, while touching on aspects of gender within Gaelic games and soccer, does not see notions of nationalism and national identity that are created by, and linked with sport, as gender-specific.

The book presents the following key arguments:

1 That nationalism as an ideology has been studied from a very narrow and elitist perspective in Ireland.

2 That there is no single nationalism in Ireland, but several nationalisms. Irish nationalism is constantly transforming and there can never been any closure or end to Irish nationalism. As conditions change, or external factors such as developments in the media or international relations, question society's understanding of Irish nationalism, one or several of the nationalisms will transform themselves to adapt to the new situation.

3 That sport has been ignored as a method of seeking to understand Irish society or history, and its importance has been overlooked with regard to definitions of nationalism.

4 That the GAA has, throughout history, championed a highly traditional ideal of Irish nationalism. In doing so it has played a key role in the political changes that have transformed Ireland, and has provided great support for those within its own community. However, as we approach the end of the twentieth century it is clear that the GAA, although a highly successful sporting body, is struggling to come to terms with an outdated and idealized notion of what it means to be Irish and what the nation should be.

5 . That soccer, although playing second fiddle to Gaelic games until the mid-1980s, has recently had a profound effect on notions of Irish nationalism and identity. While the nationalism that emerges from soccer may be regarded as an evanescent nationalism, its existence represents fundamental shifts within Irish identity.

The final conclusions of the book stress that sport and nationalism are inextricably linked and play a key role in defining Irish nationalism and notions of Irish national identity. This role, as with the very nature of Irishness, is constantly in a state of flux as sport is such an ever changing vehicle for the transmission of both ideology and identity.

2 / Nationalism

Perhaps the central difficulty in the study of nations and nationalism has been the problem of finding adequate and agreed definitions of the key concepts, nation and nationalism.[1]

Across much of the contemporary world, we are witnessing a supposedly welcome revival of nationalism ... Flags, languages, symbols, grievances long suppressed or supposedly forgotten have now been revived.[2]

Nationalism[3] has been one of the most resilient of modern ideologies. While the nineteenth and twentieth century have witnessed the rise and fall of the ideologies of Marxism, communism and fascism amongst others, nationalism has survived, and some would argue, has prospered.[4] But what exactly is nationalism?[5] The aim of this chapter is to lay the groundwork for the discussions that follow. The ability to discuss the links between sport and nationalism in Ireland, which is the aim of the book, relies on a clear picture of what nationalism is and how it functions. The chapter will explore the general debate that has raged around the concept of nationalism and pick out the key areas that will be useful here. This general theorising will then be located firmly within the historical past[6] and the contemporary reality of Ireland. By uncovering what is meant, and what has been meant, by both the idea, and the phrase 'Irish nationalism', it will be possible to discuss sport in a far clearer context.

DEFINITIONS

The word nationalism conjures up all kinds of images in the popular mind. In recent years many commentators have thrown around the word nationalism when discussing the upheavals in the former Yugoslavia. The battle scenes that raged around small, previously anonymous towns, were, when broadcast around the world, accompanied by commentary that referred to the forces of nationalism. The nationalism in question could be Serbian, Croat, Bosnian or even ethnic Albanian, but no matter what variety it was, nationalism, it appeared, was a dirty word and dangerous force.[7] A similar discourse followed the collapse of the Soviet Union and the eastern bloc nations in the 1990s. In the wake of the old order, what would follow? Again, commentators were quick to point towards the spectre of nationalism as a force that would fill the ideological void. It was nationalism that was once more seen as a subversive and threatening force. How would the newly freed East Germans destabilize a unified Germany with their nationalist fervour? Could a virulent German nationalism threaten the whole of Europe? Links were made across history that sought to find parallels between the new Germany and the Third Reich. The Third Reich was seen as a horrific accident from the depths of time that had been so destructive to so many millions of people, and a part of history that had to be avoided in the future. The force behind that destruction was fascism, which, many argued had at its roots the force of nationalism. In the contemporary world, as in the historical, it appears on the surface that nationalism is a bad thing. Football hooligans are nationalists, racists and skinheads are nationalists, and aberrant politicians such as Russia's Vladimir Zhirinovsky or Australia's Pauline Hanson are nationalists.

Is nationalism really that bad, or indeed that simplistic? Is it even real?[8] Most writers have agreed that nationalism emerged and became a dominant force in the western world in the second half of the eighteenth century. Some, such as Adrian Hastings, have argued that we should be more adventurous and seek the origins of nationalism in the fourteenth century. Hastings suggests that nationalism is not centrally linked to the idea of the nation-state itself, but instead should be seen as 'deriving from the belief that one's own ethnic or national tradition is especially valuable and needs to be defended at any cost'.[9] Within this statement, for Hastings at least, is a nationalism that is identifiable in a period before the arrival of the formalized nation state. This is a nationalism that can be located as far back as the fourteenth-century English wars against France. While seeing the merits in Hasting's arguments and noting them as another way of viewing the history of the formation of nationalism, the discussion here will accept the majority verdict. Nationalism, as an ideological expression of identity and political aspiration, was a product of the second half of the eighteenth century, and most commonly linked with the key dates of the American Declaration of Independence (1776) and the outbreak of the French Revolution (1793). It was at this point in history that nationalism, although it may have existed in some form prior to that period, was formalized and articulated as a way of explaining who represented the nation.

With this historical watershed in mind it is necessary to examine the way in which academics have dealt with the issue of nationalism. While this is an important discussion in the context of arriving at some level of appraisal of what nationalism is, it should be remembered that academics write about how they view the ideology from the perspective of detached investigation. For them nationalism is ultimately a value-free term. Nationalists, and the manner in which they behave, give its meaning to it. How any two given nationalists arrive at a rationalisation of why they belong to and represent their nation and its aspirations may well differ greatly. Indeed, it may not be rationalized at all by the individual into any coherent argument as to why they are what they profess to be. With this division between academic debate and what might be called 'the reality of nationalism' in mind, it is worthwhile examining the four broad overviews academics have formulated as to how nationalism has developed, or, to put it more simply, the four theories.[10] These theories do not explain or seek to define exactly what nationalism is, but illustrate how the major groups of theorists have arrived at the point where they seek to explain the historical origins of nationalism. Briefly, these are as follows:

1 *The primordialists*[11] Writers on nationalism who take the primordialist line have argued that nationalism is rooted within the land. For them, there is genuine physicality to the notion of the nation. It belongs not only in the mind of the individual, within songs and literature, but can be clearly identified as a homeland that is lived in by the members of the nation. The primordialists see nationalism as an ideology that has been as long-standing as peoples have had, throughout history, a clear notion of an identifiable homeland for themselves. Any group that has longstanding connections with specific areas or regions will display this type of nationalism, and will use various anthropological and archaeological justifications in support of their rights. Essentially, primordialists champion the view that nationalism is the product of ethnicty which can be rooted in history.

2 *The modernists*[12] argue, quite simply, that nationalism is a product of the modern age. While they accept that nationalists may seek to justify themselves by using historical artefacts, traditions and other identity forming tools from the past, nationalism itself is a direct product of the transformations that took place alongside the destruction of feudal society. For modernists, nationalism takes hold as capitalism creates a new culture. Technologies such as the printing press[13] and new forms of transport standardize society in such a way that the power of formalized religion is broken down and new social structures emerge to create a unitary sense of identity. The writers who support the modernist interpretation may disagree on the exact train of events or the specific components which create nationalism, but they are agreed that nationalism provided, and continues to provide society with a basis around which social unity could be built.[14]

3 *The statists*[15] have argued that the production of nationalism is wrapped up in the idea of the state. The states that have emerged across the

world and throughout history have come into conflict with other nation states, and such competition has thereby necessitated the use of nationalism as a justification for the wars that they fight. The way in which the different nation states have developed over the course of time and the impact that the forces of change has had on them have affected the nature of any one nationalism. This explains why Britain, as a nation which modernized early and relatively evenly has developed a state nationalism which is closely tied to the nature of its long tradition of parliamentary democracy. A situation that contrasts starkly with post-First World War Germany. In the post-Versailles Treaty chaos Germany was poorly led by a weak middle class. The ensuing financial collapse of the late 1920s allowed for the emergence of an authoritarian nationalism that was seen as the only plausible way of modernising the nation. In these examples it can be seen how the statists see nationalism as a direct product of the overriding political ethos of the nation state. Eric Hobsbawm and Terence Ranger have supplied a politically driven version of the statist case.[16] They have argued that the state (which will be under the control of an elite), will use invented traditions, such as public commemorations and monuments, as a way of allying the masses to the force of nationalism in support of the state.

4 *The political mythologists*[17] have examined nationalism from a far more esoteric angle than the others. While the three preceding groups have understood the force of nationalism through something that is tangible, that is, the homelands, modernity or the state, the political mythologists locate the ideology within ideas that are imagined or mythical. These ideas are ones that have been articulated in many different forms across history, although usually they are proposed by the elites within any given society. The mythology will present an image of the nation that, while not existing, will be a common currency for the majority of the society, and may often be formalized through civic commemoration.[18] The basic aim of the mythical or imagined nationalism was to motivate the whole of society around the idea of the nation. This is done through a shared sense of community and a similar belief in the values of the institutions of the state.

Within these four different approaches can be found a welter of ideas that can be applied to the history of any given nationalism. The problematic for theorists is that the actual development and history of nationalism in any country has always been different. There are always various key, or shared, elements that are seen as central to the development of nationalism, but the fabric or detail of any one variety will always be unique. All the different theoretical overviews explained above that may suggest why nationalism emerged, can be applied to the Irish experience and will be discussed later.

In the same way that there is academic and theoretical debate surrounding the causes and development of nationalism, there is an equally vivid debate which surrounds the central issue of what nationalism is. Ernest Gellner defined nationalism as,

> primarily a political principle, which holds that the political and the national unit should be congruent. Nationalism as a sentiment, or as a movement, can best be defined in terms of this principle. Nationalist sentiment is the anger aroused by violation of the principle, or the feeling of satisfaction aroused by its fulfilment. A nationalist movement is one actuated by a sentiment of this kind.[19]

Gellner is suggesting a very clear notion of what nationalism is. It is an ideology which, in his definition, is clearly linked to the political structure of any given nation and its territorial and cultural aspirations. One of the problematics for such a classical definition as Gellner's is that it fails to allow for the ongoing changes within the world. It is a definition that is fundamentally linked to the emergence of nation states in the nineteenth century, and, as such, belongs to a world of imperial powers and high politics. It is the nationalism of jingoism and war. How does such a nationalism fit in with the development of global politics, mass communications and marketing? Is the force of nationalism still concerned with the matching of the political and the national?

The difficulties imposed by Gellner's definition, so clearly the product of a reading of nineteenth-century politics, are duplicated in the approach taken by Moses. In seeking to understand the force of classical black nationalism, Moses argued that the period 1850 to 1925 witnessed the high point of that concept. It was during this time that black nationalists were most forceful in their belief that African Americans should create a state and a culture for themselves. Moses stated that

> the essential feature of classical black nationalism is its goal of creating a black nation-state or empire with absolute control over a specific geographical territory, and sufficient economic and military power to defend it.[20]

Moses offers a clear and succinct definition of black nationalist aspirations that could be applied to any aspirational nationalism. All nationalisms strive for their own territory and the ability to defend such. However, in the same way

that Gellner's definition is rooted in a specific historical place and is not therefore easily transferable, Moses' aspirational definition is equally problematic.
Can an aspiration be the source of an ideology? If the black nation state never
comes into being, does this negate against any statement or desire of black
nationalism? Can nationalism exist without the reality of the nation state?

Isaiah Berlin offered a useful, if all encompassing, ideal of the nationalist,
that begins to offer bridges between the historical and aspirational nationalism already detailed. Berlin suggested that the nationalist had four beliefs: in
the need to belong to a nation; in the relationships between all the elements
that make up the nation; in the nation because it is their nation; and in the
supremacy of their nation against all other claims.[21] Berlin offers a key link in
seeking to understand what nationalism is. He brings the desires and beliefs
of the individual into the equation. This is an important step as one of the key
ideas that is put forward in this work is that there is no single nationalism. As
an ideology, nationalism works on a variety of levels and is shaped by a multitude of forces. It is not an historical continuum. If the individual identifies
with a vision of the nation that is not a simple replication of the official
nationalism of the state, does that invalidate the belief of the individual? It is
the contention here that nationalism, is multifaceted, and can encompass
many different notions and ideals of what it is without fracturing. As Peter
Alter stated,

> an initial conclusion could run like this: nationalism does not exist as
> such, but a multitude of manifestations of nationalism do. In other
> words it is more appropriate to speak of nationalisms in the plural than
> of nationalism in the singular.[22]

The multi-layered and differential nature of nationalism is an idea that has
been pursued in the work of Walker Connor. He has argued that there are
clear links between the pronouncements of political leaders and the mythical
components of nationalism, such as common ancestry. In understanding these
components, political leaders have been able to engender support for their
own party or government, and they have also harnessed the different ideals of
the nation that belong in the hearts and minds of the people in their propaganda and policies. That such links exist, and can be found, is clear within the
case of Irish sport and nationalism, and will be explored later. But why have
some theorists who have sought to define nationalism struggled to make the
link between the multifaceted aspirations, demands and dreaming of the individuals that compromise a society, and the ideology of nationalism? As
Connor has argued, this is a result of the 'intellectual's discomfort with the
nonrational and the search for quantifiable, and therefore tangible, explana-

tions'.[23] Any definition of nationalism, no matter how general, must not shy away from forces that cannot be 'pinned down'. In essence, definitions should not be scared of the non-definable.

Another problematic in defining nationalism is, not simply that it is multi-faceted, but that it is now such a long-lived ideology. If it was an ideology that had been relatively short lived the production of any agreed definition would have been problematic enough, as has been the case with fascism, but nationalism has now had an identifiable existence of at least two hundred years. Across such a time span an ideology cannot be static, it will be constantly changing. As such, nationalism cannot be defined as the same single entity across history. Nationalism may be more virulent and more successful during times of political crisis, or else it may be a problematic ideology when it is seen as being in decline.[24] At other times it will exist peaceful as an ideology that is part of civic respectability[25] or as part of day-to-day banality.[26]

There are several questions that any definition of nationalism must attempt to tackle, or at the very least allow space for. Some have been covered in the preceding discussion, but are worthy of clarification. First, how do we measure actual nationalism? Who or what is representative of nationalism? In trying to answer these questions should we examine the literature of a nation, look at its history, watch its television, or examine its political extremes? Or should we simply examine the pronouncements of its political leaders to understand what its nationalism is? If we do that, how do we fathom what the nationalism of Joe or Joanna Average is? Second, we have to consider whether nationalism is a perception, something transient and artificial, or whether it is a reality? Is it invented by politicians and intellectuals or is nationalism a real experience which can be lived by the individual? Finally, if nationalism does exist in one or more of these forms, is it merely a symbolic and transient representation of the idea of the nation or is it central and permanent?

In attempting to take on board all the points that have been made thus far, it is time to suggest a model of nationalism that can be used for the remainder of the book. I would argue that nationalism should be understood as:

> a multifaceted expression of identity which, while having some common constituents, functions as both a mobile and historically contested ideology. It can be either formalized, imagined or challenged by forces, groups and individuals both within, and outside the projected vision or reality of the nation.

So what does that actually mean? When broken down into its constituent parts the definition is suggesting the following. First, that nationalism is not a single entity, it is multifaceted and can function at several levels. Nationalism does not have to be the preserve of a governing intellectual elite, but can equally be defined and shaped by other forces, such as the individual, the people, the media, customs, traditions, gastronomy, sporting styles and so on. While viewing nationalism as multifaceted, the definition accepts that there are certain core elements within nationalism that have been both recognized at the theoretical level and exist in practice. These common constituents, which are often seen as 'real', include ideas such as an identifiable geographical area for the nation, a shared or common language, history, race, tradition, customs and so on. Nationalism, it has to be remembered, is not static. The definition suggests that nationalism be seen as both mobile and historically contested. Put simply, nationalism has to be seen as an ongoing project. The nationalism of mid nineteenth-century Britain, a land of heavy industry, rapid change and global empire, cannot be compared to the nationalism of a late twentieth-century Britain that is profoundly affected by the demands of multiculturalism, globalisation and European integration. Nationalism, and the process that produces it, has no closure. There is no end to nationalism. It may change and transform itself, but it cannot be static. That ability to transform is as true for nationalism in history as it is for the contemporary.

The second major point, that nationalism can be formalized, imagined or challenged by different forces and groups, is the key to understanding how broad a phenomenon nationalism is and has been.

The idea of the nation at the legalistic level of formalisation depends on its very existence. Catalan or Welsh nationalists may dream of a Catalan or Welsh nation, but these simply do not exist. For the formal nationalist the nation has to be recognized. In the fall out from the collapse of communism the various new nations that emerged sought to legitimize their existence by making the nation formal. This involved the creation of legal machinery, such as a parliament and judicial system, applications to join or to be recognized by the United Nations, NATO or other politico-military bodies of internationalism, and the minting of national coins, the designing of the new nation's flag or the penning of an anthem. At another, maybe less important level, but central in the context of this book, new nations have also sought to be formally recognized by international sporting bodies such as the International Olympic Committee and FIFA. The formal creation of the nation will normally be accepted by the majority of the population, especially if it is the end product of a period of national struggle. It is important to remember however, that formal nationalism is not necessarily the 'rightful' nationalism. At the time of its creation or through its existence, any formal nationalism may be challenged. The Irish did not accept themselves as part of the formal Union with Great Britain during the late nineteenth and early twentieth century, and sought to free themselves. Basque separatists do not see themselves as part of the formal Spanish nation. The new nation of Belarus, although accepted by the international community as a formal nation, is now led by a president who, along with many of his compatriots, views his nation as a white elephant. Many in Belarus would trade their formal nationalism to be part of the USSR once more. Formal nationalism can also be challenged by the individual or groups such as members of the diaspora who have emigrated through economic necessity and still see their connections with 'home' as more important than their recognition of their host nation.

The imagined nation works at a far more general and less specific level than formal nationalism. The imagined nation ties together the members of a nation in a fashion that is real but non-specific. The nation can be imagined by its members, and is created at many levels. The imagined nationalism may consist of factors such as a common heritage, a shared ethnic background or shared values. It does not actually matter if these imagined commonalities are not real or that they never existed. It is enough for the members of a nationalism to believe that they are real and that they existed. An individual living in New York will have a list of beliefs and values that make them American. Another person living in Los Angeles will probably have a different list. There will be, however, certain common features that both individuals see as making them American, even if that is as absurd or ephemeral as Mom's apple pie and the importance of watching the Pro Football game with friends and family on Thanksgiving day. Countless different forces, such as the media, the popular imagination, music, literature, customs and so on, feed the creation of the imagined nation. At times imagined nationalism can be harnessed by the formalized state to bolster governments and political regimes. It can be used by a wide variety of groups, such as the marketing industry who will pander to the imagined to sell more products.[27] Finally it can be the preserve of the individual.

The challenge to nationalism can exist at several levels, and works, as with the formalized or imagined nationalism both within or outside the projected vision or reality of the nation. For the nation that exists, the real nation, challenges can come from those who wish the ideal of nationalism to change. Such challenges and transformations have taken place, or else have been requested, in the United Kingdom in recent decades. This has taken place as certain groups have demanded that nationalism become more inclusive. The argument presented was that existent nationalism was too wrapped up with images of war and empire, and had not moved on to adapt to a postcolonial and multicultural ideal of nationalism that was more inclusive. Challenges come from groups that seek to create a new nationalism and nation, if they believe that their inclusion has previously been denied to them. A classic example would be the movement towards Indian liberation from Britain after the

Second World War. Indian nationalists challenged the colonial ethos, the reality of the British-Indian nation, and sought instead to champion their projected vision of an independent India. Such challenges often incur the wrath of the formalized nation which seeks to deny the wishes of those who seek their own nation, as has been the case in East Timor whose nationalist aspirations are denied by the Indonesians.

That then is a working ideal of nationalism for the purposes of this text. An ideology that is constantly changing, functions on a variety of different levels and has no single variety. With this in mind, it is necessary to examine what Irish nationalism is, how it has been treated by academics and theorists, and what has shaped it.

IRISH NATIONALISM

A straightforward challenge that might be made to the majority of Irish historians is to ask how far they have understood the broad nature and appeal of nationalism and the forces that lie behind it. The history of Ireland is littered with references to nationalism as an ideology, as a phenomenon, as a cultural construct and so on, but it appears that within all these references nationalism is taken as a norm. The very word nationalism is enough to impart the knowledge of exactly what is being spoken of. It requires no further probing, no defining, no understanding.

One of the main reasons for the relative lack of exploration that has been shown by Irish writers, I would argue, has been the ongoing Irish history that still has a violently expressed nationalism at its heart. John Hutchinson, in his fine overview of the writing that has centred on Irish nationalism, argued that the very nature of Irish history, coupled with the political and intellectual climate that produced revisionism, is to blame for the narrow focus of Irish writers.[28] He argues that there is a need within Irish history writing for

> a willingness to embrace comparative perspectives and to conceptualize the history of modern Ireland as part of the human story. An 'internationalisation' of historical practice may achieve considerably more than a corrosive scepticism by lessening the claustrophobic intensity with which the Irish are wont to examine themselves.[29]

There is much truth in Hutchinson's argument. As explained at the beginning of this chapter, there is a fascination with nationalism when it is subjectively seen as a bad or destructive force. It may be a fascination that is more prevalent in the media or the popular mind than it is within the mind of the academic, but it does exist. The history of Ireland, and that of Northern Ireland in particular, has brought about a huge interest in the history, or rather the story, of Irish nationalism. The streets of Belfast and elsewhere in Northern Ireland have provided constant images of bombings, destruction and hooded men with guns. The fascination has fuelled an avid market in the literary genre and increasingly in Hollywood, for books and films that tell the story of terrorism. Terrorism is equated with nationalism, and in the high street book shops the 'true' stories of Ireland's nationalist warriors and killers compete with the 'real' stories of Nazi killers and concentration camp horrors.[30] I would argue that the high street is the place where the fascination with a virulent and violent nationalism is played out in the extreme. At a more considered level, within books and newspaper editorials there is an equal desire, indeed demand, that nationalism be explained. The fascination with nationalism stems from the following:

1 Irish nationalism, as a violent force, has existed throughout the century.
2 Until recent years the problem of violent nationalism was seen as perpetual and unable to be solved.
3 The Irish and Northern Irish experience of violent nationalism has become the *bête noire* of international terrorism.
4 It is the only long-standing nationalist terrorism that exists in the English speaking world, especially important in the context of the huge Irish-American market.
5 To many, nationalist terrorism is repulsive and objectionable, unfortunately to many others it is interesting, trendy and some would even argue sexy.

The problems that stem from an ongoing and fascinating nationalism that is viewed solely in terms of its terrorist and violent abilities, has a profound effect on the writing and study of Irish nationalism. Liberal-minded academics have attempted to sever the links between Irish history and its contemporary terrorist manifestations. In doing so they have had no choice but to delve more deeply into Ireland's violent past. The difficulties of writing about Irish nationalism are clearly compounded by its multifaceted nature. Within the island of Ireland there exists both an extreme political and paramilitary nationalism that seeks to achieve a thirty-two county Ireland through the use (or at least the threat of) violent means, and a formalized nationalism of the Irish Republic that stresses plurality, co-operation and democratic means. The roots of the latter are to be found, however, in an historical expression of the former. Writers of Irish history have to contend with a nation, the Irish

Republic, which, although democratic and peaceful since its foundation, achieved freedom from Britain through violent struggle. The existence of such a history obviously gives succour to those who pursue the battle for national freedom in the north of Ireland. Do historians therefore, write a history that could be seen as legitimising violent contemporary Irish nationalism, or do they seek to destroy such links? This is the dilemma which I believe, is central to the manner in which historians have treated Irish nationalism.

George Boyce and Sean Cronin have written the two major historical overviews of Irish nationalism.[31] Both books are excellent histories of the broad nationalist history of Ireland. Boyce begins back in pre-Christian times and works his way through to the contemporary period, while Cronin, although beginning later with the United Irishmen, again works through to the modern north. Boyce wrote in his preface that 'this book is mainly about Irishmen thinking aloud about their politics: a disagreeable habit, but one which they share with other nations'.[32] This short statement sums up quite brilliantly the substance of both his own book and that of Cronin: politics. Irish nationalism exists, it would appear, only in the long history of political movements, organisations and governments. While not wishing to appear critical of either work, the approach is indicative of most writing on Irish nationalism, an obsession with the only two things which Irish nationalists have ever seemed to do: politicize or write (in an ideal world they do both like Eoin MacNeill). Both the politicians and the literary groups are seen as representative of Irish nationalism. The academics who write about Irish nationalists are content to see the ideology in the same terms as the nationalists themselves. Irish nationalism is essentially primordialist. The Irish land-mass is clear and definable. An island, rich in history inhabited by a Gaelic people. The course of nationalism, indeed the course of Irish history, resonates with a desire to recapture the homeland, the ancient idyll. Such rhetoric features in the speeches and writings of the United Irishmen and Wolfe Tone, Young Ireland, the Fenians, the Gaelic League, the Irish Republican Brotherhood, the early twentieth-century Irish Republican Army and the Fianna Fáil of Eamon de Valera. It is present in the works of Yeats, Synge and Russell. Although the rhetoric of literary nationalism, and the actions of the political nationalists, are at times assessed in the context of their understanding or practice of modernity, Irish nationalists are rarely viewed as nationalists of the modernist school. Some writers, such as Tom Garvin, have examined the ideals behind the nationalist revolutionaries of the late nineteenth and early twentieth century, and have thus arrived at a more statist view of the ideology.[33] Garvin's recent *1922: The Birth of Irish Democracy* is especially important in that it addresses the move away from the idealism of primordialist nationalism towards the realism of a nationalism that had to become formalized as part of the state-building mission.[34] Richard Kearney has provided a useful coverage of the political mythologist concept of Irish nationalism. In examining the political, literary and cultural history of Irish nationalism, he was able to comment that:

> without mythology, our memories are homeless; we capitulate to the mindless conformism of fact. But if revered as ideological dogma, and divorced from the summons of reality, myth becomes another kind of conformism, another kind of death. That is why we must never cease to keep mythological images in dialogue with history. And that is why each society, each community, each nation needs to go on telling stories, inventing and reinventing its mythic imaginary, until it brings history home to itself.[35]

Kearney, although recognising political mythology within nationalism and national history, still allows for the transference of myth and history to the service of the primordialist view of nationalism. Myths and ghosts stalk Irish history, all of them in the service of an image of the Irish nation and a definition of Irish nationalism. Despite the revisionist texts of Ruth Dudley Edwards[36] and Tom Dunne,[37] who have sought to reinvent the role of the heroes of the Irish nationalist pantheon, they are still with us. Writers of history, have to discuss the life of Pearse, have to seek to understand what 1916 meant and how it came to form the basis of the revolution that would create the new state. In doing so, Pearse and his compatriots, the dead heroes who loom large in Irish history, survive. The nationalist figures of the past therefore dominate the agenda of the present, they control how Irish nationalism and history is written about, and while they may be dismissed, they cannot be left out. As Joseph O'Connor noted

> Irish history is full of ghosts. Tone, O'Connell, Connolly, all appear in Irish ballads as ghosts ... We name our streets and our railway stations after these ghosts. Heuston Station, Cathal Brugha Barracks, Pearse Street, Connolly Station. Part of the problem with Ireland is that everything is named after someone.[38]

It is difficult to see how Irish history can escape the problem. Nationalism has become a Gordian knot. It is easier to evade the problem than solve it. As George Boyce rightly commented, 'little wonder that the historian retreats hurriedly into the last refuge of the non-social scientist: the definition of a nation as a group of people who consider themselves to be a nation'.[39] Despite the wealth of excellent work that has been carried out in Irish history in the last few decades, the predominant focus for understanding nationalism has remained the long history of political and literary elites. There has not been, with the exception of the occasional outstanding work, a move into areas such as social history as a way of understanding nationalism and nationalist sentiment.[40] Within such history the understanding of nationalism is underdeveloped and narrowly focused. In the context of political and literary history it is largely taken as a given, a norm. Although this norm, the aspiration of a unified and united sovereign state with a common heritage, history and culture, has been widened to include different aspects of social and economic history, the norm survives. As Patrick Maume has written

> nationalism has provided the central theme of much Irish historical writing. Yet the point at which its Irish history begins continues to be debated. The issue can in part be resolved by distinguishing between national consciousness, an awareness of belonging to one nationality rather than another, and nationalism, a political philosophy and programme for action built round the proposition that national consciousness finds it s only proper expression in the achievement of the nation state.[41]

Despite Maume's incisive distinction, the bulk of Irish history writing belongs to the category of nationalism rather than that which discusses national consciousness. So what then is Irish nationalism? By examining the nature of contemporary nationalism in Ireland in the context of history it is possible to reach an answer. As will be demonstrated Irish nationalism is not the preserve of a single type, but is a multifaceted concept in line with the definition offered earlier.

CONTEMPORARY NATIONALISM

Joesp Llobera suggested that Irish nationalism was an interesting variant on the usual shape and form of the ideology. He suggested that Ireland should be viewed as a third way in the understanding of nationalism[42] or, as he termed it, the Irish model of nationalism. This model was built around a nationalism that was constructed to encompass the dream and ideal of a culturally defined nation and associated with an identifiable and historic territory within a state. Llobera chose Ireland as his model as it represented 'the case with the utmost complexity in terms of relations between an oppressed nationality and its oppressor'.[43]

The role of Britain in arriving at an understanding of Irish nationalism, indeed the history of Irish nationalism, is of key importance. The works of Irish historians over concentrate on the political and literary constructions of Irish nationalism. In view of Ireland's long, and often troubled, relationship with Britain this is more than understandable. It has long been argued that Ireland cannot be understood without reference to the role of Britain in its history. Ireland and Britain were linked formally under the Act of Union from 1800, but the Irish had been under British control for far longer. The nineteenth century is littered with tales of famine, nationalist uprising and coercion. The British are held, in some quarters, as being responsible for the famine of the 1840s, and it is here that many of the roots of the modern nationalist struggle can be located.[44] A domiciled Irish population worked in harness with its world-wide diaspora to undermine the strength of British rule in Ireland. The struggle dominated the late nineteenth and early twentieth century, and culminated with the legalistic, but altogether problematic, division of Ireland in 1921. The Anglo-Irish relationship is of profound importance to any understanding of Irish nationalism. It affects the direction of nationalism politically. But, possibly more importantly, it also shapes the nature of that nationalism, as the Irish often seek to define themselves in a manner that is oppositional to the British, rather than in their own terms. Irish nationalism is not an ideology merely shaped by the aspirations of a small nation, but coloured, if not governed, by the experiences of colonialism and post-colonialism. As Llobera concluded,

> the [Irish] model refers usually to small national units that try to break away from an existing mulitnational state or empire, rather than small states coming together to form a larger, nationally based state. The objectives of the nationalisms against the state vary from cultural demands to autonomy, from federalism to outright independence. In theroy all units can progress from cultural demands to demands for independence.[45]

In understanding the nature of Irish nationalism (and later its relationship with sport), recognition must be made of the welter of different relationships that have affected it. As stated earlier, nationalism is multifaceted. The causal factors behind nationalism are equally varied. The many different types of Irish nationalism have not only been self-defined, but have also emerged as a result of definition against the 'other'. In the Irish case the 'other' has comprised countless different forces. The geographical closeness of Britain is hugely important, and this relationship has been central. Other forces have also been of vital importance, and have, since independence, become more prominent. If the multitude of forces that affect and feed into notions of nationalism are outlined, then it is easier to understand how and why nationalism itself is so varied.

In the nineteenth century Irish nationalism was driven by a desire for freedom from Britain. Irish nationalists dreamt of a free and Gaelic Ireland that functioned across all thirty-two counties. To bolster the dream, nationalists looked to Ireland's long history, to its high kings, its saints and scholars.[46] There had once existed an Irish Ireland that was free and prosperous. The dreamings of this past were relocated to the nineteenth century as a juxtaposition to the contemporary land of poverty, emigration and famine. The simple concept of mid and late nineteenth-century nationalism that is outlined above was, in practice, promised by a welter of different organisations using a variety of different methods and appealing to divergent sections of the population. Politically, the solidly respectable and constitutional parliamentary groups led by Parnell, and later Redmond, understood the dream but rationalized it in a radically different fashion. They held that national freedom could only be won through the British parliament, and debated long and hard whether such a freedom would lead to complete separation from Britain and her Empire. The more radical factions within the political, such as the Fenians and the Irish Republican Brotherhood, both of whom were supported by fanatical Irish-Americans who believed the dream could be a reality, sought to remove Britain from Ireland completely. They were prepared to use violence, indeed any method that would bring about the Irish Ireland of their hearts. Underneath the political were a whole host of different cultural organisations such as the Gaelic League, the Gaelic Athletic Association and the Ancient Order of Hibernians. Into this melting pot of movements and opinion formers can also be thrown such influential bodies as the Catholic Church, esoteric movements such as the literary revival, and processes such as the growth of literacy, the spread of newspapers, a slow breakdown of parochialism and the impact of foreign customs and fashions. Ireland was a nation that was witnessing profound change, albeit in the confines of a seemingly unchanging rural and agrarian landscape. The individual, the ultimate arbiter of whether the dream of a nationalism would be followed, was undergoing a change in perspective. The world of the individual had altered rapidly in the mid to late nineteenth century. Those living or working in the cities, or in rural areas, were witnessing a slow modernisation of how things were done. They would experience occasional times of severe hardship. The majority of parents would put a child onboard an emigrant ship. They would receive letters from foreign shores, would hear news of different cultures, of hardship, success and of grandchildren they would never see.[47] A profound personal tragedy, that of losing children to a foreign land, led to a fascination for experiences and events outside of Ireland. Across the land people learnt that there was something beyond the lives that they had, and the nation they lived in. Horizons and perceptions were transformed in the period following the famine in a manner that is difficult to fathom. The changed individual, the individual who was still dealing with the issues of land, of unemployment and lack of opportunity, had to decide which projected vision of the nation that they stood behind. There was not, however, one vision. There never has been, and there never can be. Nationalism is so personally driven, so widely shaped and directed by a multitude of forces that it is impossible to see a unitary notion of political nationalism.

Even with a seemingly simple, and in the wake of the famine and the dislocation that followed, understandable, dream to pursue, nineteenth-century nationalists were multifaceted in both their approach to, and their vision of the nation that they believed could be achieved. The early twentieth-century nationalists were no different. At the political level there were divisions and disagreements as to how an independent nation could be achieved and what shape it would take. There were ideological battles between Redmond's belief that the constitutional path was the only way that Ireland could achieve its freedom (a freedom within the Empire), and the more radical visions of the Irish Republican Brotherhood, the Irish Citizen Army and Clan na Gael; all of which were challenged by the force of Ulster Unionism. Into such divisions was planted an event of proportions that no Irish nationalist could have forecast, nor could have judged the effects of. The First World War transformed Europe, if not the world, and had a concomitant effect on Ireland. Redmond allied with the Empire, the Unionists pinned their colours to the flag, and radical nationalists stayed at home and executed the Easter Rising. The bloodshed of the Western front destroyed a generation across the whole of Ireland in the same fashion as it did across Europe. The dislocation in what might be considered 'normal' life was huge. Sons, brothers, uncles and nephews never came home. Families, farm workforces, university classes and office numbers were decimated. The actions of the 1916 insurgents added to the chaos that the war caused in Ireland. The executions of the leaders of the Rising, the imposition of martial law, controls on the press, and the imprisonment of a host of men and women identified as nationalists, all served to change Ireland forever.

The effects of the First World War were mirrored elsewhere in the world. Franklin Knight noted with respect of the Caribbean:

> nationalism and class consciousness gained major impetus in the inter-war years. Like the Bolivian Indians after the wars in the Gran Chaco, the West Indians who returned after service in the European war theatre agitated for change. And their agitation coincided with a

number of other factors which together contributed toward hastening
the end of European colonialism in the Caribbean.[48]

After the war, events conspired with personal tragedy, and the altered
perception of the individual's view of the world to transform Ireland in a
manner comparable to the Caribbean. Where the pre-war period had seen a
fierce debate surrounding the future shape of Irish nationalism and a steady
growth in the forces that affected it, the post-war period ushered in a period
of rapid change and, it could be argued, total chaos.

While it may be possible to examine the revolutionary period in Ireland to
the Anglo-Irish Treaty of 1921 and to plot the reasons behind the military
success of the IRA or the appeal of Eamon de Valera, Arthur Griffith or
Michael Collins to the Irish people and to assess the effect of Ulster Unionist
political action on the psyche of politicians in Westminster, it is hugely difficult to understand what held the whole process together. To put it more
simply, as John Hutchinson has been able to do, 'Why nationalism?'[49] That
the Irish people were held together by a bond that enabled the forces of the
IRA, Sinn Féin and Dáil Eireann to bring about national freedom, is undeniable. But if that force was nationalism, what kind of nationalism, and how did
it work? Were the Irish all united by the same vision of what the nation should
be? Was it the same dream that had existed in the nineteenth century?

It is clear that the politicising and propaganda of Sinn Féin played a large
part in creating a vocalized model of the nation that all nationalists could rally
behind. However, as the work of David Fitzpatrick[50] and Peter Hart[51] show,
Sinn Féin and the IRA were both organisations with wide agendas that kept
many people loyal to the nationalist project by either promising other political gains or, at times, through the use of intimidation and fear. Even in the
political vision of nationalism there is schism and divergence, no unified
reason as to 'Why nationalism?' The disagreements that surrounded the signing of the Treaty in 1921 and the vicious Civil War are further evidence that
the goals of nationalism were divergent. Alongside the political, there was the
continuation of a lively cultural nationalism. This existed at the 'high' cultural level of literature, literary journals, drama and quality journalism, and at the
'low' cultural level through sport, social organisations, parties and dances. In
the revolutionary period, any grouping of people would have been profoundly affected by the events of the day. Every medium, every meeting, every experience culminated to shape the individual vision of nationalism. In the
revolutionary period 1918 to 1921 nationalism was at the centre of Irish life,
but it was as multifaceted and intangible as it has ever been.

Since the foundation of the Irish Free State in 1921, the shape of Irish
nationalism and the forces that feed it, have continued to change. The first

government of the State, Cumann na nGaedheal, embarked on a very formal process of state building, seeking international recognition and putting in order the nuts and bolts of a new nation, such as an army and police force. While achieving much, the government of the 1920s were, by their own admission, the most conservative revolutionaries ever. After having fought a bloody war for the nation, Cumann na nGaedheal abided by the terms of the Treaty and 'forgot' about Ireland's six northern counties. It did not pursue an active policy with respect of the language issue, nor did it seek to separate Ireland from its economic dependency on Britain. While the Cumann na nGaedheal government have to be applauded for their pragmatism, it has to be noted how radically they altered the practical direction of nationalism in the context of the revolutionary aims of Sinn Féin. The Fianna Fáil government of the 1930s and 1940s changed direction and, although failing in many of their goals, did attempt to repackage many of the dreams of an Irish Ireland that was rurally based, Irish speaking and Catholic. In the context of a modernized industrial world the dream was untenable, but the activities of Fianna Fáil, and the levels of support that they were able to engender demonstrate how alive the dream was.

In last thirty years Irish nationalism has been in a constant state of flux. With the onset of the troubles in Northern Ireland in the late 1960s two very different nationalisms have emerged that exist at the political level, which are then also internally fragmented. They are nationalisms that are very divided and different. One version of nationalism has traditionally been championed by bodies such as Sinn Féin, the Provisional IRA, the INLA (and more recently by organisations such as the Real IRA) and has preached a thirty-two county nationalism. It was a nationalism that, while accepting the reality of modernism and the modern world, sought to rediscover and re-enact the political dreams that were championed by the 1916 insurgents and the revolutionary Dáil of 1919. It was a nationalism that is essentially priomordialist but accompanied by a wealth of political mythology, and surrounded by an intense debate as to whether its battle was one against imperialism or of coming to terms with postcolonialism.[52] The other version of nationalism is liberal and inclusive. It is the nationalism that has been represented by the government's of the Irish Republic since the mid 1970s. Although it had held onto articles two and three of its constitution (those that lay claim to the territory of the north), the government had sought co-operation with Britain and with the representatives of Ulster Unionism as a way of finding a solution to the problems of Northern Ireland.[53]

These are obviously very basic, and, by necessity, political ideals of contemporary nationalism. They do show how different, and indeed competitive, two variations of the same self-proclaimed nationalism can be.

During this same period the number of factors that have affected notions of nationalism, at all levels (not solely the political), have increased dramatically.[54]

So, as we approach the end of the twentieth century, what does it mean to be Irish? What is contemporary Irish nationalism? I would argue that all individuals that profess to be Irish would have a clear answer as to which political vision of Irish nationalism they believe in. Some will undoubtedly favour a thirty-two county Ireland, and there would be many arguments as to the best way that this should be achieved. There are also many who would consider themselves Irish nationalists but who are content to remain within a Northern Ireland that is linked to Britain (albeit with qualifications as to the structure of that society). Many that profess to be Irish nationalists will not even live on the island of Ireland, but will be spread across the globe as part of the world-wide diaspora,[55] but even they will have an answer or opinion as to the political and geographical structure of the nation.

The political construction of the nation, and the idea that nationalism is solely linked to the question of whether Ireland is made up of twenty-six or thirty-two counties, is but one part of contemporary nationalism.

In recent years there has been a proliferation of political nationalisms within, and connected to, the Irish peace process. There has been the constitutional northern nationalism of the SDLP, the republican nationalism of Sinn Féin, and the new trend towards that non-party allied nationalism that can be found amongst members of the Women's coalition.

At the state level both the Irish Republic and Northern Ireland have been opened up to a myriad of different forces and agencies. The constant pressure to find peace since the Anglo-Irish Agreement of 1985 has thrown up countless cross-border bodies that have created new paradigms of nationalism within institutions, such as the civil service or the police. Irish nationalism has also been affected at the state level as a result of the integrative nature of European Union. The Irish Republic has been a keen supporter and an active member of the European family.[56] It has, during the years of its membership, learnt to see the nation in a context that stretches far beyond its own national borders. European money has contributed towards road building, farm subsidies and other capital schemes that are visible to the whole population. In thinking of itself as European, the Irish state has shown its people that it is part of a larger common unit. Within the wider Europe, the Republic has had to jettison much of its tendency towards insular parochialism, and view a wider picture. This places the Republic in the context of other nations and their affairs, and opens the door to the forces of globalization. Such external forces have a wide-ranging effect on Irish nationalism.[57]

The election, in 1990, of Mary Robinson, to the presidency of the Irish Republic, had a profound effect on notions of Irish nationalism.[58] Robinson was not only one of the first Presidents who had not taken an active part in the Irish revolution, but she was the first woman President. Equally important was the fact that she was a member of the Labour Party, and not the chosen candidate of one of Ireland's two main parties, Fianna Fáil or Fine Gael, both of whom had such long and contentious histories that linked them with the years of revolution and civil war. Robinson was the catalyst for much soul searching that took place in Ireland during the 1990s. She was a high-profile, but essentially apolitical, president, who was prepared to use her office to spark debate rather than remain a purely ceremonial figure. Robinson was a staunch supporter of the role and place of women within Ireland. The period of her presidency brought the acrimonious debates that surrounded the abortion and divorce debate issues to a head, and both were the subject of referendums that produced a 'yes vote' in favour of liberalisation. Commentators were quick to suggest that without the galvanising effect of the Robinson presidency such referendums would have not been possible, and that the debate that surrounded the abortion and divorce issues were symbolic of a strong modernising and secularising theme within Irish society. The label 'modern Ireland' came into political and popular usage as a shorthand method of representing the depth of change within the Republic.[59] Robinson's other great target for attention was the difficult history of Ireland's famine and the ensuing emigration. Robinson was prepared to ask the Irish people who and what they were. She clearly identified the Irish diaspora as part of the nation. In Robinson's mind the nation was not geographically determined, but consisted of a world-wide network of people who professed a shared Irish heritage and culture. Her attitude to the diaspora, coupled with her commitment to the ongoing search for peace throughout her presidency, marked her out as a modernizer of the very idea of Irish nationalism. She attempted to include everyone within her vision of the nation. That vision was built on an equality for all sectors of society and did not explicitly support any single ethos or ideal of the nation. She supported the Church in that she was a Catholic, yet encouraged the referendums into the sensitive issues that led to the final break between Church and State. She supported the nationalist community in the north of Ireland by visiting Belfast, yet did not ally herself with any ideal of republicanism; in fact she also attempted to be highly inclusive in her attitude towards the unionist mindset. It will be many years until the full legacy of the Robinson years can be understood as many of the changes that took place were not officially directed by her as she had no legal or political powers in her position as presidency. What is of great importance, however, is her clear vocalising of a new, inclusive and modernized Ireland that sought to come to terms with its long and difficult history.

As the end of the twentieth century draws nearer the whole concept of Irish nationalism is being remade.[60] There exists in Ireland a wealth of different types of nationalism. Outside of the island of Ireland there are various types of nationalism and national identity that are to be found amongst those who are part of the Irish diaspora and those who profess links with the Emerald Isle at a whole variety of different levels. There are different cultural, popular cultural and artistic notions of Irish nationalism and identity. These are played out in small bars in Boston and may have a more virulent republican nationalism attached, or else may be observed in stadiums and large theatres as *Riverdance* crosses the stage. The dancers may not even be of Irish birth, but they represent, to those watching, a version, indeed a vision of what the Irish nation is about.

Within the Irish Republic there currently exists a very positive and self-believing nationalism which accepts the forces of change that have impinged on nationalism in recent decades. Irish people have coped with the force of modernity, have come to terms with their own nationalism that exists in the context of a wider Europe and enjoy the wealth that the success of the Celtic Tiger has afforded them, itself a product of the forces of the global business market. To be Irish in the 1990s and to proclaim such a nationalism is unproblematic. The sea change in attitudes in the Republic has led to a separation in many minds between the two Irelands. The south is straightforward; good-time people that are content with their self image. It contrasts starkly with the more problematic 'battling' nationalism of Northern Ireland. Even this is changing as the peace process manages to deal with and overcome each problem that is set in its path. As northern nationalism jettisons its link with the bomb and the bullet, it will fall into line with a nationalism that is more inclusive and less aggressive. The Republic's nationalism is underpinned by the relative prosperity of the diaspora overseas who are now settled and integrated with their host communities. There has been a slow decline in the numbers of emigrants who could be classed as the 'Irish on the lump' or 'the Mick on the make'. The Irish abroad are no longer seen as the problematic transient drunken workforce that was such an English construct of the nineteenth century. As they have transformed themselves into the Ryanair generation of young professionals,[61] so the nationalism of the Irish has been perceived differently. It is no longer a belligerent and hostile nationalism that is locked into a history of grievance and terrorism, but one that is both civic and banal, a nationalism that is little different from most other nationalisms in the western world.

There are a huge number of variables that affect the construction of Irish nationalism across the island of Ireland and amongst the diaspora. The effect of European and US media has been great, especially in the satellite age. With the changes that Séan Lemass ushered in during the 1960s, and the ending of de Valera's insular vision of Irish society, there has been an end to the relative isolation of Ireland. Once the Irish politicians accepted that Ireland could not be an independent, Gaelic, rural idyll perched on the edge of Western Europe ignoring everyone else, its position in the world changed significantly. With the opening of Ireland to a whole host of different forces, with the ending of isolation, the nature of its society had to shift. Challenges to the old order and the growth of secularisation broke the mould of what Ireland was. It is no longer a nationalism dominated exclusively by the official views of either Church or State, but one that includes the individual and a plethora of different forces. There has been a steady breaking of links between the north and south of Ireland within cultural mind: although one may be seen as violent and the other peaceful, the existence of the former no longer shapes the vision of the latter. The confidence of the diaspora and changes in transport and communications technology have affected the distance from home, and as such the diaspora now has a more instance impact on the nature of the Irish nation. There has even been a downturn in the numbers joining the diaspora due to success of the Celtic Tiger and the peace dividend, both of which have had a profound effect. The peace process has had a great impact on ideas of inclusion and cultural togetherness that have even been enshrined in official documentation, such as the Joint Framework Document. The recent history of nationalism in Ireland is, like British culture, 'not fixed and impervious to change', and, as a result, 'sports and entertainment are important sites of nationalist activity'.[62]

A survey, such as that offered above, has to make some broad statements that will be the cause of disagreement. The aim of such an outline was not to demonstrate beyond all doubt what Irish nationalism now is. The aim was to illustrate how multifaceted Irish nationalism has been throughout the twentieth century and the huge variety of forces that have impinged on it. To understand fully the importance of the place of sport in Ireland, and its role in creating or sustaining notions of Irish nationalism, the widely varying ideal of nationalism itself has to be understood.

3 / Sport

As the days went by, the news from Ireland [during the 1990 World Cup Finals] was more and more astonishing. Everybody told me I was insane to be in Cagliari with the fans. At home, it was one big party: little old ladies learnt the intricacies of offside; when Ireland drew with England it was like the Pope's visit in the confines of your local bar.[1]

Like almost everybody else in Scotland [during the 1978 World Cup Finals] I had bought the mug, the T-shirt, got drunk and sang 'Allie's Tartan Army' on the tops of buses. Once again there was hope in Scotland, once again we were on the march. For the first time since the last time (RIP Billy Bremner et al.) we were a nation once more. Nationhood is awarded to us every four years. For ninety minutes at a stretch, us raggedy Scotties with a Whitehall father put away our political immaturity and rise above our traditional Scottish heroes who themselves were all children (Peter Pan, Wee McGregor, Oor Wullie) ... Thus, for one moment every four years, the kilted and non-kilted alike, we stand at the very threshold of eternity, with our heads held high.
The moment, of course, passes.[2]

The World Cup, along with the Olympic Games, is one of the biggest and most important sporting events. The global television audience for both events runs into millions, and the passion aroused is immense. Ireland's qualification for, and subsequent success at, the 1990 World Cup Finals, was the source of great pride for the Irish nation and brought about a common sense of purpose across the country. Italia '90 also led to sponsorship deals for the Irish team, a regular linkage between products and soccer, a feeding frenzy within the media concentrating on both the Irish team and the effects of their success on the Irish nation, and for many, a dislocation of normal life (who could work when there was a game on?). Similarly the World Cup has had a profound effect on the Scottish nation. Regular qualifiers for the Finals, the Scottish always seem to fail. The expectations, the hopes and dreams are always there, and every time they are shattered. The regularity of failure never dampens the enthusiasm in Scotland for soccer or for the World Cup. It is a national passion, eleven men in blue who can represent a nation that, although now having a parliament, does not officially exist in the eyes of institutions such as the United Nations, NATO or the IOC.

The aim of this chapter is to explore the reasons why sport is worthy of examination and to explain its broad functions within society, to understand why a nation, whether aspirational or formalized, can get so excited by eleven men kicking a ball around or any other sporting pursuit. If the role of sport, and its appeal to large sections of society is understood, it is then possible to tackle the often thorny question of why the link between sport and nationalism has been so important across history, why it has been so resilient and how it actually operates.

THE ROLE OF SPORT

Sport, or so it seems in the contemporary age, is everywhere. As Mark Dyreson has noted specifically in relation to the US, but a comment that could be true of most nations,

> most Americans know more about sport and sports than they do about politics, science, religion or their own Constitution. They discuss sports with friends, relatives, and strangers with more passion and conviction than they do any other subject. 'Who won the game?' breaks more silences than any other imaginable query.[3]

In soccer, not only are there the traditional match days of Saturday and Sunday, but with the advent of satellite television and the demands for something to broadcast, 'live and exclusive', there are now the match days of Monday, Tuesday, Wednesday, Thursday and Friday. For the totally fixated soccer fan there is also a wealth of analysis programmes, highlights of classic games and quizzes. If suffering withdrawal, the fan can always watch the games from far-flung corners of the world in the middle of the night. Soccer may be, within Europe at least, the worst offender in offering blanket coverage, but other sports, indeed all sports, are just the same. Gaelic games have live matches on television, highlights programmes, preview slots, and page after page in the printed media. There are pundits, experts, ex-players, county chairmen, 'real' fans, all of them squashed into the special sections of Monday morning's paper, expressing their views on the most recent game, the next game and any controversy that may be rumbling on. The Americans have the same fixation with American Football and baseball, the Australians with Australian rules and the Japanese with sumo (and increasingly soccer and baseball). Michael Jordan and the Nike swoosh are the most identifiable symbols of the modern age alongside the McDonalds logo, the name Coca-Cola and the alternative world that is Disney.

Millions of people around the globe will travel at least once a week to their local stadium, ground, arena or local park to watch their team or representatives playing the national, regional or local sport. The thrill and the passion is the same for the Cork City fan in a crowd that barely scrapes into four figures, as it is for the Barcelona fan surrounded by one hundred thousand fellow devotees. The devotion, the hopes and fears are the same for the green and red bedecked Mayo fan watching their team in a Provincial final, as it is for the Green Bay Packers fan that wears a cheese on their head for the Superbowl. All the spectators in any given ground are usually accompanied by a television crowd of some description, be it as live or through highlights, or a radio audience that can span the globe. The media is crucial in understanding the historical and contemporary impact of sport on society. From basic reporting in the print media, through the days of mass radio audiences for live transmissions, down to the current domination of satellite television, the media and sport have had a reciprocal and highly profitable relationship. The media, in whatever form, takes the battle of the sports ground or arena direct into people's homes. For a nation such as Australia, sport obsessed, yet spread over a large geographical area, the media, and television in particular, is centrally important in taking sport to everyone within the nation. Sport on the small screen provides a common link and focus, a catalyst for universal expressions of identity (in this case an Australian one) for people that may live thousands of miles apart and have little else that is common or national. Geoffrey Caldwell noted:

> Even as I write this article, the ABC is broadcasting from 11 a.m. to 6 p.m., on television and radio, the full day's play of the five days of a Test Match between Australia and the West Indies … The ABC is transmitting to all parts of Australia the spectacle of the Australian nation duelling with another. With a mass of partisan spectators offering appreciative and emotional support, Test cricket provides a peculiarly intense form of national drama or sports theatre.[4]

The central role of the media in feeding sport to the world, and the catalyst that it is for the transfer of sporting functions to the masses, is vitally important.[5] There is nothing that cannot be endorsed by the famous sports person, not a television chat show that they won't be invited to appear on, and not a single newspaper or magazine (not matter how serious it may claim to be) that will ignore the importance of sport. It may be transient, temporary and fickle, it may at times be boring, appear strange or stupid to the outsider, but sport has been with us, in its various forms, for centuries. To ignore it, its importance within our historic and contemporary societies, or to marginalize its many varied functions, is to be blinkered, naive and selective. If, as historians or social commentators, we are prepared to take seriously the experience and value of trade union movements, of religions, of political extremes, or any other movement of the masses, then sport cannot be ignored.

Colin Tatz has argued that sport is 'everywhere'. In his view sport is a central and highly pervasive force in most societies. He is, I would suggest, quite right in arguing that 'we spend a great deal of time, energy, emotion and money on sports'.[6] Be it reading the newspaper, workplace conversations or during a televised event, we all become self-appointed experts, and all of us who are interested in sport, will invest our emotions in our favourite team, the underdog or the fortunes of the big name star. At the national level we invest our attachment in the national squad in international tournaments. The development of international competition has a long history, and one, with the passage of time, that became increasingly important. Following the national squad does not perform the same function as watching a local representative in a national competition. The local may be a source of great pride, and will underpin notions of regional identity. The local may, if successful, place sport into the position of being a big business and may even encourage greater productivity and inward investment in local industry.[7] Eric Hobsbawm touched on the role of the local as a means of identity formation and group cohesion. He argued that soccer in England in the late nineteenth century allowed the supporters of different industrial cities and conurbations to underpin their local culture and identity through ritual rivalries. Although soccer, because of its ability to also transcend the local and construct the national, had a dual function, Hobsbawm also argued that specific regional sports such as rugby union in South Wales or cricket in northern England also constructed and underpinned the local.[8] The national squad, however, is the carrier of national prestige. If competition takes place between nations, then nationalism and national identity are factors. If successful, the national squad are fêted in the media and will bring about a feeling of good will within the nation. Governments have, especially in the post-1945 period, realized this, and have invested heavily in sportsmen and women that compete at the international level. This trend may have reached its hiatus within the totalitarian regimes of the former East Germany or the USSR, and continues as part of communist China's desire to prove itself 'better' than the decadent west, but all countries have invested in their various national sporting squads. It is at this level that the function of sport enters its most clearly political phase. Bodies, such as the UK Sports Council, may exist to encourage and underpin the development of sport as a pastime or, to improve the health of the entire nation, but the over-concentration on the activities of the elite athlete demonstrates that national sporting bodies have nationalistic agendas. Are the newly founded UK Sports Academy or the older Australian Institute of Sport concerned with the health of the nation, or obsessed with counting gold medals and proving that 'we' are better than 'them'? Once set along, it is difficult to get off the path of attempting to 'buy' national prestige through sporting performance. For governments that seek to underpin the ideal of the nation and its standing within the world by counting gold medals or trophies, the function of sport changes dramatically. Sport, rather than an arena for the expression of friendly competition between nations, can become a yard-stick of the nation's success or failure. The more that is invested in the elite athletes and sports stars of any given nation so that they can achieve the morale boosting victory, the more any failure is accentuated to the detriment of the original goal of national pride.[9] The demand for sporting success is made by those groups wishing to underline the ideal of a unified identity, hence its problematic relationship with politics.[10] The whole linkage between sport and the construction of an identity has been spelt out most clearly by John Bale, who noted that

> whether at local, regional or national level, sport is, after war, probably the principal means of collective identification in modern life. It provides one of the few occasions when large, complex, impersonal and functionally bonded units can unite as a whole.[11]

Sport then, has historically, and within contemporary society, played a varied and important role. It is a form of national popular culture, a forum for the creation, expression or maintenance of senses and ideals of identity, a form of business, and a central point of focus for groups within and outside of any given society or nation. It is a massive subject that plays, and has performed many functions within all societies around the world. Max Horkheimer has even suggested that as 'modern civilisation [is] threatened on all sides ... sport has become a kind of world in itself [that] we should stake our hopes on'.[12] As important as sport may be, it must be remembered that, 'international sport is like an iceberg; a small part consisting of the Olympic Games and other world championships is seen, but most international contests go unnoticed by Press or people'.[13] One of its most important functions to be considered here is the link between sport and nationalism. While obviously conscious of the huge importance of the global sports events in forming such links, any coverage must be attentive of the huge variety of other arenas in which sport and nationalism meet and are formulated.

SPORT AND NATIONALISM

> Who cares if anyone remembers who finishes third – try telling the Croatians that their bronze medals [at the 1998 World Cup Finals] mean nothing. The title of the third best team in the whole world might not be enough for Brazil but for Croatia, a nation which didn't exist 10 years ago, it is patently a huge honour.[14]

> I take athletic competitive sports very seriously indeed … as they seem to produce more bad feeling, bad manners and international hatred than any other popular movement.[15]

Sport is, and always has been, inextricably linked to the forces of nationalism and identity.[16] It should be noted at the outset that, although nationalism is a political force, it is quite distinct from politics.[17] Politics is a discourse concerned with the practice of forming, directing and administrating the state and other political units. Politics will use or adapt nationalism and a variety of other ideological forms, but has no intrinsic ideological basis in itself. All politics and political systems, be they democratic or totalitarian, will function within the nationalist sphere. Nationalism represents the values, beliefs and self-image, amongst other things, of peoples who declare themselves as a common group. At the nation-state level, Jean Leiper has suggested that

> nationalism may well be explained as the attitude that the total reputation of a country can be enhanced through sport success because the citizen's pride is heightened and the world's respect is promoted. Politics, in contrast, is the magnification of a nation's international power and influence particularly in nonsport activities by the manipulation of the sporting event.[18]

With the genesis of modern codified sport and its spread across the globe, sporting associations and organisations predominantly ordered themselves into national groupings. Clubs would always exist at some local, county or provincial level, but the arbitrators of disputes and the makers of rules would be a national body. As national bodies sprang up around the world, it was perhaps inevitable that they would seek to measure their performance against each other. The idea of the international fixture or competition was born. The nation-state as the natural unit of sporting competition was reinforced by the development of the great universal sporting bodies at the end of the nineteenth century, personified so perfectly by the Olympic movement (and if it hadn't been the Olympics, there would have been a different contest that would have emerged so that nations could seek to bolster their self-image and international reputation).[19] The rationale for such sporting competition is located in the very thinking of Victorian society, a thinking that was widespread across the late nineteenth-century industrialized world. Society at that time was built on competition and rivalry. There was competition within the education system, in industry, politics and between nations. To transfer such competition and rivalry onto the sports field was a natural development. As has been argued, 'a belief in collisions, collisions of political parties, religious sects, industrial firms and teams of sportsmen was the light to illumine the broad road of social progress'.[20] The playing of sport, its formalisation and codification and eventual transference into international competition was, I would argue, as inevitable as the scramble for Africa or the pre-1914 arms race. To build a society on the basis of an industrial revolution that is underpinned by a rampant capitalism is to encourage competition and make it the norm. Such competitive instincts are then transferred to every facet of life and every organisational structure be it the shop floor, the boardroom, the cabinet office, the battlefield or sports field.

At the end of the nineteenth and the beginning of the twentieth century, the nations of Western Europe were locked into a colonial, strategic and military struggle that would give rise to the carnage of the First World War. During that period a common, if not all-pervasive, experience within most nations was one of excessive patriotism and jingoism, and at times a virulent nationalism that was expressed in forms that were to the detriment of other nations. National characteristics became hugely important and, perhaps understandably, the characteristics of home were considered good and worthy, while those of the foreigner were dismissed as corruptive and decadent. Into such an atmosphere was thrown sport, a pastime and event that aroused such great passions even at the local level. Organized at the international level, with all the feelings of patriotism and jingoism that accompany expressions of national identity, sporting competitions between different countries were bound to provide a focus for expressions of identity: sometimes positive, at times antagonistic.[21] The reality of international competition may be summed up thus:

> [the] embellishment of outstanding sports performances with the trappings of patriotism occurs in all societies. Nowhere is sportpolitics more clearly evident than in modern international sports. Here, worldclass athletes and other sports personnel emerge as little more than political foot soldiers, front-line troops in assorted cultural and ideological struggles camouflaged under the pageantry of international competitions.[22]

In sharp contrast, the cosy idealism that is often pushed forward by the self-appointed defenders of sporting Corinthianism denies the historic links between sport and nationalism. Too often those who offer banal comments on the apolitical nature of sport are blinkered as to the functions of sport. While they are prepared to indulge and engage with an industry that can offer wealth and glory, they seek to deny that such an important part of society should have political and identity-forming values. Comments such as, 'true sportsmen only wish to compete against the best in the world, a situation no longer possible because of differing political ideals',[23] are unhelpful and unrealistic. What has been surprising is how often the leaders of international movements such as the Olympics have backed the supporters of such idealism. Avery Brundage in particular was a keen proponent of the view that sport is completely free of politics. Surely part of the frission and spark that sport provides is because it is us against them, their decadence against our purity, their wealth against our poverty, or their aggression against our weakness. Sport is political, and has a long history of political intervention and value judgements. Through its political nature sport is symbolic of nationalism. Eric Hobsbawm has argued strongly that sport has to be viewed in the context of national struggle, an overriding trend whose origins he locates in the inter-war period.[24]

A problematic factor is that while most people would accept that sport and politics generally, and sport and nationalism specifically, have been closely linked throughout history, there has not been a wealth of work that has examined such. As Brian Stoddart noted

> while in recent years there has been an increase in the number of works devoted to what is loosely described as sport and politics, little has proceeded from a base in political theory. It has been overwhelmingly descriptive, seizing upon sport as an interesting political sidelight or political issue ... Much of the writing on sports politics, then, might fairly be described as incident based, providing little in the way of continuing momentum or accumulating knowledge.[25]

With its foundations in the later decades of the nineteenth century, a period of colonial expansion and diplomatic and military competition between nations, it is perhaps hardly surprising that codified sport became so closely entwined with the politics of nationalism. While the 'sport as a substitute for war' metaphor may seem overstated at times, the history of sport in the twentieth century does nothing to make the expression obsolete. Through the Olympic boycotts, the campaign against apartheid, the bodyline test series between Australia and England, and a host of other examples, sport has never escaped its political function. It is a function, I would argue, that is interwoven with nationalism.

But what are the actual links between sport and nationalism? For the purpose of the remainder of this book, a clear idea of how the two ideas are interlinked, must be explained. The definitions and processes listed below should be understood in the context of the definition of nationalism that was offered in chapter two, and should address the concerns of Brian Stoddart relating to works on sport and politics. By rooting the ensuing discussion of Irish sport in the context of an ideological appreciation of how nationalism functions, the work should provide more than an incident-based description. Put more simply, this text, and the notes on the links between sport and nationalism set out below, seek to develop an answer to the most straightforward questions asked in relation to sport and society: What is it? How did it develop? Why is it so important in contemporary society? What should we do with or about it?[26]

The nationalism that is connected with sport is:

1   *Constructed by many different forces.* The nationalism that is expressed through sport can be a nationalism that is constructed by either the state, the individual, the fan or spectator, the media, the athlete, the national governing body of any given sport, the team or even the style in which a team plays.

2   *The manifestation of a variety of different types of nationalism.* It can be a nationalism that is political, religious, cultural, media-constructed, historical, banal, individual, aspirational or formalized by the existence of an actual state.

3   *Both real and imagined.* Those parties that wish to create or identify a nationalism connected with sport can observe the real, that is, a team or individual in national uniform, standing under a national flag, singing an anthem and competing as a recognized nation in an international competition; or they can imagine a nation of common or shared characteristics. This imagined nation might be represented by the manner is which a team plays, the idea that the players involved share common elements with the nation watching, that is, that they are 'our boys and girls'.

4   *A force of either creation or reflection.* Sport can either create a nationalism (or at least sustain a non-formalized variety) thereby giving it a voice and a focus as with the case of Irish nationalism and the Gaelic Athletic Association, or can reflect and project the nationalism that already exists within the formalized state. An example of the latter might be the use of sport as a vehicle of nationalism by the former East Germany during the Cold War period.

5   *Both positive and negative.* In its positive mode, sport can bring together different groups within the nation, project a strong and positive image

of the nation to other countries, and provide a meeting place for antagonistic nations that may be (at times) politically value-free. In its negative mode, sport can demonstrate weak and disunified images of the nation, can be the focus for violence, may exclude groups within the nation, or project negative images of the nation to the outside world or through defeat in competition.

6 *Can be transient and temporary.* Through sport we become transfixed by the ninety-minute image of the nation. Nationalism in sport is often created only as long as the game, event or tournament lasts. The nation can become fixated by sporting nationalism, it creates national cohesion and gives cause for celebration, yet it is a nationalism that is often not permanent. It is a nationalism that will only thrive as long as the team survive in a tournament or while they succeed. Inevitably, all representatives of the nation will lose and the transient nationalism provided by sport will pass.

7 *An evolution not an invention.* Sport is predominantly located in a history of organized rules, associations, leagues, competitions and so on. Such rules and associations have a place within the history of the nation and will have been the product of or affected by long-term political, religious, economic, social and cultural forces. Thus sport has to be viewed as having an evolving past that is firmly located in the development or understanding of the nation and its nationalism. Sport cannot be successfully transplanted or forced on a nation without being adopted or adapted to demonstrate national traits and thereby coming to represent the force of nationalism.[27]

8 *Multifaceted and multilayered.* As with nationalism itself, the constructs of nationalism connected with sport can be representative of many different themes, groups and ideas, and are formed and shaped by a multitude of different forces.

With an understanding of how the nationalism that is connected with sport functions, and how it might express itself, it is worthwhile exploring some of the specific examples of how nationalism has impinged on sport. By exploring specific national examples it is possible to demonstrate how multifaceted the nationalism that connects itself with sport is. In addition to the national examples, there is a host of broader questions that need to be asked. By questioning the use of, and understanding the debate that surrounds, nationalist symbolism (such as the playing of national anthems at sporting events), the sheer scale of the linkage between sport and nationalism becomes apparent. Such linkages are not merely incident based, nor are they solely represented by the high-level political games that were played out on the sports field during the Cold War. Sport and nationalism are interrelated in a variety of ways, some extreme and obvious, some subtle or ephemeral. By illustrating such linkages and learning to see how broad the connection can be, the subsequent central coverage of sport and nationalism in Ireland can be understood far more clearly, as it will be digested and appreciated from the perspective of diversity.

In 1948, in the wake of the Second World War, London hosted the Olympics. While the 1948 games were seen as a great success, the very hosting of the games generated a serious debate in Britain that revolved around the nation's sporting prowess and the prestige connected with such. Britain's post-war Labour government was restructuring society in a radical fashion around the concept of the welfare state, the withdrawal from the colonies was in full flight, and the economy was in a state of flux. In 1948, as Norman Baker has convincingly argued, Britain was entering a period of intense dislocation and uncertainty. Despite having won the war, how would Britain cope with the peace? One of the constants in society that the state and the individual looked to for succour in a time of uncertainty was sport. As Baker noted, 'sport was neither seen as irrelevant nor unassociated with the more serious issues facing post-war Britain'.[28] Politicians demanded that the Olympics be a success from an organisational point of view as this would demonstrate the continuation of Britain's pre-eminent position in the world. More importantly though, was sporting performance. There was a fear that 'Britain's generally poor sporting form would hold good at the Games and the host nation would thus be embarrassed'.[29] By hosting, and subsequently performing well at such an important event as the Olympics, the British could comfort themselves that no matter what upheavals were changing their world and the nation's place within it, Britain still led the world in sport. In 1948, sport served a vital function in giving the British people and her politicians a nationalism that, although different to the nationalism that had created the world's largest empire, they could still rally to. A nationalism that underpinned a sense of superiority within the world, and one that allied the state with the people through the success of sporting endeavour. The processes that linked sport and nationalism which took place in 1948 were witnessed again in 1953. At a time of even greater post colonial crisis and in the period leading up to Queen Elizabeth II's coronation, the British nation rallied round the conquest of Everest as a successful sporting victory over other nations. Reaching the peak of Everest reinforced within the British mind that the unique national traits that had given birth to the world's largest empire were still in existence, even though the empire itself was slipping away. By getting to the summit of Everest first the British reaffirmed 'the spirit of amateurism, gentlemanly sportsmanship, the ability to deal with "backward" races and places, English reserve and common sense'.[30] At times of crisis and self doubt, sporting success can clearly bolster the force of nationalism.

The emerging politics of the Caribbean offer a further example of the important links between sport and nationalism. In 1964 Gary Sobers was appointed West Indies cricket captain. At the time he was under contract to the South Australian Cricket Association, and his release from that contract was not certain. A leading Caribbean politician, Eric Williams, appealed directly to the Australian Prime Minister for the release of Sobers from his contract. While no doubt driven by a desire that the West Indies should have the best available captain, the appeal to the highest echelons of Australian politics was couched in nationalistic terms. Williams argued that Sobers, and the ensuing success of the West Indies cricket team, was essential in bringing cohesion to the emergent nations of the Caribbean region.[31] Sport, in this instance, was vital in under-pinning the evolution of a nationalist identity, that was seen as essential in ensuring the postcolonial future of an emergent nation. While it is clear that emergent nations can define their nationhood through international sporting competition and bring domestic cohesion and common identity through sport-ing success, this is not always an easy process. The West Indies cricket side had performed well in international test series, but it took time before they achieved the moral boosting and epoch making victory against the English, their ex-colo-nial overlords. Some commentators have argued 'for developing countries sport ... provides an area in which it is relatively simple to compete with industrial-ized nations'.[32] I would suggest that in the era where modern sport increasing-ly functions as a media-based big business, it is very difficult for emerging nations to compete with the industrialized world. Emergent nations, and the nationalism that is attached to them, have successfully used sport as a way of demonstrating their 'arrival' on the world scene. This is vital for understanding the use of sport by emerging nationalisms in the historic, but is an idea that needs more careful attention when applied to the contemporary. Ireland is an excellent illustration of such a pattern. A separate Irish Free State soccer team was formed at the time of partition, yet not recognized by the other 'home' nations. Until the 1950s, the Irish Republic was denied the morale-boosting victory over England. It took until the late 1980s before the Republic's team could even be considered a world-class side, yet if their record in the first half of the 1990s is considered in isolation, they are one of the top ranked teams in the world. In understanding the importance of the Irish national soccer team, it is necessary to differentiate between the first symbolic success of the nation, and sustained sporting success.

What is more noticeable is the use of sport by nationalisms that are well established, indeed they are recognized and formalized, but which exist in the shadow of other larger units. Two examples suffice to illustrate what is a highly common form of nationalism, but obviously the political and sporting relationships between Ireland and Britain are part and parcel of this theme. Typically illustrative are the comments by a Canadian minister in 1962. Driven by a need to improve the nation's health and fitness, a campaign to encourage sport was launched. Wary of the Canadian's lack of distinctive national identity in the face of the all pervading influence of US culture, the Minister commented that 'Canadian participation in international competitive events is emerging as an important aspect of a growing spirit of nationhood'.[33] Sport offered the Canadians a way of establishing their credentials as better than, and distinct from, the US. It was, and still is, a nationalism that is highly attractive as it clearly allows Canadian nationalists to laud it over their American counterparts.[34] Of similar value is the case of Sweden. As a small nation perched on the northern extremes of Europe, Sweden has struggled to find a clearly identifiable identity within Europe, and, has also had problems in breaking away from a conglomerated Nordic identity. To find an identity, and to stress a clear sense of nationalism, sport has been of the utmost importance to the Swedes. Billy Ehn explained that

> nothing awakens Swedish national feeling so easily and strongly (at least among men) as sporting success. Glorious history, royalty, a splendid army, democracy and the welfare system, ancient ideals and traditions, Volvo and other great companies – none of these things can measure up to sport in providing bonds of national solidarity or in creating collective consciousness of one's country.[35]

Alongside those nations struggling to break free from a larger national unit that overshadows them, have been those nations that cling onto what can be called 'nation specific' sports. Although Joseph Maguire has argued that 'it is increasingly difficult to sustain the notion that a single sport represents the nation',[36] there are countless examples that illustrate the opposite. Obviously one of the best, most often cited and most relevant examples is the continued success of Gaelic games, but around the globe one only has to observe the ongoing popularity (yet very isolationism) of American football, Aussie rules or pelota to realize that nation-specific games have thrived, and continue to thrive, thereby form a central part of a national culture. In doing so they create a particular ideal of the specific nationalism of their nation, as the nation-specific sport will be value-laden and representative of only one national grouping.

As sporting competition has developed, it has, as already described, used the nation-state as a basis of organisation. As a result, sport has utilized the paraphernalia of the nation. Sporting events are loaded with symbolism. Athletes and teams wear national colours, they stand for a national anthem and play their sport under their national flag. Spectators and fans copy this behaviour and seek to adopt the symbols by painting their faces with the colours of the nation, wearing the national strip and singing national songs. The various sporting bodies in the Irish Republic have been exemplary in their use of the national colour of green in their sporting strips, the shamrock as a national emblem, the tricolour as the national flag and *A Soldier's Song* as their anthem. The followers of Irish teams and sports stars are vociferous in their use of national colours, emblems and songs. This has been most notable at international soccer matches, but has also been a feature of those support- ers following individuals such as the runner Sonia O'Sullivan, the boxer Steve Collins and the swimmer Michelle Smith. The use of such symbols is often seen as an expression of official nationalism, as indeed it usually is, but at times this can change. In 1968 the American sprint medalists Tommie Smith and John Carlos used the medal ceremony to stress an unofficial, or aspirational nationalism. While standing for the national anthem and recognising that it was 'their' flag being raised, the two athletes offered a raised glove salute as a way of drawing attention to the plight of black Americans. While not attempt- ing to deny their American nationality, Carlos and Smith wanted to stress the rights of the black American nation, the denied other. Smith summed up his identity thus, 'people recognize me as a fast nigger but that still means I'm nigger', while Carlos said, 'we are great American athletes for 19.8 seconds; then we are animals so far as our country is concerned'.[37] The formal nation- alism of a sporting event such as the Olympics seemingly has no room for the aspirational, and some argued, the undermining and unofficial nationalism of black America. Both men were sent home in disgrace for bringing politics into the Games. Their offence was that the anthem had been 'used as a vehicle of protest [rather than] as a glorious affirmation of national unity'.[38]

Carlos and Smith are important as they offer one of the rare examples of athletes taking control of their own nationalism and identity. A constant ques- tion in any study of sport and nationalism has surrounded the role of the athlete. What is their role in the creation of an identity? What responsibility do they have towards nationalism? Whose nationalism do they represent? Their own, or that of the official nation state?

The athlete, it has been argued, is unable to free themselves from the iden- tity of another larger unit. The individual is always located within a wider identity, 'even the lone runner cannot escape his association with club or town, county or country. The member of a team inevitably sinks some of his indi- viduality in the group'.[39] At the international level the athlete will represent the nation-state. Any regional identity that they may have is subsumed to the nation. As the representatives of the state it is therefore understandable that assumptions about the nation, its culture and its values are drawn from the exploits, behaviour and demeanour of the athlete. 'A competitor … is some-body representing the prowess of athletes in a given country, their physical strength, agility, nimbleness, sometimes even gracefulness and charm'.[40] With the exception of athletes such as Carlos and Smith, the individual competing in international competition cannot (indeed, will not), free themselves from a nationalism that is constructed by the state. The athlete is not the lone gambler who breaks the bank, but is an individual whose victory (or failure) is embedded with values such as 'patriotism, national pride, honour'.[41] These are values that cannot be escaped from, as even if they are denied within the nation, they are values that are assumed from outside. Athletes that represented nations from the former Eastern bloc were seen from outside as representative of communism (and thus likely to be taking drugs, likely to cheat and so on), irrespective of whether the individual athlete supports or opposes communism on a personal level. One of the difficulties for a work such as this is to extrapolate the individual from the various other forms of nationalism that revolve around international sport. Should we dismiss Wayne McCullough's 1988 Olympic success as being representative of the Irish Republic because the athlete in question is from Northern Ireland? Should we remove Michelle Smith from the list of heroes who have represented the Irish nation because of questions that relate to her alleged use of performance enhancing drugs? Or should we only celebrate true grit performances like that of Davy Langan? He was playing soccer for the Irish Republic in October 1981 and suffered an injury that would prematurely end his career. But for those who are proud to represent their nation like Langan,

> pain is relative to the surroundings a person is in. When Langan got hurt in Lansdowne Road, it didn't feel the same as it did elsewhere. With the green jersey on him, the crest of the three shamrocks over his heart and adrenalin surging through his body, he wouldn't have seen any option but to continue.[42]

While there are those local heroes who personify the national spirit like Langan, and are celebrated for doing so, it must be remembered at all times that the nationalism of any sporting representative may not be the nationalism solely of the nation state, but may be symbolic of a multitude of different nationalisms.

Symbolism in sport is important as it can be used in a many ways. Those who claim that sport and politics don't mix are 'like the alchemists … [they] don't or won't understand the nature of their ingredients. They will not concede that the mixture is mixed and inseparable, that their ideal is not real but fool's gold'.[43] People who utter such slogans fail to see that the very fabric of sport is, through its symbols, linked to politics and nationalism. Those who oppose the linkages between sport and nationalism fail to see that such a mix is central to the success of modern sport. While the playing of the national anthem at a basketball game under the auspices of the NBA in America may elicit little response because of its weekly familiarity, the national anthem is central to the pageantry of the Superbowl final in American Football. That said, 'the song has come to be equated with sports, as if the game could not proceed if the anthem were not played'.[44] The Rugby World Cup in South Africa in 1995 demonstrated how central symbolism is. The flag of the new South Africa flew constantly and was used in a high-profile fashion, and allusions to the rainbow nation were regularly made. Would those who wish to separate sport from politics see the South African World Cup as a bad thing? Do they wish to go back to the past where sport had been used by the government 'to keep a people divided'.[45] Did the quite obvious use of symbolism in sport to underpin the creation of a new nation and to generate the racial harmony that had been absent from apartheid South Africa, lead to a degeneration of the sporting spectacle as it was so closely allied to the politics of the nation's new nationalism?[46]

The political symbolism of sport is clearest in the Olympic arena. As an organisation, as Allen Guttmann has explained, the IOC has denied the political role of the Olympic Games and stresses instead its social role. Yet, 'to ring the stadium with a hundred flags of a hundred different nations was *ipso facto* an implicit political statement'.[47] To ring sporting events with flags, to drape sportsmen and supporters in the very fabric of the national flag, is to create a symbolism that links sport with nationalism in a manner that no one, but the most ardent idealist, can deny. Three times Avery Brundage, former President of the IOC, suggested that the national anthem and flag-raising at medal ceremonies be abolished, but every time he was defeated. To be considered a nation is to possess the symbolism of national flag, membership of the UN, a national airline and an Olympic gold. Why would IOC members, especially ones from recently formed nations, jettison the very symbolism that denotes that they have arrived on the world stage?[48] A medal results in coverage, a place on the podium and a position on the medals table during the Games. The nationalistic symbolism of sport is needed by aspiring and new nations so that they can be recognized on the world stage, by established nations so that they may demonstrate their strength and prowess, by the media so that they can construct a national battle that can be sold, and by the individual so that they can cheer on their compatriot.[49] One of the Irish nation's first heroes in the period after independence was Dr Pat O'Callaghan. At the 1928 Amsterdam Olympics O'Callaghan won the Irish Free State's first ever medal, a gold, in the hammer event. O'Callaghan's victory was celebrated widely in the Irish press and he was given a hero's welcome on his return home. The victory, at only the second Olympics following independence, instantaneously placed the Irish Free State firmly on the world stage in a way that other events or actions could not. O'Callaghan was granted leave from his job as a doctor in Clonmel Mental Hospital to travel to Los Angeles to defend his Olympic title.[50] This he was able to do successfully, and he remained Ireland's most successful Olympian until Michelle Smith in 1996.

Clear political linkages between sport and nationalism are of central importance to struggling or marginalized states. The Romanian decision to break the Eastern bloc boycott of the 1984 Los Angeles games engendered external celebration and recognition of their country. 'As their team paraded around the … Coliseum track, people sitting in those sections noticed that many of the Romanian athletes were crying with joy, overwhelmed by the crowd's reception'.[51] That such cheering in the heightened environment of the Olympic arena produced tears, when others of the political persuasion have boycotted, is understandable. It created an ideal of Romanian nationalism that while supportive of a political ideal of the nation, stressed an independence from the larger bloc that functioned under the Soviet Union. Internally it created a far more extreme and politically celebratory notion of what Romanian nationalism was. 'Government broadcasters boasted that the victorious athletes had dedicated their victories to their President, or were inspired by the 40th anniversary of Romania's liberation from fascism'.[52] While such needs as the Romanian desire to support their regime exist, sport will utilize symbolism for political gain, and thus the many varied forces of nationalism will feed off sport.

The Olympic Games have obviously been the most longstanding and contentious arena for the expression of nationalism through sport. They have been so successful in allowing for agreed and regularly expressed forms of national identity as 'the modern Olympics provided the intellectual classes and the masses with common subject matter'.[53] The whole Olympic ethos was built, at the time of its foundation, on ideals of nationalism. Baron Pierre de Coubertin, the founder of the modern Olympics, was driven by twin goals, both of which were concomitant with nationalism. As a French national he was driven by a desire to 'bolster the morale of French youth after the debacle of the Franco-Prussian War', thus satisfying the domestic political demands of nationalism, while, as someone aware of the tensions inherent in international relations at the time he also sought to develop an event that would 'lessen, not end, tensions between nations through athletic competition'.[54] With origins that located sport so clearly in the midst of competition between nation states, with all the accompanying symbolism of anthems and flags, it is difficult to see how the Olympics could ever be free of nationalism.[55]

As time has progressed, the Games have become an important media event. An event of such scale, played out in front of a world television audience, is an ideal medium for the projection of ideological values. Any nationalism wishing to gain political, cultural or identity-forming capital, has, therefore, viewed the Olympics throughout the twentieth century as an ideal forum for the projection of its image or beliefs. As one notable commentator observed, 'athletes continue to be perceived by the spectators as representatives of their race, religion or nation rather than as symbols of human possibility. Most spectators seem to need the opportunity to identify with someone who represents them'.[56]

The central role of the Olympics as a forum where new nations can gain acceptance is clear in the number of nations taking part.[57] In Antwerp in 1920, the first Olympics after the First World War, 29 nations competed. By the Berlin Olympics of 1936, the number of nations taking part had steadily risen to 49. Much of the inter-war rise can be understood in the light of the growing acceptability and permanence of the Games, and the comparative ease of international travel as the century had progressed. The inter-war years did not witness the glut of nation creation that was such a feature of the 1940s and 1950s, and more recently of the 1990s. Indeed, Ireland is fairly unusual in that it was a nation that did emerge and was formally established in the inter-war years. While colonial nations within the British Empire sought to equalize their relationship with the mother country, none of them looked (or were able) to break free and establish themselves as newly independent nations. In the post-Second World War era the situation changed dramatically. The post-war peace treaties redrew the world map and created new nations in a manner that the Versailles Treaty of 1919 had failed to do. The post-1945 era also witnessed the collapse of the British Empire and the emergence of a wealth of newly independent states. The two factors combined to produce a huge increase in the number of nations looking for IOC approval. Once that had been granted, the new nations aim was to actually compete in the Olympics. At the London Olympics of 1948, 59 nations to part, and by the time that the Rome Games of 1960 came round the figure had leapt to 83. In the wake of the new nationalism that accompanied the collapse of communism, and the ending of cold war hostilities, the number of nations that travelled to the Atlanta Games of 1996 hit an all-time record of 197 nations. The central importance of the Olympic Games as a sporting event, as a globalized carnival, and as a method of being identified as a nation is clear from such figures. What is also clear is the political power of the Olympics in stressing and reinforcing ideas of nationalism. The figures for the 1976 and 1980 Games were respectively a woeful 92 and 80 competing nations. Both were beset by political boycott as a result of African and then cold war politics. The force of many different state nationalisms was stressed by boycott: the explicit refusal to recognize the rights and existence of other nations. The 1980 Games in Moscow were the most political ever and a melting pot for the extremes of state nationalism that had emerged as a result of the renewed cold war struggle. The USA and USSR spent much energy during that period in demonising each other and denigrating the values of their respective state nationalisms. One US commentator noted that the Moscow Games,

> were the first held in a totalitarian country since 1936. The USSR is totalitarian in that it seeks to control every aspect of its citizen's social life. Leisure and recreation are as important to the Communist Party as production quotas and political education.[58]

Comments such as these clearly demonized the USSR. They are constructed to reject the Soviet political system and the nationalism that it attempts to enforce through sport, and to repudiate that system as it rejects the positive and righteous views espoused by the American political system, so perfectly encapsulated by the American dream. What is noticeable about the process of state-sponsored nationalism within the Olympics, indeed all sporting events, is how transient such ties are. The US rejects the Soviet political system and its accompanying nationalism in 1980 and celebrates its own values (the American dream), values which, in 1968, were not extended to Carlos and Smith.

The power of boycott and the impact of the twin forces of politics and nationalism had profound effect on the Olympic movement in the wake of the 1976 Games. In an effort to combat the political and nationalistic forces that were playing havoc with the Games, the Greek Prime Minister suggested that the Games return to their spiritual home on a permanent basis as a way of avoiding the devastating effect of national jealousies.[59]

The very hosting of the Games had become an issue of nationalism. In granting the Games to any given city, the awarding committee of the IOC has to take into account many political and national variables. In doing so the threat of boycott can be avoided. By examining the political stability of any prospective host nation the IOC also becomes aware of any national groups within the host nation that may seek to derail the Olympics for political capital. To host the Olympics is a great source of pride. The Sydney delegation celebrated like victorious athletes when the 2000 Games were awarded to them. No doubt the opening ceremony in Sydney in 2000 will reflect and project an official version of the Australian nation, one that includes native creatures and the native population, yet fails to deal with colonial history, the destruction of the aboriginal way of life or the ongoing issue of native land titles. The Olympics hosts, irrespective of how their athletes perform, will project a nationalistic vision, a construction of their nationalism (usually the official nation state version) onto the Games through the opening ceremony. However, the official nation state nationalism projected by Olympic host, may be challenged from within. The 1988 Olympic Games held in Barcelona had to try and accommodate the official nationalism of the Spanish nation state as well as pacifying the demands of the Catalonian population based in and around the Olympic venues.[60] Nationalism is not a single force. International bodies such as the IOC, who only recognize and work in tandem with the official nation state, have to be aware, as everyone should be, that there is often more than one nationalism, and one version of nationalism contained within the state.

In addition to the complicating factors caused by nationalisms within nations, any exploration such as this has to be alert to the process of globalisation. In itself it is a huge topic, and one that has received much attention, yet in many ways the ongoing debate does not present a clear ideal, or consensus, as to how the process of globalisation functions and how it has affected society. Joseph Maguire has offered a useful exploration of the process of globalisation and its effect on the question of identity within sport.[61] He argues that the process of globalisation should be understood as a process whereby 'people's living conditions, beliefs, knowledge and actions are intertwined, to varying degrees, with unfolding globalisation processes'.[62] The medium for such globalisation varies, but relies on the transference of a multitude of ideas from one part of the globe to another. This can be done by the transferral of customs, leisure style, gastronomy, music, through experiences such as tourism and obviously through sport. However, while it is clear that certain trends conglomerate to form the globalisation that we speak of (McDonalds, Coca-Cola, indeed some would argue the process of Americanisation rather than globalisation), there is a deep seated need to preserve the national against the global.[63] The rise of the global leads to the restatement of the national. In sport the rise of the global, that is, the success of global events such as the Olympics or the World Cup, or trends towards the spread of sports such as basketball, is counterbalanced by the preservation of national games like Gaelic games. Also, while a European identity may have emerged in golf's Ryder Cup, in other sports there is a keen desire to preserve the national in most sports and not to encourage the transnational unit. Most importantly, as Maguire has argued, the resistance of the globalisation process in sport (as elsewhere) leads to a desire to recapture past times and previous glories through the use of wilful nostalgia.[64] Britain is often used as an obvious example of wilful nostalgia in sport. As a nation it has attempted to recapture a glorious imperial past, confident in the knowledge that the British were the best at all the sports of the world. This is a process that is common elsewhere, including in Ireland. In times of crisis and self doubt, the Irish nation has attempted to cling to the values of Gaelic games as being central to an Irish identity. It is a nostalgia that employs the great players and glorious matches of the games in an attempt to rationalize and reconcile the forces of modernity with the belief in a self comforting past.

One of the forces that has been concomitant with the development of sport, its central place in the popular mind, the centrality of international competition and the linkage between sport and nationalism, has been the media. The media, in all its various historic and contemporary forms, has been a feature of all sports. The national media in any given country has played a pivotal role in presenting a justification of nationalism in sport.[65] The press, television and radio are transmitters of the simple values of our boys and girls against the rest. The media, as with its views on everything else, is shaped by ideals of national stereotypes, superior values and a will to win or be the best. In sporting events, the commentators of live events on television or radio, or in the written reports of the printed press will protect and celebrate the nationalism of its own nation at the expense of the outsider. The media, in creating national stereotypes that the viewers, listeners and readers at home can follow and buy into, create a nation that is commonly shared by those who follow sport. The examples of this process are countless. In Ireland the construction of good and bad images of the home nation and the opposition are equally plentiful. In rugby union, the *Times*, has created a welter of images that stereotype the Irish for their British readers.[66] In boxing the *Belfast Telegraph* sought to divert the success of Wayne MacCullough, a Protestant from Belfast who won silver at the 1992 Olympic Games under the Irish tricolour, away from the nation that he represented, and locate it instead within a mainstream unionist identity.[67] The global press joined together in celebrating the behaviour of the Irish fans during the 1990 World Cup. The fans were universally praised for the celebratory spirit, a spirit that was contrasted with the negative stereotypical images of the English fan as hooligan. The Irish press went as far as to praise their own fans as being superior to the famously boisterous behaviour of those supporters of Latin and South American supporters.[68]

Even when not directly reporting an actual sporting event the media will still present images that are specific to the nation. On both stage and screen, media forms are used to represent and glorify the sporting nation. An excellent example, discussed at length by Richard Fotheringham, is the Australian film *Gallipoli*. Against the backdrop of the carnage of the First World War, soldiers are shown playing Australian rules football near the Sphinx. As Fotheringham makes clear, this is a scene that is unlikely to have taken place as the Gallopli troops were predominantly drawn from Western Australia, at the time a non-Australian rules state. However, the scene is used specifically to engender a sense of Australian nationalism. The period when the film was released in Australia overlapped with a concerted attempt to 'make the one game Australians have invented a symbol of Australia itself', and, in depicting the game of Australian Rules the film offers a vision of 'the relationship between the sporting prowess and national identity, patriotism and colonial self-sacrifice'.[69] To combine the idea of the construction of national images and nationalist discourse with the factor of globalisation, one needs look no further than Asa Briggs. The contemporary period is witnessing an age 'of satellite and multinational conglomerates' that could be seen as the agents of globalisation, yet as Briggs makes clear, 'the nation, tribal or not, remains the main unit both in sport and in communications and that in each nation both are part of distinctive cultural complexes'.[70] The national media will peddle national myths and stereotypes and thereby will aid, support and underpin ideals of nationalism. Therefore while the global, in the form of Sky or CNN may project non-Irish images and sports into Irish homes, RTE and BBC Northern Ireland will continue to project Gaelic games to the same televisions. The national will coexist with the global ideals of nationalism and these will sit alongside internationalism. The All Ireland final will be shown by RTE and consumed across Ireland by a partisan audience who will respond to and understand its nationalistic prejudices and traditions. They will be accompanied by a global Irish diaspora watching Irish satellite channels such as Setanta Sport or Tara TV who will react to the same identity-forming messages as it gives them a taste of home. In addition the game will be shown at odd times of the day in far-flung corners of the world and on aeroplanes on programmes such as *TransWorld Sport*. This global audience will observe a piece of sporting parochialism that they may find enchanting, exciting, violent or plain boring, and will no doubt make some fleeting generalisation regarding the Irish character based on the sport they play, but that audience will be on the receiving end of the national going global.

From the discussion and illustrations that has formed the central part of this chapter, it is clear that sport is inextricably linked to the force of nationalism. The nationalism that is expressed or formed through sport is varied and serves a variety of functions, but as the specific examples from history demonstrate, the two cannot be separated. With such close linkages being so apparent, it is clear that Irish sport will be no different. Why should it be? Ireland's history, as was shown in chapter two, has been threaded with references to, constructions of, and actual demonstrations of, the power of nationalism. Ireland, its sport and its nationalism are thus common partners with a long history. John Hunter has crystallized this general enquiry into as single question by asking, 'is sport being appropriated by countries in the search for a new national identity?'[71] This has special resonance for Ireland. As notions of its national identity have changed over the decades, and have constantly shifted in respect of its relationship with Northern Ireland and Britain, sport has been a perpetual mirror for the search of new forms and expressions of identity. A crucial element in understanding the history of sport and nationalism in Ireland is the whole status of Northern Ireland. Hargreaves and Ferrando's examination of the 1992 Barcelona Olympics explained how Catalonian athletes formed the majority of the Spanish team. When victorious the Catalonian's, as part of the Spanish team stood for the Spanish national anthem, under a Spanish flag and in front of a member of the Spanish royal family. As a result of the symbolic process of victory celebration 'Catalonia was thus symbolically subsumed within the greater Spanish nation-state'.[72] To understand the force of nationalism within sport, its aspirations and at times its rootlesness, is to appreciate the Catalonian example. Codified sport gave rise to international sport that took as its basis for the nation state. Nations without nation states were therefore lost between the cracks. Northern Ireland, for all its complex history is in the same position as Catalonia. While many residents of Northern Ireland are happy to see themselves as British and thus have a nation state in sport, many others see themselves as Irish, yet are subsumed by another larger unit. The history of sport and nationalism in Ireland that is turned to in the following chapters, not only charts the official state nationalism that has existed in Irish sport, but also examines the pre-1921 period and the modern troubles as an illustration of aspiring nationalism.

4 / Gaelic games

It [the GAA] arrested an important aspect of the peaceful penetration of Ireland by English culture and began the cultural revival that led to the political revolution of the 1913-1922 period, in which it played a major role.[1]

The All Ireland finals in football and hurling are events which define autumn in our culture, great gatherings of the clans, afternoons when a farmer in Mayo will sit down to watch the same game as a labourer in the Bronx or a displaced schoolteacher in Sydney. Once upon a time, winning an All Ireland medal in September virtually guaranteed you a seat if you ran for Parliament the next time there was an election. That era has passed maybe, but the social phenomenon of the All Ireland series continues to grow.[2]

Boom! Boom! Boom! Let me here you say Jayo! JAYO![3]

The Gaelic games of hurling and football have been is existence for well over a hundred years. However, that is only the period of time that they have been played under the auspices of, and regulated by, the Gaelic Athletic Association. Many traditionalists argue that the origins of the games stretch back into the depths of time, and sit in the long history of Ireland alongside such legendary figures as Cú Chulainn (who was reputed to have been a useful hurler). Hurling was recognized by the ancient Brehon law, while manuscripts dating as far back as the twelfth century mention a game that has similarities to hurling. The Statute of Kilkenny in 1366 made laws that would stop the English colonists present in Ireland from playing the game of hurling as a way of preventing them from developing degenerate Irish habits.[4] By 1884 the situation had reversed, and the Gaelic games, including hurling, were reinvented and formalized by Michael Cusack and the founders of the GAA in an attempt to halt the spread of degenerative English habits amongst the Irish.

Within the very story of Gaelic games, and the history of the GAA, there is much hyperbole, many ideologically constructed tales and a wealth of contradiction. The various quotes at the beginning of this chapter are an attempt to illustrate the heterogeneous nature of the GAA's history and its function within contemporary Irish history. For a traditionalist such as Marcus de Búrca, the GAA has performed a vital, indeed central role, in the construction of the Irish nation that is firmly planted in the years of post-famine chaos and the decade of revolution. Tom Humphries, while acknowledging that Gaelic games can have political function in propelling a local star into the Dáil, prefers to stress the communal nature of the games. The annual pilgrimage that begins on a cold field in late winter, that yet may end in glory at Croke Park in September, is a pilgrimage that is a key to understanding the sporting ties that bind Irish society. It is a shared and commonly understood part of Ireland's history and culture. A force that offers a safe haven where one variety of Irish nationalism can be found, though not necessarily one that is political or that still has to tie itself to the upheavals of the late nineteenth and early twentieth centuries. The final quote, the screaming chant of the Dublin supporters standing on Hill 16, is a mixture of the popular culture of the pop music chart, the imported culture of the soccer terrace and a celebration of Ireland's first Gaelic games superstar, Jason Sherlock. Sherlock was 'the greatest marketing and recruitment tool the games ever possessed'[5] and signified the resonance of a modern commercialism that, it appeared in the mid-1990s, had finally caught up with Gaelic games. But what are Gaelic games? What do they, and what have they, signified within Irish society? Most importantly, how have the games that have been so clearly located within the years of nationalist uprising and revolution been represented, and how do they contribute to the formation of Irish nationalism and national identity?

These are difficult questions to answer. The aim of this chapter is to examine the history of Gaelic games generally, and of the GAA specifically, in the context of Irish nationalism. There is obviously a wealth of sporting endeavour that has taken place under the auspices of the GAA over the decades. At local, county and provincial level there are stories of legendary matches to be retold, famous players such as Christy Ring or Teddy McCarthy to be remembered, as well as the wealth of personal recollection and storytelling. There is the story of Bill Doonan, a footballer from Cavan, fighting his way through southern Italy in the Second World War. One afternoon Bill Doonan left his post and disappeared. He was found up a tree 'on the side of a steep hill and [he] seemed to be in a trance. And in a way he was, for after much effort and experimentation, Private Doonan had eventually homed in on the commentary of the second half of the All Ireland football final between Roscommon and Cavan from Croke Park'.[6] Bill Doonan is, as Breandán Ó hEithir suggested, the true spirit of the GAA. It is the enthusiast, the supporter or the lover of the game, that will give any sport its unique place in the hearts of the wider society. Ian Prior summed up the appeal of Gaelic games in the modern sports age by stating,

> in a sporting world where players change allegiance for the price of a hospital wing and satellite television holds fans to ransom, there remains in Gaelic games vital proof of a purer idea.[7]

To understand the GAA and Gaelic games is to understand the sociability of the Gaelic crowd, be it hurling or football. The games induce a great feeling of fraternity through a combined passion, a common language, an enjoyment of physical endeavor, of a pint after the match and of friendly rivalry. This book does not seek to explore this part of the GAA experience, but for anyone who wishes to understand it they should read Breandán Ó hEithir,[8] or more simply travel to any Gaelic ground. This chapter has to look beyond the colourful characters and the classic matches, and try and understand why the GAA has been so successful in projecting an image, so that it is seen as an integral part of the very definition of Irish nationalism. The aim here is to examine the GAA's own beliefs, and also explore how others perceive it as an organisation, and how they interpret those beliefs. Such a survey will offer a way of understanding the types of nationalism that the GAA has represented and how these can be located within the wider scheme of Irish nationalism.

ORIGINS

According to Irish legend the first battle of Moytura, fought about 2000 BC between two rival races, was preceded by a fierce hurling match between two teams of 27 aside drawn from the opposing forces; the casualties were buried under a huge cairn.[9]

Every year a battle for potatoes was supposed to take place in the autumn between the fairies of Cnoc Áine, led by Áine, and those from Cnoc Fírinne, led by Donn Fírinne. The fight took the form of a cross-country hurling match and the victors carried off the best of the potato crop to their side of the country.[10]

Whether located in the ancient battles of Moytura, or found in the annual fairy battle of Munster, the roots of Gaelic games have always exerted a fascination for those who follow the games. William Sayers has argued that the seventh-century law document, *Mellbretha*, which listed some 25 Irish sports offered the most detailed coverage of ancient sport in Ireland. Sayers believes that such a document, primarily concerned with sports judgements and the legal liability of participants, 'can lay claim to be the earliest work in a European vernacular to treat games and sports in a legal framework'.[11] The work of Sayer's is valuable as it traces the various literary and archaeological fragments that depict men training in sport. Within the literary texts there is a clear linkage between the masculinity of youth and their sporting prowess, from which stems their ability to become warriors. *Mellbratha* is viewed as a document that places sport at the base of a series of progressions through which a boy must travel through to become a man. Children aged between one and twelve years are listed in the document as playing with balls and sticks (an early reference to hurling?), from which they graduate to the use of weapons in later life. It is within this progression that the legends of Cú Chulainn and his *Boyhoood Deeds* can be located. Sayers concludes that 'one aspect of the function of sport in a society marked by chronic intertribal raiding seems clear enough – physical training and the whetting of competitive instinct'.[12] Such language is similar to arguments that were made in favour of Gaelic games during the nineteenth century, except that the intertribal raiding had been replaced by British occupancy.

The written history of Gaelic games in its pre-codified period is really quite sparse.[13] The various literary sources of the National Library in Dublin, and the artefacts of the National Museum have been searched through in an attempt to give the games a clear linear history that stretches from Cú Chulainn to Michael Cusack. While some writers have apparently managed this feat, such as Art Ó Maolfabhail's, *Camán: 2,000 Years of Hurling in Ireland*,[14] most serious historians would recognize that such work is driven by a political, rather than historical, agenda. As will be shown later in this chapter, the history of Gaelic games and its role in Irish life has been a political battleground. Since the inception of what might be called 'the modern' Gaelic games in 1884, elements within the GAA have seen one of the major functions of the Association, and the actual games, as being the support of political nationalism. To justify such a function the supporters of Gaelic games have turned to history as a way of proving conclusively that their case has a long and valuable pedigree in the annals of the Irish past. By examining the work of Marcus de Búrca,[15] one of the staunchest historian supporters of the GAA, I would argue that concrete linkages between the past and the present are difficult to make, and when made, become highly problematic.

In the introduction to his centenary history, de Búrca seeks to locate the modern GAA in the long history of Ireland. While accepting that this is a brief exercise in the context of a much longer book, it clearly highlights the difficulties in illustrating a clear continuum in Gaelic games from the pre-Christian era down to the late nineteenth century. The fragments that exist are used by de Búrca to trace a history of hurling that begins with mention of the Brehon Laws, leaps forward to the legend of Cú Chulainn and onwards to St Colmcille's dealings with a hurley in the fifth century. From this the story roles forward to the Statues of Kilkenny in 1367 and the 1527 Statute of Galway, both clear attempts to ban hurling. From the sixteenth century the narrative shifts wholesale to the eighteenth century. Here, de Búrca argues, it is clear that hurling was in a healthy state and widespread across the island because of the numerous mentions of the games that can be found in the records of that period. For football, de Búrca offers more of the same. He acknowledges that mentions of the game pre-1600 are practically non-existent 'because of the universal use of the English verb "hurl" to describe the movement of a ball'.[16] Details are given of games played in Dublin in the eighteenth century, and de Búrca argues that the game flourished in the nineteenth-century decades leading to the famine. Both hurling and football were seriously disrupted by the famine, indeed de Búrca goes as far as to argue that 'amongst the major casualties of the famine were the field games and other traditional pastimes of rural Ireland, which in many areas suffered an irreversible decline' and while the forty-year period from the end of the famine to the foundation of the GAA 'probably saw the [the games] nearer than ever to extinction, native games did not die'.[17]

The problem with such a potted history as that offered by de Búrca (and a host of others), is that it gives the impression that there is a clear linkage between the games of Cú Chulainn and those of the modern GAA. The fact that a king of Ossory listed bronze hurleys amongst his precious items at the end of the fifth century does not equate him to the exploits of the legendary 1980s Galway hurler, Gerry McInerney. All sports historians have had to try and deal with the difficult problem of where modern codified sport emerged from. Gaelic games evolved in their modern form in 1884 under the auspices of the GAA. The reasons for the foundation of the GAA are many and varied. They owe much to the nationalism that existed in late nineteenth-century Ireland, but the origins also owe a great deal to the whole process of codification and organisation that was an ongoing part of sporting life in the whole of Britain, of which Ireland was a part. To try and equate a modern, organized and rule-driven game with the sport of the pre-famine period in Ireland is fraught with problems. Marcus de Búrca is absolutely correct in using the examples he does to demonstrate that hurling is recorded as having existed in Ireland across the centuries. But is it really hurling? Hugh Dan MacLennan, the leading authority on the history of Scotland's native game, shinty, has dealt with a similar issue to that which plagues the history of hurling. Although he has located countless archival descriptions of a game that looks or sounds like shinty, is it actually shinty? MacLennan concluded that true origins of any individual variant of any game with club and ball were difficult to locate and imprecise. He suggested,

> another conclusion, which would seem to be legitimate, is that not only were all these games, which were played with a 'clubbe or hurl batte' indigenous, but they all derive from one common ancestor, to wit from the game to which such frequent reference is made in the Celtic story. Thus hockey, golf, cricket, stool-ball, trap-ball, tip-cat: et hoc genus

omne, no matter by what names they are now differentiated, no matter what modifications they may have suffered in the lapse of centuries … all reveal an unmistakable community of origin … [but] we may not be able to point to the exact date at which any one emerged from the parent stem and acquired a distinct form and individual existence.[18]

In the light of MacLennan's argument, can we simply believe that hurling existed in Ireland in splendid isolation, when the origins of so many other games with club and ball are difficult to locate? I would agree that de Búrca is correct in his assertion that a game of club and ball existed in the pre-famine centuries, but would suggest that caution be practised before these games are given the name hurling and linkages made between past and present.

The case of football is similar. Across Europe (if not the globe) the pre-nineteenth century period is awash with references to different peoples playing games that involved kicking or carrying an inflated sphere that eventually evolved into a ball. From these different forms of ball games emerged a whole host of different modern sports, all dependant on different national histories and the impact of ludic diffusion. To suggest that Ireland would be different and that it would generate from day one its own identifiable game, with a singular heritage, is a highly suspect line of argument. Ireland shared, along with many other nations, a history of a mass ball game. In Britain and elsewhere in Europe this is identified as folk-football, a game which, when codified, becomes Association football or soccer. I would suggest that Ireland has exactly the same game. A mob-style game that involves large groups of men trying to propel a ball in one direction or another towards a goal. The game would have been chaotic, rule free, and involving massive numbers of men. At the point of codification, and for clearly political reasons, Cusack invents Gaelic football as a method of preserving national characteristics and national identity. To suggest, however, that Cusack is building Gaelic football on an identifiable game of the past that has shared features is doubtful. Cusack took the Irish experience of folk football, an experience that was identical to the mainland British experience, and created Gaelic football. In this Gaelic football has identical origins to soccer. It is not a game of clear origins with national characteristics and a long history, it is a game that is part of parcel of the late nineteenth century obsession with rules and organisation.

To place the development of hurling and football in context, a concept of Nancy Struna's is worthy of elaboration. She argued that we should not see the hobbyhorse as the first bicycle, but should understand its invention in the context of the time. What the inventors of the hobbyhorse were attempting to do was to duplicate the movements and style of their normal form of transport, the horse, into a more modern form, hence, the hobbyhorse.[19] We are always too quick to look for the long history, to find a straight line between our past and ourselves. I would suggest that this is what the adherents of the GAA have done. In searching for the roots of the Gaelic games, they see everything with a ball, or with ball and club, as football and hurling respectively, in the same way that others have seen everything with two wheels as a bicycle. They cannot see these ancient games as something different, a product of their times. In assessing the origins of Gaelic games, we have to understand the Ireland of the 1880s. In doing so it is possible to see a clear division between the games of folklore and the modern sport. It is also in the late nineteenth century where the links between sport and nationalism can be located in a valid fashion, as opposed to the primordialist ideal of the long history. Those that see Gaelic games in the records of the past two thousand years, also see an Irish nationalism across that period. For them, Cú Chulainn was not only the first Irish sportsman, he was the first Irish nationalist. Such primordialism is possible to understand, but one that is unhistorical.

Mark Tierney wrote in the GAA's centenary year of 1984 that

> for some people the GAA is like the shamrock, a symbol of Faith and Nationhood, and it is difficult to think of the year passing by without the great gatherings at Croke Park or Semple Stadium.[20]

For over a hundred years the GAA has had a central place in Irish life and society that stretches beyond that which is normally reserved for a national sporting body. As Tierney makes clear, the GAA has a function that goes beyond that of a mere sport but is a symbol of something more profound. How was that possible? No matter what kind of ball games that the annalists and newspaper reports describe in the long history of Ireland, it is clear that some kind of games did exist, and appeared to be thriving in the pre-famine period. In the period that followed the famine the presence of sporting pursuits across the Irish landscape clearly declined. The sports that were popular can be classified as English, that is cricket, soccer and rugby, but even these seem to have a very regionalized and social group specific following. How did Cusack manage to establish an Association in 1884 that would spread so rapidly and so successfully?

To understand the origins of the GAA, is to understand the historical context of the period. The 1880s were a highpoint in the organisation of Irish nationalist politics and culture. In the wake of the dislocation that the famine caused, a new breed of Irish intellectual emerged who was not content to allow Ireland to continue its existence within the Union. The link with Britain, it was argued was the basis of all Ireland's problems, and until that link was severed, Ireland would have no peace. Importantly, the leaders of the different nationalist groups were able to transfer their ideas to the wider population, thereby engendering a far higher level of support and uniformity of action amongst the Irish people than had ever been possible in the past.

The 1870s witnessed a sea change in the politics of Ireland. Prior to this period Irish separatist politics had struggled to gain a genuinely popular foothold and had, at the high political level, been the reserve of an elite social grouping. The 1870s witnessed the emergence of the Fenians as an organized, popularly supported and radical group with clear objectives. The general atmosphere of discontent was bolstered by an ongoing struggle over the issue of land ownership and tenancy. The Land League headed the land struggle. Led by Michael Davitt, the Land League gained widespread support across the whole of Ireland with the exception of Ulster. Importantly, the Land League had its own newspaper, *United Ireland*. This was an essential source of funds for the organisation, and also formed the basis for a network of support around Ireland, kept supporters informed of the major issues and protests and allowed for the spread of a nationalist ideology that was linked to the land. Papers such as *United Ireland* are vital in understanding the spread of nationalism and a nationalist agenda in Ireland during this period. On the strength of better communications, increasing literacy and the relative cheapness of printing newspapers, a welter of politically linked newspapers and campaign sheets emerged to spread the word.

Underpinning all moves to change the power structures in Ireland was the Catholic Church. As the only genuine national movement in the 1870s, the Church had the potential to make or break any movement of the masses. As the majority of priests in Ireland came from the ranks of the small farmers and tenants, their natural sympathies were with organisations such as the Land League. As these movements transferred their one-issue politics into a larger crusade that was connected with the aspirations of political nationalism, so the priesthood, and thus the Church, followed and supported.

On the back of all this ferment, Charles Stewart Parnell emerged as the chairman of the Irish Parliamentary Party (IPP) in 1880. Under his leadership the IPP would be galvanized into a genuine political force within Westminster politics. The Parnell stewardship of Irish political aspirations within the constitutional sphere would lead to Gladstone's conversion to the cause of Irish home rule, and the return of 86 Nationalist MPs to Westminster at the 1885 election which was followed by the presentation of the first Irish Home Rule Bill in 1886. Parnell's electoral and political success was underpinned by the organisation of a political party machinery across Ireland. The years of the 1880s saw the forces of nationalism predominantly rally around Parnell's constitutional vision that home rule could be won from Westminster. Such a vision was hugely popular and was constructed in such a way that it became an incredibly broad church. The land leaguer, the fenian or the IPP elite could all find something within Parnell's message that was to their benefit, and so worthy of their support.

It was perhaps inevitable that in such a rapidly changing political and social period that questions would be asked of the nation's culture. On the back of the famine years, the land war and the political vocalisation of home rule, a cultural revival began that expressed the thoughts, dreams and feelings of a Gaelic Ireland. There has been an over concentration perhaps on the literary and linguistic revival that took place during this time, but it is within this rapid period of change, of confident self expression, that the emergence of the GAA can, and should be located.

The cultural revival was necessary to underpin the emerging demands for political separatism from Britain and to provide the myriad of nationalist movements with a definite identity to rally around. While home rule was a clearly stated and commonly understood political concept, it was difficult to for the Irish people to identify with this concept while it remained an abstract goal. The cultural revival played a key role in providing the Irish with an identity. John Sugden and Alan Bairner have argued that the lack of collective identity around which political movements for national independence could be constructed led to the realisation that they would have to 'create the cultural preconditions for independence by reviving and popularising an identity which was distinctively Gaelic and separate from that of the British'.[21] By linking together the common canons of what might be loosely termed a generic Irish identity, that is a 32-county Ireland, the Catholic faith, the Irish language and an Irish culture, the nationalist movement could provide, through its cultural wing, a commonly recognized form of belonging. Such an identity, which was explicitly nationalist, appealed to a combination of real political goals and the revival of a lost or mythologized Ireland. All the appeals to this form of a commonly shared, and some might argue, idealized notion of Irish nationalism and identity, were not solely couched in the promotion of things Irish, but the rejection of anything British. The removal of the British from Dublin Castle was not enough. The cultural nationalists recognized that to fully mobilize opinion behind their goals, indeed to achieve those goals, all elements of British rule had to be removed from Ireland. This included British habits, customs, language and their sports.

Sport had become an increasingly important feature of the British presence in Ireland. In the nineteenth century there had been a steady growth of cricket clubs across all parts of Ireland. The sport was a firm favourite in the Dublin Universities, grew steadily in schools and was underpinned across Ireland by the presence of various British garrisons and by the Anglo-Irish elite. Rugby union had a steady following amongst the Protestant and Anglo-

Irish population of Ireland, but really flourished in Ulster. Soccer had a great following as a direct result of British importation, a topic that will be discussed later, and other sports such as hockey and tennis grew steadily across the whole island. While it is clear that many of these games were, in the main, the preserve of elite strata of Irish society that identified itself with the Union, the mere presence of such games was an offence to the cultural nationalist movement. If young Gaelic manhood had no Irish pursuits for their leisure time, they would be forced to play British games. Once they had gone down this road, how could they be true Irish nationalists?

It was this thinking, an awareness of the political situation in Ireland, a belief in the need for a cultural nationalist agenda and an alertness that British sport was coming to dominate in Ireland, that drove the founders of the GAA. From their first meeting the founders were motivated by a nationalist agenda. They clearly wanted to create an Irish sporting body that would halt the spread of British games within Ireland, and eventually replace them altogether. Such a process could also underpin the various movements of political nationalism.

The forces behind the foundation of the GAA are important to understand as they reveal much about the linkage between sport and nationalism in Ireland at the time, and how visions were shaped for the future. The GAA was formed against the backdrop of a political nationalism, both constitutionalist and militant, which it backed and who's aspirations it shared. In this the GAA was displaying the statist ideal of nationalism, a belief that Ireland should formally exist as an independent thirty-two county nation. Within the GAA there was also room for another nationalism, the nationalism of culture. The two (political and cultural nationalism) are clearly linked and underpin each other. However, it is also important that they are viewed as distinct entities. The GAA could perform a central function in creating and sustaining an Irish identity without relying on the success of political nationalism. In the early years of its existence the GAA was a solid supporter of Parnell's vision of a constitutionally achieved home rule. In 1900, with the rise of John Redmond, and the electoral process whereby the Irish were left holding the balance of power, the GAA was again highly supportive (officially at least) of the constitutional route. As the period of revolution gathered pace in the years surrounding the First World War, the GAA was linked, both within the popular and Dublin Castle mind, with the forces of radical nationalism. A shift had taken place in the variety of political nationalism that the GAA would support, but political nationalism was still the primary goal. In the years following the fall of Parnell however, and at other points in its history, the GAA has been invaluable in sustaining cultural nationalism, thereby giving the Irish people an identity. At that time there was no unified political nationalism that seemingly had any chance of achieving success, or to which the Irish could rally. The GAA should thus be seen as a chameleon of Irish nationalism. As with other sporting nationalisms, the GAA can represent either different specific forms of nationalism or else a combination of types. The Association has reflected the political history of Ireland and the endless debate that has surrounded the shape of the nation. At times it has been able to stress a strident political nationalism, at others it has retreated to the invaluable role of supporting a cultural nationalism.

What is fascinating about the GAA as a sporting body, driven by a desire to represent and reflect a variety of Irish nationalist forms, is that it has used the lessons learnt from British sport to become an effective medium. As will be explained later, the GAA, in expressing a range of unblemished Irish nationalist traits that involved the outward rejection of all things British, adopted wholesale the British model of codified sport and sporting organisation, and an intensely British ethos toward sport.

What then were the actual origins of the GAA?[22] The Association was founded on 1 November 1884 in the billiard room at Hayes Hotel in Thurles. A short meeting attended by a small group of men agreed that the Gaelic Athletic Association for the Preservation and Cultivation of National Pastimes would be formed. The driving force behind the meeting was Michael Cusack, an amateur athlete and proprietor of a small college in Dublin. Cusack's enthusiasm for sport did not stop with Gaelic games, and it is known that he had played British games such as cricket. Cusack was certainly a nationalist. He was not active in nationalist politics at any involved level, but had been a supporter of the Fenians, and by 1884 was full-square behind Parnell's crusade. Cusack had prefaced the Thurles meeting with letters to *United Ireland* and the *Irishman*.[23] The letters revealed the true nature of Cusack's nationalism and the motivation for his attempts to set up the GAA. The letters pointed out that any political movement of national freedom, clearly a reference to Parnell's work, could not progress unless it also built a system that promoted the national games. Cusack is, I would argue, driven by a desire to create a cultural nationalism that would accompany political nationalism. He believed that any successful political nationalism would be an empty gesture unless there was a culture to accompany such. Put more bluntly, why fight for an Irish nation if there was nothing that is Irish left? Marcus de Búrca outlined Cusack's letter as a simple thesis of which he was justifiably proud. Cusack argued that

> national pastimes were an essential element of a thriving nation, and any neglect of them usually began in urban areas. Not only had this been happening in Ireland, but the rot was now also starting to spread

to the provinces. The reason for this decline, he believed, was because people hostile to national aspirations controlled Irish athletics. Accordingly, the time had come for the masses to take control of their own pastimes and to draft rules for this purpose.[24]

The response that Cusack elicited is interesting as it came from Maurice Davin, a famous Irish athlete of the time.[25] In a letter to *United Ireland*, Davin pursued the sporting ramifications of Cusack's plea, and closed his letter, 'if a movement such as you advise is made for the purpose of reviving and encouraging Irish games and drafting rules & c., I will gladly lend a hand if I can be of any use'.[26] Davin is following Cusack's lead and seeing the 'Word on Irish Athletics' as just that, a plea that relates to the preservation of national games and pastimes, not a nationalistically driven political agenda.

At the meeting in Thurles however, the very shape and future of the GAA was changed at a stroke. Three of the seven men who attended the meeting, John Wyse Power, Joseph K. Bracken and F.R. Moloney, were all members of the Irish Republican Brotherhood (IRB), a radically minded political and highly secretive nationalist organisation aiming at the expulsion of Britain from Ireland.[27] From this very first meeting the GAA was infiltrated and, at various times, controlled by, the forces of the IRB. The GAA was not unique in this, the IRB believed that any outlet or manifestation of nationalism should be utilized in the fight against the British. The actual history of the IRB–GAA relationship is long and complicated, has been fully covered by W.F. Mandle[28] and does not require detailed attention here. The central point is that alongside Cusack and Davin's vision of reborn national sports as the backbone of cultural nationalism, sat a blatantly political organisation that aimed at using the GAA for its own purposes. In addition to the secretive infiltration of the GAA by the IRB that would result in an altered agenda for the Association from the cultural to the political, there was also a shift that would have ramifications for public perceptions of the GAA. The meeting agreed that three leading figures should be approached so that they might become patrons of the Association. The three men approached were Archbishop Croke, Charles Stewart Parnell and Michael Davitt, and all three accepted the invitation to become patrons of the GAA. The fledgling organisation had half as many patrons as it did founding members! What is of central importance is the publicity that surrounded the appointment of the patrons. While the Thurles meeting elicited little comment in the press, the letters from Croke, Parnell and Davitt agreeing to become patrons were reprinted in the *Freeman's Journal*, *United Ireland* and the *Irishman*.[29] All the letters were supportive of the GAA, the reasons behind its foundation and all the patrons wished the Association well. The most memorable letter and the longest, that of Archbishop Croke, has become a central plank of the GAA's ethos. Croke attacked the growth of English habits within Irish society and warned that unless the situation was resolved and a return was made to Irish sports and customs then there would be no Ireland to speak of in the future (a process he feared would take only twenty years). He ended his letter

> deprecating as I do such dire and disgraceful consummation, and seeing in your society of athletes something altogether opposed to it, I shall be happy to do all that I can, and authorize you now formally to place my name on the roll of your patrons.[30]

Croke's letter, and the selection of the actual patrons, placed the GAA firmly alongside the major manifestations of political nationalism in Ireland at that time. Croke as a campaigning bishop, and an outspoken advocate of the land campaign, was clearly identifiable with the type of nationalist aspirations that come across so clearly in his letter. The two other patrons, Parnell, as leader of the Irish Parliamentary Party, and Davitt, as member of the IRB, leader of the National Land League and nationalist MP, were equally obvious symbols of Irish separatist politics. In choosing such patrons, a move that was bound to court public and media attention, the GAA was to become inextricably linked with the force of political nationalism, even though Cusack and Davin's original vision for the Association, although supportive of Irish political aspirations, was fundamentally concerned with the generation of a cultural nationalism that would underpin, rather than serve, political nationalism.

The failure to separate the sporting GAA from its politicisation process is evident not only in reports of the period, but also from the views of Irish historians. Press comments on the GAA in the 1880s and 1890s give much space to the Association's links with politics, while Dublin Castle paid a great deal of attention to their activities. Considering how public the GAA had become as a result of its selection of patrons, and how its agenda was politicized because of IRB involvement, such attention is perhaps unsurprising. What does create problems, especially in the light of this work, is how generically historians have viewed the GAA as a solely political organisation, preaching only one form of nationalism. Historians of Ireland have given the GAA little space in their work, and the few snippets that are available offer only generalisations as to the GAA, its structure or its functions. While it is understandable that the comments are brief in these works as they are 'long' histories, the ability to ignore sport as having any value is staggering. Comments by writers such as Roy Foster that 'movements like the Gaelic Athletic Association traditionally had a large Fenian overlap'[31] are undoubt-

edly true, but is this all that there is to say about the place of a movement
that attracts such a high level of support? It also contrasts, especially in such
a work as highly and quite rightly praised as Foster's, with the entries and
details that surround the organisation of, and individuals involved in, the
Gaelic League and the literary revival. F.S.L. Lyons makes some broader
comments relating to the Association, but the major thrust of his argument
relates solely to the impact of the GAA on the force of political nationalism.
He concludes that, 'the connection between the GAA and the extreme wing
of the nationalist movement was never lost'.[32] Probably most indicative of
the whole attitude to the GAA is that taken by Terence Brown in his *Ireland.
A Social and Cultural History, 1922-1985*.[33] While acknowledging that
Brown's chronological period is outside the years of the foundation of the
GAA, I would suggest that the Association, as the major provider of sport
and because of its cultural resonance should have an important place within
a work dealing so explicitly with social and cultural history. With the exception of a single line of text that relates to the GAA and its struggle to make
inroads into the recreational life of urban areas in the 1970s, Brown
completely ignores the Association. The whole historiographical approach
to the GAA has been problematic. In between total omission and selective
acknowledgement of its function as a carrier of political nationalism, the
GAA has not been understood in a wider context. This, I would suggest, is a
result of IRB involvement, the selection of patrons and the GAA's own
protection of its image at times: it has wanted to be seen as a bastion of political nationalism.

The foundation of the GAA was inspired by a need for 'Irish people to
take the management of their games in[to] their own hands'.[34] From its very
inception, the GAA, as with the Gaelic League in later years, has to be viewed
as a cultural organisation dominated and driven by the demands of nationalist
politics and identity. The GAA could not exist, let alone prosper, in the late
nineteenth century in isolation as a sporting body. To succeed the nationalist
card had to be played by the GAA, and in turn, the debate surrounding Irish
nationalism would shape the GAA. Sugden and Bairner highlighted the effect
of the nationalist question on the GAA, stating 'the political dimension which
runs through the GAA is both subtle and complex, reflecting the nuances of
Irish politics in general, both in terms of relationships with Britain and in
terms of manifest divisions within the nationalist community itself'.[35]

The early years of the GAA up to 1922 are dominated by two themes: the
implementation of the ban, and the links between the Association and the
IRB. Both of these themes allowed the post-independence GAA to manipu-
late their past and create an image of a sporting movement steeped in nationalist heritage and myth, an image that has been relocated in the modern

North. The notion of myth used here can be defined as one, which although originally self created by the GAA through manipulation of the facts, is part of a wider mythical Irish nationalism prevalent in Irish life until the advent of historical revisionism in the 1960s. The GAA's view of history has remained unchanged by revisionism, and has instead been further elevated by their self-perceived role at the forefront of the nationalist struggle in the North. In fact Peter Quinn, the President of the GAA in 1992, went so far as to attack revisionists for denouncing Irishness.[36]

The GAA introduced three major bans, the merits of which were debated on countless occasions over the years, and only finally abandoned in 1971 (and later replaced by rule 21 prohibiting members of the British Army from playing any part in the GAA). The first ban introduced in 1885 meant that athletes competing under rules other than those of the GAA would be ineligible to compete under the auspices of the GAA. The second ban, introduced in 1887, excluded members of the Royal Irish Constabulary from membership of GAA affiliated clubs. Both these bans were lifted shortly after their introduction, but the spirit of both were combined and reintroduced in 1905. The new ban stated that 'persons who play rugby, soccer, hockey cricket or any imported games shall be suspended for two years from date of playing such games, and this rule to take effect from 1 February 1905. That police, militiamen and soldiers on active service be prevented from playing hurling or football under GAA rules'.[37] The spirit behind the introduction of the bans in the 1880s and 1905 is incredibly difficult to reconstruct. Throughout the post-independence years while the ban was questioned by different sections within and outside the GAA, the supporters of the ban worked hard to promote the notion of the ban as central to the success of both the Association and of Irish nationalism. Works such as Brendan MacLua's *The Steadfast Rule. A History of the GAA ban* are steeped in nationalist rhetoric, and must be seen in the context of a GAA traditionalist attempting to halt the momentum which would lead to the 1971 removal of the ban. Mandle[38] and de Búrca[39] are equally guilty, albeit to a lesser extent, of viewing the history of the GAA and that of the ban in terms of the debate of the late 1960s and early 1970s, which constructs the ban in a way far removed from the original impetus. The work of Paul Rouse[40] is central to any understanding of the bans, as he explains the ban in the context of the late nineteenth century, not that of the latter half of the twentieth century. The ban has to be seen as an instrument to ensure the success of the GAA as a sporting body. It is a tool to ensure standardisation, popularity and self-preservation, and is part of the broad Victorian standardisation of most sports at the time, most notably association football in England. In the Irish context this attempt at standardisation and self-promotion has to be set against the dominant mood of the time – that of nationalism. Again this needs qualification. Is the late nineteenth and early twentieth century nationalism in Ireland predominantly constitutional, or is it something more radical? Until the events of 1916, nationalism has to be viewed as predominantly constitutional, echoing the spirit of Parnell and Redmond. The radical forces of nationalism such as that of the IRB and later that of Sinn Féin are present but not predominant. Thus, as Rouse stated

> the GAA's choice of nationalism as its justificatory philosophy was inevitable given the prevailing political climate at the time of its foundation. The nationalist rhetoric employed by its leading officials, the choice of its patrons and, indeed, the association of the GAA with a wide range of nationalist causes were all part of an attempt to achieve the correct popular approach. This approach was intended, not just as a counter to the rhetoric which attended English pastimes, but was also designed to enhance the appeal of the organisation amongst the section of the community most likely to support it – the nationalists ... the ban, which was increasingly portrayed in the twentieth century as epitomising the GAA's commitment to a nationalist ideal, held no such associations when it was initially introduced for administrative and organisational purposes within two months of the establishment of the GAA.[41]

The introduction of the ban was to ensure the popularity and success of the Association, and in response to the political spirit which dominated Irish life at the time. It was not introduced as a statement of political ideology. Every major cultural enterprise in late nineteenth- and early twentieth-century Ireland including such diverse areas such as the literary revival, the Church, and the Gaelic League had to enter into the rhetoric of nationalism to ensure a level of popularity. What is important in any understanding of the GAA and its portrayal of nationalism in recent years is that the introduction of the ban is now projected by the Association as a definitive act of ideologically defiant nationalism, not as an act of expediency during the late nineteenth century. As an ideological act, the spirit of the ban became an article of faith for the GAA. The ban jettisoned in 1971 was replaced, again for political and ideological reasons by rule 21. The debate to remove it from its constitution is proving as difficult and painful for the GAA as that of 1971.

The other major theme, which dominated the early years of the GAA, were the links between the Association and the IRB. In many ways it is these links which enabled the whole history of the GAA to be reinterpreted in the post-independence era. Without the interference of the IRB into GAA affairs, issues such of the ban could not have been given the nationalist credo which they later achieved. The historical accidents, which transformed Ireland in the period 1912 to 1922, allowed for the creation of a nationalist history. The IRB was undeniably vital to this version of events, and as such, the custodians of the GAA could use their links with the IRB to ride on history's coat tails into a position of centrality.

The IRB began to take an interest in the GAA during its first months of existence. By 1885 the Cork IRB man J.E. Kennedy had joined the GAA executive, and by 1886 John O'Leary, the President of the IRB was appointed as the fourth patron of the GAA. Despite a battle for control of the GAA between the IRB and the Church, and conflict over the issue of Parnell in 1891, the IRB emerged victorious. As Mandle stated, 'the survival, followed by the revival, of the GAA was wholly due to the Irish Republican Brotherhood ... [and] by 1914 the GAA could claim to be the single most important institution (outside the Church) in the country, its place in Irish life and Irish nationalism assured'.[42] Up to 1914 the GAA, although dominated at the higher levels by IRB elements, was succeeding across the country solely as a sporting movement. Clubs spread to every parish, and the championships became mass spectator spectacles. As a national movement, with thousands of nationally minded Irishmen as members, the GAA was inevitably bound to feature in the upheavals of the period 1912 to 1922. During the Home Rule crisis of 1912 it is evident that many of the GAA clubs across the country formed the nucleus of the local Volunteer movements and that members were routinely armed and drilled. This support of the Volunteers is again symptomatic of a general nation-wide move of nationalist support, and is not IRB led. The events of 1914 support this idea. When the GAA split, along with the rest of the country, between the Redmondite National Volunteers and the IRB-dominated Irish Volunteers, it was the constitutionalist Redmond, and not the radical IRB faction, which received majority support from the GAA members. Thus, despite the domination of the GAA executive by the IRB, the Brotherhood had little control over the loyalty of the membership. As with the introduction of the ban, the impetus for the rank-and-file GAA man to join Redmond was a broad based practical notion of nationalism which seemingly had tangible results, rather than the radical minority view of the IRB. The GAA was not, as it was projected in the post 1922 era, the mass-based spiritual home of physical-force nationalism (which reached fruition following the events of 1916), but rather it was the home of populist national sentiment. Such ideas make a nonsense of Mandle's statement, 'that the GAA provided, as it always intended to provide, the muscle for the Easter Rising of 1916'.[43] If the GAA was so central to the Rising would they have organized an annual congress for the same day? History has decreed that the 1916 Rising should be seen as the great heroic gesture for Irish nationalism – the watermark between Imperial servitude and national freedom. That the GAA was dominated at executive level up to 1916 by the IRB is undeniable. Equally undeniable is the fact that the British saw fit to arrest thousands of GAA men in the immediate aftermath of the Rising because of their supposed sympathies for the rebels. However, the men who actually took part in the Rising were committed physical-force national-ists. As such they were likely to have joined any movement with nationalist credentials, be it to cement their own identity or as a cover for recruitment into the IRB. Thus to state that 'many members of the GAA had taken part in the Rising'[44] is too strong. The same sweeping statement could be made in relation to members of the Gaelic League or the Catholic Church. The rebels of 1916 were physical-force nationalists intent on making a stand for their cause. They also happened to be GAA men: this does not mean that the GAA was a physi-cal-force movement. The GAA was as divided as any other national-based movement during wartime, and, in particular over the question of 1916. It is nationalist history, which has decreed the rank-and-file of the GAA and the IRB were indivisible, rather than any hard evidence.

The War of Independence served to create further myths which could be used by GAA traditionalists in later years. As a functioning national movement the GAA was undoubtedly used as a cover for nationalist activity, and its rank-and-file members were no doubt committed to the wider cause of nationalism. For the Association the need to survive and function was paramount during the period of upheaval. The staging of the Dublin-Kildare challenge game in November 1920 was an attempt at normality, and the 5000 spectators who attended would have no doubt been glad to see a ball kicked at Croke Park for the first time in weeks. The attempt at normality had catastrophic results. The IRB planned and executed its biggest coup of the War of Independence that day. It was the GAA who paid the price in the short term for such a coup, yet perversely it ensured their nationalist reputation for years to come, a price and a reputation they played absolutely no part in shaping. The GAA did not know the activities the IRB were planning for that day. The match was used as a cover by Michael Collins to transport his men to Dublin and destroy the British spy network. The British reaction resulted in Bloody Sunday, the legendary attack on Croke Park which ended in thirteen deaths, including the Tipperary captain Michael Hogan (permanently immortalized by the Hogan Stand at the ground). The atrocity placed the GAA centre stage and had a greater impact than Collins' activities of the morning. The GAA knew noth-ing of Collins' plans, and at lunch time, on learning of the morning's events, considered cancelling the game. The GAA chose sporting normality and went ahead, thereby making themselves an obvious 'nationalist' target in the minds of the British bent on revenge. From such a vicious attack with such dreadful results it is obvious that myths would emerge. What is instructive for this chapter is the construct which the days events have been given. The two major historians of the GAA have placed such an emphasis on the days events that the GAA is portrayed as having colluded with the IRB and having fully supported such actions. De Búrca concluded,

> None of the three [Nowlan, O'Toole and McCarthy – GAA officials] can have been surprised at the discovery of some 30 revolvers scattered around the ground that evening; far from suggesting that some of Collins' men had come to escape detection, these weapons served only to confirm that the men of the GAA were in the forefront of the struggle ... the GAA was justly proud of the recognition by the British, implicit in the selection of the target for the reprisal, of the Associations identity with what one of the shrewdest observers called, 'the underground nation'[45]

Mandle is equally direct, stating, 'the Croke Park shootings bestowed a martyr's crown on the GAA that it wore with ostentatious pride'.[46]

As with the ban and the relationship with the IRB up to 1916, Bloody Sunday had its primary roots with the GAA's need to function as a sporting body. It held a game in the middle of a war, and unfortunately external forces overtook such a gesture. By being a national movement, amongst whose number were Collins and his gunmen, the GAA was able to claim the mantle of a centrally important nationalist movement. The GAA did not achieve lasting fame and recognition because of the sporting exploits of its members, or the organisational skills of its committee men. It achieved fame because a handful of its members were active in fighting a war of independence, and whose actions impacted massively on the organisation as a whole. The GAA itself did not plan, or were even party to the IRB's plans, but the vague connection between nationalist violence and national sport allowed for martyrdom and legendary status.

In the post-Independence era the GAA claimed its place at the heart of society. It could profess to have been central in the development of nationalist activity by being one of the first to institutionalize a ban on alien culture and alien uniformed personnel. It could claim to have been a front for the heroic IRB, and the evidence of the post-Easter 1916 internment of its members placed it at the heart of the GPO myth. Probably most important was Bloody Sunday which allowed it to be a victim at the hands of the brutal British and a martyr to the nationalist cause. The GAA's policy of neutrality (as far as was practically possible) during the Civil War, did the Association nothing but credit, and ensured 'that its pre-political function [was] more or less inverted from a traditional position of antagonism towards the state to that of outward and ideological supporter, whereas the GAA had been formed in the 1880s as part of a campaign of resistance against British hegemony, by the late 1920s it had become a vital part of the institutional infrastructure of the fledgling Irish Free State'.[47] The Civil War years saw the GAA mirroring the same splits as the rest of Irish society; within the Association there were pro-Treaty men and anti-Treaty men, and the period of the Civil War, following as it did the upheavals of the War of Independence, meant that sporting events continued to be held at irregular intervals and on an *ad hoc* basis. The hierarchy of the GAA was dominated throughout the Civil War by men who supported the pro-Treaty administration, but their decision not to call a special congress to discuss the political situation meant that any wider splits within the Association were not given a public airing and outwardly the Association gave the appearance of neutrality.[48] There was one group in county Clare who broke from the GAA in protest against the execution policy of the pro-Treaty administration and some key anti-Treaty figures left the GAA and turned their attentions to politics, but the overriding story of the Civil War period is one that allowed the GAA to show loyalty to the new government, thereby ensuring its position at the heart of the new state.

After 1922 the GAA posed as the third strand in the nation behind State and Church. Both religious and political leaders had to be seen at Croke Park on All-Ireland finals days or else their credibility would be dented. The GAA was immensely powerful, and continually reiterated its central place in the struggle for independence – a reputation gained, as we have seen, by accident rather than by design. The custodians of the GAA forgot about their true actions in the period 1884 to 1921, and propagated the myth that they were somehow central to the cause of nationalism. During the inter-war period the two leading Gaelic games journalists pursued the myth. P.D. Mehigan (Carbery) claimed that

> like the martial spirit of the race, Hurling was at its lowest ebb when Michael Cusack brought together that pioneer band of seven in a Thurles Hotel one dark November day in 1884. Famine, oppression, ruin, almost despair had possessed the anguished land. Like the fiery cross of the highland dams, a blazing camán reappeared on every hill. The Irish nation was reborn.[49]

P.J. Devlin was equally poetic stating that

> the grip of the native ash draws impressionable young hearts back to the soil and atmosphere of Gaeldom; fortifies them against national submis-

sion and racial perversion. It imparts a spirit of self-reliance, a yearning for a deeper intimacy with native glories and history ... the mountain ash had its mystic place in ancient Irish rites, fashioned as a lithe camán, it is the symbol of physical fitness and national integrity today.[50]

The GAA was portraying a romantic and mythic notion of nationality which stressed sporting physical fitness as a route to securing national self determination. Links such as these between physical fitness and national strength were not unique to the GAA or to Ireland. The experience of the Boer War and later the First World War, began a widespread debate in Britain over the links between the fitness of society and the ability to wage a national war. Similar concerns were expressed in Europe and America. During the 1930s the various fascist regimes and movements across Europe, as well as Soviet Russia, became obsessive about the links between fitness and national strength. The most obvious example being the Nazi regime.[51] Successive presidents and publications restated the centrality of the GAA in the process which led to the emergence of a self-confident national state in the post-Second World War era. Alf Ó Muir, president of the GAA in 1966, claimed the spirit of 1916 as the GAA's own when he spoke of the GAA's heritage as a central cultural and political organisation in the State. He said

> what thinking man could say that the time is ripe to depart from the spiritual heritage which, as shown in 1916 and the years after, backs up and sustains great national endeavour? Who would say that there is not likely to be in our future any national endeavour – either economic, cultural or political – which might require the backing of pure patriotism? If there are such people, have they not heard of the current economic necessity to buy Irish, of the cultural necessity to restore the symbol of nationhood, of the political necessity to bring back a fourth green field? There is need of patriotism in Ireland still'.[52]

In commemorating the Easter Rising's golden jubilee Ó Muir wrote, 'it is not outside the bounds of possibility that, at some time in the future, the red blood may have to flow again to call the Irish back to the knowledge that they have "a country of their own". Only true, everyday patriotism can give life'.[53] The GAA historians of the post-war period took much the same angle. They used quotes and sources that backed the notion of the GAA as a movement making and defining history and nationalism. This process has to be understood in the context of the onset of the modern troubles, and the belief amongst many GAA followers that the period of revolution was to be replayed in the north of Ireland, and that the Association must be seen to be fulfilling its historic role. Séamus Ó Ceallaigh in his 1977, *Story of the GAA*, inserted countless quotes at the base of each page of text glorifying the links between the GAA and nationalism. These included quotes from Pearse stressing the importance of Gaelic games for the future of Ireland, and this from Michael U. Ó Donnchadha, president of the GAA between 1952 and 1955:

> Now, we of the Gaelic Athletic Association, and those of other nation-al bodies and groups associated with us in the struggle for an Ireland Gaelic and free, must stand together henceforth and present a solid front of unyielding hostility to all forms of foreign aggression and infil-tration. Let every Gael of us renew his pledge to prove steadfast and loyal to the lofty principles of patriotism which we profess. Let us inculcate our young Gaels with the noble idea of unselfish service to the nation. Let us convince them that the playing of our national games and the use of the Gaelic tongue are positive acts of patriotism, just as meritous and just as effective contributors as the ultimate triumph of the Gael as were the deeds of military valour of our Flying Columns in the War of Independence. On the active loyalty of Ireland's youth today depends the survival of all that is good and noble and national and Gaelic in Ireland.[54]

In the Free State and later in the Republic, the GAA stood as a movement projecting unblemished nationalist credentials. As a sporting body they did not have to deal with political realities, but instead chose to preach an insulat-ed and isolated notion of nationality. This whole notion of nationalism, steeped as it is in the events of the late nineteenth and early twentieth centu-ry, has been challenged across the board in recent years in the South, yet the GAA has failed to respond to the forces of modernism and revisionism.

Having established how the origins of the GAA became so instantaneous-ly and seemingly continuously embroiled within debates surrounding their objectives and the nature of the nationalism that the Association projected, the discussion has to move on. There is a need to examine the nature of the histo-ry of the GAA as it has been presented by supporters of the Association and by historians. Such an examination demonstrates quite clearly that the GAA has been labelled as having credentials that are allied solely with the defence of the ideal of a thirty-two county Irish Republic.

HISTORICAL ROLE

The GAA has, as previously discussed, played a highly significant role in the history of Irish nationalism. It was founded at the height of the late nineteenth-century Gaelic revival and from its position on the cultural wing of the nationalist reawakening it was able to move centre stage and play an important part in the Irish revolutionary period, which culminated with the foundation of the Irish Free State in 1922. Mandle summed up the role of the GAA during this period by stating 'it is arguable that no organisation had done more for Irish nationalism than the GAA'.[55]

The view put forward by Mandle is undoubtedly valid, but it is symptomatic of a general problem in the approach which historians have taken towards the GAA. Historians who have explored the emergence and growing popularity of the GAA have always examined the Association through the medium of political upheaval, emergent nationalism and state building. As a result a consensus history has emerged which places the GAA at the heart of Irish nationalism yet fails to examine the wider context within which the GAA operated and the non-political reasons behind its success as a sporting body. A problematic, as outlined in the previous chapter, is that the written history of sport does not fully interrogate the theoretical linkages between sport and politics. Too often studies have been merely descriptive, allowing for the creation of an incident based history. Such history, while valuable and worthwhile, does not lead to a full understanding of the complexities of any given case. What remains instead are a series of snapshots that are welded together to produce a seamless chronological history. This process is unsatisfactory. It excludes much important detail beyond the mere sporting, and fails to contextualise the narrative.[56] The history of the GAA has become a story dominated by incidents crossing the boundaries between sport and politics so that the two have become inseparable. Within this history there has been an absence of any theoretical understanding of nationalism and little constructive use of the developing ideas of sports history as they have emerged over recent decades.[57] There is also an absence of work that attempts to explore the history of the GAA within a cultural context.

The aim here is to critically examine the written history of the GAA that stresses the role of sport as part of the nationalist mission. While accepting many of the views present in this consensus nationalist history, an attempt will be made to widen the focus for studying the GAA. By examining the ethos of the GAA in its early years it is possible to observe that alongside the political rejection of West Britonism and the embracing of Irish separatism, there is a belief within the hierarchy of the GAA that it is a sporting body which must operate outside of a solely political context. This belief seeks to establish the GAA as a popular sporting body promoting codified games. The genesis for such ideas was the English model of sporting organisation that was taking root across the globe during the late nineteenth-century period. The whole process was imbued with a strong sense of muscular Christianity, also a predominantly English ethos. While not dismissing the primacy of Irish nationalism within the GAA's early success, questions need to be asked of the narrowness of this view. Instead, the popularity of the GAA as it moved into the twentieth century should be seen, as a product of both popular nationalist sentiment and as a result of English sporting principles that the GAA adopted. If accepted, this duality of motivations behind popular support for the GAA must bring into question the continued acceptance of the singularly nationalist history of the GAA.

For a sporting body that is so important in the history of Ireland and has a great resonance for the diaspora, existing as one of the few successful 're-inventions' of native traditions and pastimes, the GAA has been poorly served by historians. The bulk of the written history of the Association has been complied by GAA supporters, people who can generally be considered to be 'on the inside'. Few academics have involved themselves with a consideration of the GAA and their work predominantly revolves around the question of Gaelic games and the national struggle. Whereas other national pastimes have attracted sports historians who will examine the past through different vehicles – muscular Christianity, fair play, national and community identity, and postmodernism amongst others – the GAA written history has not developed an agenda beyond that which considers the Association's role in the emergence of Irish nationalism. Such a bold statement does not seek to dismiss or ignore the contribution that the large number of local based or specific club histories that have been written over the years have made to our understanding of the GAA. Predominantly such works have been written from a purely factual perspective and do not seek to understand the development of the GAA in any wider context.[58]

Before a consideration of those works that have been produced it is worthwhile considering why the historical focus on the GAA has been so narrow. The major reason has been the reluctance of the GAA to open its archives to general public and unrestricted scrutiny. Without access to Council Minutes and other key materials held in Croke Park it is difficult to reconstruct what debates were actually happening prior to a decision being made. This can be overcome by using key newspapers such as *United Ireland* and the *Freeman's Journal* which supported the activities of the GAA and for long periods allowed GAA officials to write the Gaelic games columns, but this is still unsatisfactory. In the search to replace 'official' GAA material that is problematic to access, historians have been driven towards government held archives. There is a wealth of information here but it all revolves around Special Branch reports of GAA activities. The problem here is that Special Branch was only concerned with the GAA as a potentially subversive body, not as a sporting organisation. Although this material is fascinating and well worthy of scrutiny, the obvious result from its use is to see the GAA as a front for radical nationalist organisations such as the Irish Republican Brotherhood and in no wider context. As a result of these logistical difficulties relating to available archive material, the history of the GAA remains a minimalist topic for the historian wishing to understand its wider development and organisation beyond the nationalist question.

It is my contention, however, that there is a far deeper malaise which holds back historical work which seeks to examine the GAA and its effects on Irish society and history in the widest possible terms. This malaise is part of wider problems present in the writing of Irish history. For decades there was one accepted nationalist version of Ireland's past which was promoted by those who had taken part in the Irish revolutionary period, the government in Dublin and the academic establishment. Since the 1960s as a result of the 'revisionist' debate, Irish history has slowly become a far more fluid subject with sections of society, especially in the Irish Republic, prepared to challenge their shared and self-conceived notions of the past. Unfortunately, but understandably in the light of the situation in Northern Ireland, this has predominantly been an academic undertaking. There has not been the same revisionism within areas such as sports history – historians and other interested parties have been too concerned with the 'big' issues to involve themselves with studying 'mere' sport as has happened in other countries. The GAA has played no part in the wider revisionist exercise[59] and historians (amongst others) have been wary of challenging the nationalist version of events so predominant in the history of the GAA. The coverage below of the written histories of the GAA will demonstrate that although much excellent work has been done, the historical agenda still remains narrowly based and ill serves such an important and consistently popular sporting body.

The written history of the GAA can be split into two categories and these will be dealt with separately here. The first is dominated by works produced by GAA members and often officially sanctioned by the Association while the second are those pieces produced by writers with a scholarly agenda.

Of those works produced by supporters of the Association, the first notable work on the history of the GAA was T.F. O'Sullivan's *Story of the GAA*[60] published in 1916 and based on an earlier series of newspaper articles. O'Sullivan was a GAA official and the book presents a highly simplistic notion of the Association's past beginning with the seven pioneers who met in Thurles in 1884 to reawaken the Gaelic nation and taking the narrative up to 1916 by recounting details of major personalities, decisions taken by the Central Council and recording the results of matches. Although there is no explicit mention of the Easter Rising, as such an inclusion would have meant that the book would not have been approved by military censors, there is an implicit celebration of the Rising as those GAA men who took part are included in the list of GAA personalities. Although not a researched history, as it is more of a contemporary account, O'Sullivan's book is important as it sets out an accepted chronology that is rarely challenged by subsequent authors. This chronology, while celebrating the games of the Gael, primarily revolves around the role of the GAA in reawakening the national spirit.

The first important consideration of the GAA published after independence was P.J.Devlin's 1934 book, *Our Native Games.*[61] Much of Devlin's book looks back before the days of the GAA and attempts to find the historical roots for Gaelic games in earlier centuries. This is an important exercise in the creation of a historical mythology surrounding the games (irrelevant of historical accuracy) as it allows the appropriation of blame for the demise of original Gaelic games onto the British. In turn this necessitates that the foundation of the GAA has to be seen in terms of an heroic underground movement which succeeded against the huge odds of re-establishing native political and cultural identity in the face of British oppression. By re-emphasising an accepted chronology of the GAA's history and reinforcing it with the weight of pre-1884 events Devlin produces the 'long' version of Irish history which was so popular within inter-war nationalist circles. This history begins with the happy and successful Gael who is then nearly destroyed by the British incursion. Despite the depletion of the Gael's strength they re-group and finally drive the British out. Within this history Devlin is successfully transposing the accepted norm of nationalist Irish history onto the history of the GAA. Chronologically Devlin's book is interesting as it dates to a difficult period in the history of the Irish Free State and of Irish nationalist history. Freedom had been won in 1922, but only partially. In the early 1930s there was a wider debate as to whether Ireland should continue to push forward and attempt to gain control of the fourth 'green field', i.e. Ulster (as enshrined in the GAA constitution) or if it should accept the reality of a divided Ireland. Devlin ties this situation back into Gaelic games by warning

> Ireland may have reached the haven of peace and freedom; but unless she is to be run aground or scrapped there, surely she should be kept sea-worthy and fit to brave the tempests when the necessity arises? The sense of loyalty lost to a nation is as fatal to her hopes as is the spirit of discipline lost on a ship. A sense of national loyalty cannot exist without knowledge of and pride in all that nationhood implies and entails. That influence is in danger of fading in the Gaelic ranks; and in the conflict between native and imported customs it is an essential element. Until we restore the natal spirit of the Gaelic Athletic Association, we

may be flattered by its material prosperity; but we cannot be assured of
its integrity or the fulfilment of its mission.[62]

For writers such as Devlin the nationalist battle had been fought but the
longer war had yet to be won. It is a theme that reoccurs constantly in the
later writings of many GAA men who record the Association's history.

One of the most crucial figures in GAA journalism during the middle
decades of the twentieth century was P.D. Mehigan who wrote under the pen
name 'Carbery'. Mehigan was a GAA loyalist and traditionalist whose involvement with the Association spanned a long period. He could look back to a
boyhood during which he had met Michael Cusack, he had lived through the
upheavals of the War of Independence and the Civil War and yet had to live
his later years in an Ireland struggling to come to terms with the forces of
modernity. He wrote two crucial texts, his 1941 *Gaelic Football*[63] and in 1946
the accompanying *History of Hurling*.[64] It is easier to examine both texts as one
as they are much the same; with the central history of the GAA being duplicated in both books. Mehigan, a close friend of Devlin, uses the same basic
chronology and history as that in *Our Native Games* and elaborates many similar themes. Taking the long history of oppression as his starting point
Mehigan wrote

> the Irish nation, physically and spiritually, touched its lowest ebb in
> 1884. Three rebellions had failed before overwhelming force. Famine
> and disease had ravished the dispirited population. There was dullness,
> lethargy and stagnation abroad; the peasantry were flying from the
> land. The old pastimes and culture of the nation were dying or dead. It
> looked indeed as if the 700 year struggle of the Gaelic nation for free-
> dom was on its deathbed. The hurling, dancing, native music – aye, and
> the Gaelic tongue itself were threatened with oblivion. Then Michael
> Cusack from the Barony of the Burren, Co. Clare, sounded his clarion
> call, and at once the nation rallied.[65]

Within such a version of history Mehigan, as with Devlin before him, accepts
the central role which the GAA played in the successful reinvention of national pride which led to the political pursuit of independence. Within this context
Mehigan is able to write some wonderfully excessive prose linking the
Association with the struggle for nationalism. Under a picture of Croke Park,
the national stadium of the GAA and the place where British soldiers killed
twelve spectators and one player on Bloody Sunday in 1920, Mehigan wrote
'Croke Park, the headquarters of the GAA is the best evidence of the wonderful strides made in Gaelic games. A bare rough patch of turf when purchased

by the central council, the national stadium has been built by the Gaels into a magnificent sports ground. The turf is ideal – drenched too in patriot blood'.[66] After re-emphasising the nationalist version of history Mehigan moves the debate forward in questioning the contemporary role of the Association. He is not as hesitant and negative over the future of the GAA as Devlin was in 1934 as the political context had changed considerably. At the time these two books were published, Eamon de Valera, the Fianna Fáil Taoiseach, was setting out his vision for the future of Ireland. Culminating in his famous 'dream' speech of St Patrick's Day 1943, de Valera envisaged an Ireland which would be self-sufficient, rurally and agriculturally centred, Gaelic speaking and traditionalist. This was summed up in a phrase from the speech when he dreamt of the countryside 'bright with the laughter of comely maidens'.[67] For GAA men like Mehigan, de Valera's ideas for the recapturing (or reinvention) of the Gaelic spirit across all aspects of Irish life was the political embodiment of the whole spirit of the GAA mission. The message of Mehigan's two books builds on a history of the GAA which expresses the centrality of the Association in reawakening the spirit of nationalism and looks forward in the hope that alongside de Valera's dream of rural idyllicness the GAA can play a second key role in the rebirth of a truly Gaelic Ireland.

E.N.M. O'Sullivan's *Art and Science of Gaelic Football* written in 1958[68] was primarily an attempt to produce a textbook for young Gaelic Football players which would teach them the importance of their national game as well as providing hints on playing and training for the game. O'Sullivan's starting point was to make the same criticism regarding writing on the GAA that is inherent in my own argument. He noted 'there is unfortunately a complete dearth of books dealing with our national games ... it is sincerely trusted that this attempt, no matter what inadequacies and short comings it may possess will, if not meet this deficiency, at least encourage others, better equipped, to blaze further this important national physical culture trail'.[68] The short fifteen-page history of Gaelic football which O'Sullivan offers begins at the start of the first millennium and works through the early legends to the advent of Cusack and the GAA. Unlike other writers O'Sullivan does not see the history of Gaelic games solely as an instrument of nationalism but stresses instead the changing nature of the games. This culminates in an appreciation of the GAA as a body that codifies and popularizes Gaelic games as a sporting spectacle rather than the more normal view of the GAA as part of nationalistic triumphalism. O'Sullivan's book is not a great historical masterpiece, but is important as it stands alone in its use of a non-political agenda when approaching its subject.

The period from the mid-1960s witnessed a shift in the way that GAA supporters wrote their history. Two major factors precipitated the change in emphasis and both reinforce a traditionalist link between the Association and Irish nationalism. The first factor was a debate that began within GAA ranks over the ban on foreign games and the exclusion of Army personnel from the ranks of the GAA. Although the ban was eventually lifted in 1971, the debate is underpinned by the work of Brendan MacLua.[70] He argues that the ban is central to the very existence of the GAA as it constantly reinforced the purity, not only of the actual games, but also of the Irish race. The second factor in changing the debate is the start of the modern troubles in Northern Ireland. As the GAA had always been committed to a thirty-two county Ireland, its sympathies naturally lay with the plight of the nationalist population.

The first major book relating to the history of Gaelic games written in the wake of the Northern troubles was Art Ó Maolfabhail's history of hurling.[71] The book traces the history of hurling from the ancient legends to the modern era and, although not an explicitly nationalist history, it does make linkages between the late nineteenth-century reawakening of the national spirit and events in the North. It is this type of history which attempts to transplant the heroic nationalism of Cusack, Davit, Croke and company into modern Northern Ireland which has assumed a position of primacy within the history written by GAA adherents and which exists right up to the present time. In a chapter entitled 'The Camán in Irish History' Ó Maolfabhail explores the use of the camán as a symbol of nationalism. He describes how Liberal home rule MPs arriving in Dublin in 1888 are met by are crowd bearing their camán's. A similar scene is enacted in 1891 when an identical crowd accompanies Parnell's funeral cortege. The 1798 centenary and the centenary of Robert Emmet's execution in 1803 are both celebrated 'solely [by] young men carrying hurls on their shoulders'.[72] Ó Maolfabhail is making clear links between hurling and the nationalist enterprise of the turn of the century, a link he reinforces and transplants to modern Northern Ireland by describing how 'Young women demonstrating outside courts of law in Belfast in 1971 carried hurling sticks as a symbol of their nationalism'.[73]

The written history of the GAA across the last quarter century has been caught up in the problems surrounding the North. The Association as a whole has to support the nationalists of the North, an ideal encapsulated by Pat Fanning, former president of the GAA who stated in 1973

> the GAA position is clear. Its historical role is not a myth. Our charter proclaims the determination of the GAA to work for a 32-county Ireland ... The allegiance of the GAA is to Ireland. That allegiance is unequivocal. The very existence of the GAA is a protest not alone against the occupation of Casement Park, but against the occupation of Ireland or any part of Ireland.[74]

Within this understandable support for the GAA members of Ulster and the constant restating of a historical mission that this implies, how can the Association ever confront its past objectively? One way, as with Marcus de Búrca's otherwise excellent history of the GAA,[75] is to ignore, with the exception of the final two pages, that the troubles exist. In taking such a decision it is easy to locate the history and the role of the Association primarily in the period 1884 through to the early 1920s where the story is one of successfully reawakened nationalism, rather than one of continuing struggle. In the most recent book on Gaelic games written by the *Irish Times* GAA writer Tom Humphries,[76] the spirit of Mehigan's 1941 text is reinvoked, and clear links again made between the spirit of the Irish revolutionary period and the struggle in the modern North. Humphries writes

> Casement Park itself had been occupied by the British Army in the early 1970s, denying the community access to its principal leisure facility. In August 1978, the mood of the north had been inflamed further when Provisional IRA men displayed weapons at a rally inside Casement Park. The ground itself is named after a Republican hero, the British traitor Roger Casement. Just one pitch drenched in so much history and emotion.[77]

In concluding this section on GAA-inspired history we see a narrative which leads us from the reawakening of an Irish nation in 1884, which concluded with Independence in 1922 and is now, within sections of the GAA mindset, being re-enacted in the North of Ireland. This history only allows for a nationalist construct of history. The whole tenor of the games is one in which the Irish nation, actual or perceived, rejects West Britonism and embraces Irishness. This Irishness is both a political ideal encapsulating all thirty-two counties, and a cultural one which embraces the legend of the Gael. Within this history the GAA can never be a sporting body, but is instead something central to the life blood of a nation, or as Humphries states,

> through a long history, during which native language and native law were driven underground, the door to freedom always remained ajar for people who could express themselves through play ... the influence of the GAA cannot be measured in units of membership or revenue, through attendance's or viewing figures. Its impact is emotional, visceral the GAA is more than a sports' organisation, it is national trust, an entity which we feel we hold in common ownership.[78]

In the light of Richard Holt's comment that 'the formation and early history of the GAA is arguably the most striking instance of politics shaping sport in modern history'[79] it is surprising how few historians have tackled the GAA as an individual topic of investigation. It is dealt with in a multitude of modern Irish history monographs[80] and then always in its political context, but I would argue that there are few academics who have turned their attention to the GAA as a specific subject. Although there is some discussion of the history of physical education in Ireland after the foundation of the Irish Free State in 1921, which is well worthy of examination, it only mentions the GAA in passing, and so has not been considered here.[81] Those examined here are W.F. Mandle, Paul Rouse, John Sugden and Alan Bairner, and Michael Mullan. In addition to the actual dearth of academic work on the GAA, there is the concomitant problem that those works which have been produced have largely supported the version of history as outlined in the previous section, that is, one that primarily stresses or examines the nationalist dynamic in the foundation and success of the GAA and does not focus equally on wider social, economic or specifically sporting reasons behind its ongoing popularity.

Mandle's book[82] is the most important work ever produced which details the history of the Association and should always be a first point of reference for anyone studying the area. Despite this the book does have real faults in terms of its focus. On the jacket it is stated that Mandle's book recognises that 'the appeal of the GAA was also partly that of muscular Christianity which at that time, was sweeping the British Empire … as a sporting body it was a great success, tapping wells of nationalism and the developing interest in sport as mass entertainment'.[83] Within this statement there is the hint of wider dynamics beyond the national struggle encouraging the growth of the GAA. Despite the hint, Mandle's book concentrates exclusively on the GAA as part of the nationalist struggle and any alternative reasons behind the growth of the GAA are restricted to a single discussion during the text.[84] Although the work is not written in the same triumphant manner as those works by adherents of the GAA, Mandle fails to explore the Association in any terms other than as a movement which is mobilized and then embraces nationalism as its sole *raison d'être*. It is a history of the radical IRB as much as it is a history of the GAA. In Mandle's opinion it seems that the GAA is nothing without nationalism and vice versa. Ideas of social changes, communication improvements, codification, the amateur ethic and muscular Christianity have no place in Mandle's history. What is surprising is that many of these themes were advanced in an earlier piece of work by the same author.[85] In this work Mandle extends his vision beyond the political dimension of the Association and embraces some of the themes later absent in his book. In one key sentence he encapsulates much that is absent four years later, writing 'but not even the GAA, founded, manipulated and sustained, first by the IRB, later by the nationalist movement as a whole, could escape the wider influences that came from its being located within the United Kingdom. The sports revolution that codified and organized so many traditional games, and invented new ones, was British, even an English phenomenon'.[86] Taking nothing away from the importance of Mandle's book, I would argue that as a total coverage of the reasons behind the inspiration for and continued success of the GAA, the earlier piece has a far greater resonance, and, as such, will be referred to in greater detail later.

The work of Paul Rouse is one of the best pieces ever published on the GAA. His article concentrates specifically on the development and retention of a ban on foreign sports and uniformed personnel.[87] By examining the history of the ban Rouse is able to demonstrate how fluid the whole debate surrounding the Association and political nationalism actually was in the period up to 1921. He shows clearly how many of the custodians of the GAA, whose work is outlined above, manipulated the past in an attempt to justify contemporary actions. As Rouse states 'the ban was seen as the ultimate expression of the GAA's intimate association with nationalism. For its supporters, the nationalist ethos implicit in the continued acceptance of the ban was essential to the growth of the organisation. Indeed, they regarded this nationalism as being of even greater importance than the games themselves within the context of the movement's progress'[88] Throughout his article Rouse, while accepting the importance of links between the GAA and political nationalism, is prepared to challenge this contention and questions whether there are wider reasons for the success of the GAA as a sporting body. The history that Rouse observes is far more contested than that put forward by GAA loyalists. Nationalism is not an all-encompassing and central life force for the GAA, but rather an important weapon in a far bigger armoury. Ultimately however, the article is still centred, albeit critically, on nationalism as the defining force in the growth of the GAA.

Sugden and Bairner's[89] book is, despite the title, essentially an examination of sport in Northern Ireland and as such has to tackle the difficult links between a nationalist history and the lived reality of the Northern troubles. It is a vitally important text, yet one which has to deal with the same problems as those as Ó Maolfabhail, how to separate contemporary manifestations and constructs of nationalism in Northern Ireland from the history of the Irish revolution and the stated aims of the GAA? The historical coverage of the GAA from the 1880s through to the foundation of the state is straight-forward and concentrates on the development of Gaelic games as a manifestation of a national sport in the context of a reawakened nation. Again, as with Mandle, the main focus is concerned with political dynamics and there is only the briefest acknowledgement of other forces which explain the success of the Association.[90] As the subject of the book is Northern Ireland, the majority of the Gaelic Games chapter concentrates on the Association during the period of the troubles. The coverage which Sugden and Bairner offer has to place the historical mission of the GAA, that is a thirty-two county nationalism, in the context of a long running armed struggle in which the IRA are fighting for the same stated aim. It is therefore entirely understandable and correct that the work examines how the activities of the GAA encroach into the politics of the Northern situation and vice versa. However, in the light of the stated aims of this book which seeks to understand the GAA in terms functioning alongside the specifically political, Sugden and Bairner's work has to be criticised in the same way as other academics', as they stress politically defined nationalism as the primary force behind the emergence and continued success of the GAA.

Michael Mullan's work[91] is important as it suggests an alternative framework for the evolution of the GAA as a modern sporting body in Ireland. Mullan accepts the centrality of the nationalist explanation but states that his economic approach 'does not intend to suggest economic factors as primary in GAA history – simply, what is presented here suggests as set of plausible social and economic connections which have been previously overlooked'.[92] Mullan's investigation of the bifurcation of Irish Sport details how economic development in Ireland, which differed from the English model of industrialisation, has a concomitant effect on the development of Irish sport. Without industrialisation key class developments fail to take place which leaves the way clear for the development of the GAA rather than an Irish adoption of so-called garrison games. Mullan's work needs greater empirical detail in order that his central argument might become definitive rather than speculative, but as with the ideas which are suggested below, by opening a wider agenda for understanding the early development of the GAA, Mullan has performed a vital service.

It is clear that the written history of the GAA sees nationalism as the major force in the development and spread of Gaelic Games. Historians who have examined the Association have hinted at wider forces which contributed to the development of the GAA, yet they have rarely been prepared to sacrifice the primacy of the nationalist explanation in favour of a sustained exploration of these other contributory forces. This despite Sugden and Bairner's comment that 'the birth of the GAA and the codification of Gaelic sports which followed can be regarded both as a nationalist reaction against English influence and as a product of the athletic revolution which had been pioneered by the British'.[93] Before the specifics of the Irish situation are examined in any detail it is necessary to highlight the well known and commonly agreed major developments that occurred in Britain during the late nineteenth century. It is then possible to observe at what level the British experience is unconsciously duplicated in Ireland, whether the British experience is specifically used as a guiding model by those who led the GAA during its early years, and if the GAA is indeed the product of forces specifically Irish.

The development of modern sport is well documented and the process which saw the British middle and upper classes take the decision that it was 'consequently considered a Christian and patriotic duty to marginalize him [the working class professional] as far as possible and to this end ... set about re-regulating each sport in order to exclude them'[94] led to the emergence of organized regulatory sporting bodies in the nineteenth century. These included the formation of the Football Association in 1863, the Rugby Football Union in 1871, the Amateur Athletic Association and the Amateur Boxing Association in 1880 and the Amateur Rowing Association in 1882 amongst others. It is important to note that the establishment of all these bodies predates the establishment of the GAA. Equally it is worth remembering that Ireland was still part of the Union at this stage so all these bodies were present in Ireland and were not just mainland organisations.

The emergence of modern organized sport in nineteenth-century Britain was a result of a combination of factors.[95] To encapsulate the main themes it can be argued that social and economic changes, such as the introduction of the Ten Hours Act, had led to an increased availability of leisure time and universal access to cheap transport was affording extra opportunities for players and spectators to follow their chosen sport across an ever-wider area. The belief that sport was good for mind and body, an ideal promoted by the champions of muscular Christianity, was encouraged in public schools and universities across the country and later passed down to all sections of society. The amateur versus professional debate, although contentious, focused minds on the future of sport and led to either compromise, as with football, or division, as in the case of rugby's Northern Union. The need to make sport, at whatever level, more accessible, less violent and more attractive to spectators produced increased levels of codification and regulation that made the majority of sports truly national.

If this simplistic history can be used to identify the emergence of British sporting norms, all of which were imbued with an imperialistic and public school arrogance, what then of the Irish experience? Whereas Britain was a modernized industrial and imperial nation by the end of the nineteenth century, Ireland (with the exception of Ulster) was still predominantly unmodernized and based around small- and medium-sized farms with agriculture the dominant means of production. The long-term effects of the Great Famine still plagued Ireland, most notably in terms of population decline 'a decline unmatched in any other European country in the nineteenth century, a decline that lasted in Ireland as a whole until the 1900s'.[96] The absence of modernising forces across most of Ireland meant that many of the social and economic changes, which would empower the sporting revolution in Britain, were absent. Although Ireland, as part of the United Kingdom, was legislated for under such key innovations as the Ten Hours Act, the nature of work was so different that the Act was relevant for only a small proportion of Irish workers. For many workers in Ireland subsistence agriculture remained the main method of work, and social changes, which led in Britain to a regimented working day and specified leisure time, did not have a great impact. The only genuine leisure time the majority of the Irish actually had was linked with Sunday as a day of worship and the observance of such was closely controlled by the Catholic Church. Religion was another key difference between Ireland and Britain. Whereas the mainland had undergone a process of secularisation and witnessed challenges to the established Church, catholicism dominated Ireland, again with the exception of Ulster. This becomes important within the history of the GAA. Whereas in Britain sport is applauded as a positive force in instilling Christian values in young men but not promoted by the Church in any sustained manner,[97] the early years of the GAA are sponsored and at times controlled by the Catholic Church. It is also important that the GAA takes for its model of organisation the Church's parish structure. In this way, not only organisation, but also rivalries and competitions are based around commonly recognized Church structures.

The class structure, as far as one existed in Ireland at the time, did not play the same role in the growth of organized sport as it does in Britain. The majority of major British sports originate amongst a public school and university elite and were then spread across the nation by former pupils and students. In turn many clubs, which were established in working-class areas, were initially sponsored by or directly connected with factories and their owners. In Ireland this situation could not exist. The only major structure similar to the public school or university was Trinity College Dublin. Generally there was not the same industrial paternalism to encourage work-sponsored sport. The elites in Ireland, predominantly made up of the Anglo-Irish, rather than encouraging common sporting pastimes as a way of instilling positive values amongst lower classes, actively distanced themselves from them. In the eighteenth century it was common practice for mass hurling games to be organized and paid for by the aristocracy as a method of facilitating gambling.[98] By the late nineteenth century, and in the face of land agitation, the effects of the famine and a loss of wealth, the landed, moneyed and small industrial elite had no interest in encouraging the leisure of the masses. The sports which these elites pursued, such as hunting or shooting, were totally exclusive to those with wealth. Any team sports such as football, rugby or hurley were conducted on an exclusive basis inside the walls of elitist bastions such as Trinity College. The separation on the playing field mirrored the separation that existed in Irish life between different political, religious and economic groups.

If the general level of modernisation and the specific nature of Irish society are seen as different to that of Britain, then how can the successful emergence of the GAA, a modern sports organisation, be explained? Undoubtedly
one of the main reasons behind the Association's success is the appropriation
of political nationalism as part of the GAA's function. This is undisputed and
has, as demonstrated earlier, been well explored by previous writers. It is my
contention that there are other equally important factors which lie behind the
rise of the GAA. These factors (codification and so on), such a central part of
the success of British sporting organisation, were harnessed by the GAA even
in the absence of a modernized society. This in turn brings into question
whether organized sport is specifically a product of modernity as has often
been believed, or if it can flourish under pre-modern conditions as the GAA
appears to have done in Ireland.

The GAA was founded at the beginning of November 1884 in Thurles
and by 17 January 1885 the first set of rules were adopted and publicized. The
speed with which a standard set of rules emerged, despite the small initial
membership of the Association, is a tribute to the foresight of men such as
Michael Cusack and Maurice Davin who had believed from the outset that
codification was central to the success of a national sporting body. Davin
wrote in October 1884

> I am much pleased to see that you take an interest in Irish Athletics. It
> is time a handbook was published with rules & c., for all Irish games.
> The English handbooks of athletics are very good in their way but they
> do not touch as many of the Irish games which, although much prac-
> tised are not included in the events on programmes of athletic sports ...
> Irish football is a great game and worth going a long way to see, when
> played on a fairly laid out ground and under proper rules. Many old
> people say that hurling exceeded it as a trial of men. I may say that
> there are no rules and therefore those games are often dangerous. I am
> anxious to see both games revived under regular rules.[99]

After the agreement of the initial rules, which would govern all the games
played under the auspices of the GAA, further changes and refinements were
quickly introduced. The initial rules promoted by Cusack were drawn from his
own experiences as a school teacher conducting games for boys and incorpo-
rated a number of features of the traditional rough-and-tumble game. As many
of the features of the old games were considered excessively violent the GAA
went through a similar debate to that played out in Britain about practices on
the rugby field. Changes were made quickly. The previously unlimited running
with the ball was reduced to not more than four steps after each individual

catch. New scoring innovations were introduced. The original goalposts with cross bars were established and contest results were determined solely on a majority of goal scores. To improve the standard and speed of play the gradual reduction of team numbers took place from the original twenty-one a side down to seventeen in 1892. This was further reduced to fifteen in 1913. The constant refinements which were introduced into the games, despite the continued battle for control of the GAA between the Church and the IRB, made Gaelic games a much better public spectacle and ensured the increasing popularity with players and spectators alike. O'Sullivan highlights the importance of the rules for the success of the GAA in this period by stating

> all the gradual evolutionary changes in the game have led to improvements in standard and to consequent increased patronage. The Association, in its first decade, suffered from so many dissensions, political and otherwise, that attendances at All-Ireland finals were far from satisfactory [yet] the unfinished replay final in 1894 at Thurles between Cork and Dublin attracted the first record gathering of 10,000.[100]

If the regulation of the new Gaelic games was so important for their success, where did the inspiration for such come from? Men such as Maurice Davin who were so instrumental in the earlier years of the Association, often had a shared past as athletes who had competed under, or at least witnessed the rules and regulations of the AAA. As Davin's letter of October 1884 demonstrates he clearly understood the need for rules if a sporting body was going to be popular and universal. The inspiration for the codification of Gaelic games is undoubtedly British, yet the image of the GAA has always been that it is a specifically Irish organisation. The contradiction is clear in the newspapers of the time. While there is the demand to reinvent Irish pastimes, there is the inherent acknowledgement of the British model as the starting point even though this has to be explicitly rejected in terms of Irish nationalist sentiment.

> The laws under which athletic sports are held in Ireland were designed mainly for the guidance of Englishmen who promote the sports of their own country; that as far as they go, these laws are good in their way so long as they are observed, but they do not deal with all the characteristic sports and pastimes of the Gaelic Race. It therefore became necessary to form an association which would resuscitate our fast fading sources of amusement and draft laws for the guidance of those patriotic enough to devise schemes of recreation for the bulk of the people and more especially for the humble and hardworking who now seem to be born to no other inheritance than an everlasting round of labour.[101]

Within statements such as these the origins of the predominantly nationalist interpretation of the GAA can be observed. Those who campaigned for
the formation of the GAA are caught in a trap. There is a successful British
model to work from, yet within the nationalist mind no facet of Britishness
can ever be embraced. This problem is sanitized in later years by supporters
of the GAA and the British inspiration for rule making put to one side. This
allows writers such as Mehigan to revise history and write

> It is true that the GAA came at a time when athletic revivals were the
> order of the day – in America, Scotland, Britain and Europe. It is also
> true that Michael Cusack and his pioneers had the revival of hurling
> and field athletics in the forefront of their minds. But Cusack sought to
> rally the whole nation in his mighty plan of social regeneration with full
> national freedom as the ultimate goal. In wide areas of rural Ireland
> Hurling was only a memory, while an Irish form of football had close
> adherents. The first President of the GAA – Mr Maurice Davin – and
> his brothers were well known footballers. And so the GAA leaders set
> about drafting Football rules to suit their purpose. They sought to
> build up the new game on the old foundations, retaining as many of its
> characteristics as possible and at the same time establishing a set of
> rules keeping the game different from imported codes that were rapid-
> ly getting a grip in the land, especially in the cities, towns and colleges.
> The GAA sought to combat such an environment and foreign influ-
> ence.[102]

The contradiction, present in the 1880s, is banished by the mid-twentieth
century in the minds of the GAA supporters. Despite this Mandle is quite
clear in his statement that 'the British model was faithfully followed'.[103] In
understanding the contemporary climate of the 1880s, and ignoring the written history of the GAA, the clear conclusion has to be that the founders and
early leaders of the Association, while promoting Irishness, had to model
themselves around a successful British experiment.

One of the major reasons behind the initial spread of organized games,
rugby and cricket in particular, in nineteenth-century Britain was the cult of
muscular Christianity and the embrace of manliness as a worthy value. As
Tony Collins has noted, 'While its origins [rugby] at the schools may be
unclear, there is little doubt as to a key reason for football's popularity among
the boys who played it or the partisans of muscular Christianity who championed it – its violent appeal to masculinity'.[104] In Britain the men who would
lead sport into its organized and codified forms were predominantly ex-public
school boys who had grown up with a set of sporting values which revolved

around the righteousness of games that were imbued with a sense of Christian and manly values.[105] The founders of the GAA in Ireland did not have public school backgrounds yet the ethos of the early years of the games clearly possesses similar values. However, as with the development of rules, the Irish adoption of muscular Christianity and manliness, although a copy British ideals, is presented as having a clearly Irish dimension.

In 1886, Revd Dr O'Callaghan, bishop of Cork stated that, 'the national game of hurling was an excellent one for Irish boys. It was a clean and manly sport that built up the frame and taught self-reliance and self-control'.[106] Statements from the clergy in support of Gaelic games were common through-out the first decade of the Association's existence. Clerical support received wide spread publicity in those newspapers that gave space to the emergence of the Association. *United Ireland* was at the forefront of this pattern as the follow-ing, one of many similar statements from 1885 demonstrates

> the GAA ought, to, from a moral point of view be hailed with welcome. It will furnish our young men with wholesome outdoor exercise, as opportunity offers, and detach them from those dangerous occasions incident to leisure time spent in towns. We commend Fr McMahon's words to the careful consideration of all who are interested in the preservation of strength, agility, morals and manhood of our people.[107]

Father McMahon's comments exhibit the central themes which were commonly used in support of the games. The activities of the GAA were applauded as they encouraged a manliness which was imbued with the values of muscular Christianity. This is further reinforced by a rejection of urbanisa-tion and its inherent dangers, while celebrating the purity of the simple rural life. The qualities of the rural over the urban are located in an imagined Gaelic past which predated the forces of West Britonism where honest hard work and toil on the land resulted in a morally superior Irish race. The adop-tion of muscular Christianity and manliness as part of the GAA's mission undoubtedly underpinned Irish nationalism in the same way that such forces underpinned the strength of British imperialism. By experiencing hard knocks on the playing field the Gaelic athlete prepared themselves for the longer-term struggle for Irish nationalist aspirations. The pursuit of muscular Christianity on the pitch, which gave the games and its players a moral right-eousness, was carried forward onto the future and imagined battlefield. This idea is not one that is later constructed in the written history of the GAA but a contemporary reality and advanced as early as 1884.

> The strength and energy of a race are largely dependent on national pastimes for the development of a spirit of courage and endurance. A

warlike race is ever fond of games requiring skill, strength and staying power. The best games of such a race are never free from danger'.[108]

It appears that the ethos of the early years of the GAA championed the values of muscular Christianity and manliness in a similar fashion to British sports. Although the inspiration is different and hedged in Irish terms, it does appear that the founders and supporters of the GAA were adopting values originally championed in British public schools.

Alongside muscular Christianity and manliness, the public school ethos, which lay behind so many British sports, championed the value of the fair play ethic. The British experience of this ethic has been well explored by Mangan[109] but has been absent from any work on Gaelic games. It is unsurprising that the fair play ethic exists in Gaelic games as it is so much a part of the introduction of rules and the supposed moral value of sport. What is important in the Irish example is that the fair play ethic is valued not only for its inherent worth, but as a way of rejecting the British construction of the Irish character. Much work has been carried out on the negative nature of Victorian constructions of the Irish race, which depicts them as having a simian appearance and possessing such negative character traits such as a tendency to violence, a lack of respect for the law, laziness and drunkenness.[110] These constructs are widespread in British journals such as *Punch* and *The London Illustrated News* and even find their way across the Atlantic to appear in *Harper's Weekly*.

Gaelic games, despite the rules introduced to control them, were violent in the same way as rugby and did not possess the gentility of soccer or cricket. As such fair play became important as a way to control the violence which could creep into the games. The newspapers of the period were well aware of how important a good attitude on the pitch was for the long-term success of the games.

> The first tournament of the season took place at Turloughmore on Sunday last and the measure of success that attended it augurs well for the reorganisation of the association and the revival and practice of its manly pastimes in the county of Galway. If there is anything that can give an impetus to the progress of the movement it is undoubtedly the assembly together in a friendly rivalry of the different clubs who wield the camán. The games were spirited and exciting and the demeanour of the players towards each other was of the most amiable and good-humoured sort. A very pleasing feature of the entire proceedings was the absence of every kind of disorderly conduct.[111]

Accompanying the celebration of the fair-play ethic as a way of ensuring the future of the games there was also the need to tackle the British stereotype of the Irish. By playing games cleanly and with good temper, despite the inherently violent nature of the hurling and Gaelic football, the GAA could dismiss the British caricature. The Victorian mind would expect to see the Irish at play descend into the violence which the British usually connected with men from the Emerald Isle. This was not the case and newspaper correspondents were delighted to report games played in good spirit and they explicitly rejected the normal construct of Irish nature.

> We trust the men of North Tipperary will not forget that nothing would give our enemies greater pleasure than to hear that the hot blood of the premier county would reach boiling point under the excitement of a game which is at once congenial and warlike and that in consequence ill feeling, if not broken heads and factious feuds, would be the necessary outcome of the revival of an ancient and time honoured pastime not unworthy of a vigorous and warlike race. We ought to take a special delight in disappointing our enemies when we can do so by abstaining from what are practically crimes against the country for which we have proven our love for by making many sacrifices.[112]

Mark Tierney echoes the tenor of such reports in his biography of Archbishop Croke, the first patron of the GAA. Tierney explains that the Irish has a reputation of being uncontrollable, evidenced by the endless coercion acts which were applied to Ireland during the late nineteenth century.[113] The British caricature of the Irish had been realized by the activities of the Fenian movement, both in Ireland and on the mainland, and outrages connected with the Land War did nothing to dispel such an image. With the advent of rules to govern Gaelic games and the intense awareness of the value of the fair play ethic the Association was able to deflect the criticism of their sports which could have easily emerged from such an accepted construct of the Irish.

I have attempted to demonstrate how the written history of the GAA is dominated by a history that links the successful growth of Gaelic games with the forces of Irish nationalism. This is only part of the picture. In the future historians who choose to look at the Association need to develop the themes which have been set out here and pursue the links between the successful development of codified sport in Ireland and the British inspiration for such. I fully accept that these British inspirations are repackaged so that they can be presented in nationalist terms, but British they are. The wider conclusions which need further examination are that the Irish experience demonstrates just how successful the British experiment with modern sport was and how easily it could be adapted in other countries in respect of 'foreign' games, and that Ireland could successfully adopt the rules, organisation and social inspirations behind modern sport without being a modernized nation. It seems that the custodians of the GAA in the late nineteenth century were indeed fighting for the cause of Irish nationalism while playing an Irish game based on a British ideal.

THE NATIONAL GAME?

While attempting to locate Gaelic games within its own historiography, and question how far it can be seen as a genuinely Irish product, this chapter has to examine whether Gaelic games are truly the 'national game'. It is clear that the games themselves and the GAA as an organisation are centrally important for the transmission of a sense of national identity and the construction of an Irish nationalism, but just how representative are these particular forms?

One of the problems for Gaelic games is that they can never be an international game. Although the Irish have organized events such as the 1924, 1928 and 1932 Tailteann Games as a form of Celtic Olympiad that have set Gaelic athletes representing Ireland against athletes from other nations, these internationalized expressions for Gaelic games have been few and far between. As a result, many of the forms and methods of nationalism in sport that were detailed and illustrated in chapter three, cannot be applied to Gaelic games. How can a sport that is devoid of genuine international competition represent the nation?

This is a problem that the GAA has long been aware of, yet one which has remained rarely addressed in practice and seemingly unsolvable.[114] Yet to dismiss Gaelic games as a medium of nationalism because it does not have an Olympics, a World Cup or even a world championships, would be foolhardy. Just because the international route is not open, this does not mean that Gaelic games become meaningless and value free. As Allen Guttmann has noted,

> traditionalists insist, however, that talk of the possible contribution of sports to nation building misses the point. For them, modern sports are a form of cultural domination and ludic diffusion is tantamount to the imperialist of hegemonic destruction of authentic native cultural forms.[115]

Gaelic games are held up as the traditional games of the Irish nation and race with a long and glorious history that stretches back into the depths of time. Yet, in understanding Guttmann's argument there has to be a realisation that the very origins of Gaelic games are problematic. On the one hand it is true that they have ancient roots that locate the games in Ireland's historic soil, yet the very organisation of the games shows all the hallmarks of a process of ludic diffusion. While not British sports, Gaelic games are run and organized on British lines, and thus they were subjected to the cultural domination of the late nineteenth century. However, as they are only an Irish sport, Gaelic games avoid the hegemonic destruction of a native culture, as the style of play, the invented history and the very isolation of the games reject the historic process of British imperialism and the more modern phenomenon of globalisation.

What are Gaelic games then? Are they the national game, and thus truly representative of Irish nationalism? Or are they a mere local affair, a sport without a national team and thus one that can stress no more than a parochial nationalism? Or, do they represent a vigorous form of nationalism, which, although having no international outlet, is fascinating as it represents Ireland's ability to avoid the forces of ludic diffusion?

The short answer is that Gaelic games are all and some of these. Gaelic games, at the time of their very inception were an invention. Although forms of hurling and football existed, Cusack, Davin and later the forces of the IRB, transformed the games into a national game from a low point of weakness in the sphere of domestic Irish sport. In this, the creation of the GAA, a sporting body with a national mission, is similar to the creation of the sporting Republic in America. As Mark Dyreson has argued

> sport was made or invented, to serve a purpose. That purpose had an intimate connection to the construction of an American team – a national identity for the United States. In making an American team, Americans invented a sporting republic ... Sport was an invention designed to meet certain political goals.[116]

The point that Dyreson makes encapsulates the purposes of the GAA perfectly. Even Cusack, cultural nationalist though he was, realized that a body such as the GAA would serve a political function in underpinning the forces of political nationalism. Once the identification with political nationalism had been made through the selection of patrons and infiltration by the IRB, the GAA existed to meet a political goal: to mobilize men and women in an Irish cultural movement that tied them to support for the vision of an Irish Republic. As has been shown, this political function is one that the GAA has performed throughout its history, and, in this respect at least, the GAA has to be seen as the national game. It is national in the sense that it sees as its function a political goal, support for a thirty-two county Ireland, the statist concept of nationalism, while also appealing to the mythic and subrational forces of nationalism by its incantation of the mythology of the fourth 'green field' idea.

One of the problems in constructing Gaelic games as representative of the nation is that, as previously mentioned, they cannot be international. While accepting that this clearly dents their ability to represent the nation as they can never, unlike soccer, field those eleven men dressed in green, Gaelic games are not a parochial form of nationalism precisely because they have avoided the international scene. International sport is highly important in the construction of national values and stereotypes as it measures 'us' against 'them'. Gaelic games cannot do this as they only measure, at the highest level, county against county. International sport, however, does have a problem. The very fact that it is global, commonly recognized and played by the same rules, produces a great deal of homogeneity. Although there can be discussions relating to national styles, no one nation can actually distinguish itself and claim that it is different in the sporting field, if they are all playing the same game. England may claim to be, as it did during the 1996 European Soccer Championships, the home of soccer ('football's coming home', so said the song), but it can only ever be a historical originator. It can never be the home, as soccer is universal. The strength of Gaelic games, the very peculiarity of its parochial nationalism, is that it allows Ireland to say to the rest of the world, 'this is us, this is our game'. This nationalism, as with the stridently political nationalism of the GAA, has its origins in 1884. Croke's letter accepting the invite to become patron, and Cusack's own rationale of why such a body as the GAA was needed, was self-definition against Britain, a desire that Ireland could say that it was different. The strength of the GAA and its ability to represent a form of Irish nationalism in the late nineteenth century, that is, one that was distinct from West Britonism, is the same strength it still possesses in that it is distinct from global sporting culture.

The root of the distinctiveness of Gaelic games lies in its self-definition against Britain. While that is an understandable motivation in the context of Anglo-Irish politics in the late 1880s, it challenges many of the common models for the spread of modern sports. It is here, I would argue, in an understanding of one of the great debates of sports history, that a real grasp of Gaelic games' place as the national game can be understood.

Johan Galtung wrote that in dealing with sport, 'we are probably dealing with one of the most powerful transfer mechanisms for culture and structure ever known to humankind'.[117] Galtung's argument is that sport, as a shared process between all genders, classes, nations and abilities, and one that is based on body language not linguistics, is the most universally shared pursuit in the world and thus the most powerful. The bulk of his argument revolves around common sports and sporting events. If his basic point is accepted, that sport is a powerful transfer mechanism, then applied to the GAA some important issues arise. Sport has all the powers Galtung mentions when competing against all the other themes within a global and nationally competitive world. Yet the GAA has no competition, internally or externally. It exists in splendid isolation. As a result it has historically been able to use all the powers of sport to transfer its own version of culture and structure, in their case Irish nationalism, to a captive audience, which until the 1960s, had little recourse to other sporting organisations.

Brian Stoddart has argued that, 'the most neglected agency in the process of cultural transfer from Britain to her colonial empire is that which involved sports and games'.[118] In the context of empire Stoddart is echoing the point made by Galtung that in history one of the most powerful forms of agency is sport. Stoddart went on to conclude that sport was not only a powerful agency for the spread of British ideas, but that the features of empire that were passed onto the colonies through sport survived into the postcolonial era. While I have attempted to show that the GAA was, at one level, part of this process as it modelled itself on the norms of British codified sport, there is one unique difference about the Irish case. The majority of colonial nations adapted British habits, cultures and structures by playing expressly British sports such as cricket and rugby, and by playing a part in institutions such as the Empire Games and the Commonwealth Games. Ireland denied this part of the British presence and its legacy. The nation did not (until late on) take to soccer and use it as a way of winning that morale-boosting victory over the British, nor did Ireland play in any great way cricket or rugby. If Trinity College Dublin and Ulster are removed from the equation, it is safe to say that the British sporting legacy in Ireland was weaker than in any other colonial nation. Such a bold statement should also be placed in the context of Ireland's geographical and constitutional position. It is not a nation that is on the other side of the globe with a small British population. It is a short hop across the Irish sea and formally, until 1921 part of the Union. The GAA is worthy of respect in that it effectively caused the failure of British colonialism in the sporting arena, a failure that other nationalist groups around the globe were unable to duplicate.

Away from the specific force of colonialism, is the greater force, especially in the minds of many sports historians, of ludic diffusion. Put simply, ludic diffusion is the process whereby sports and games are transferred to other parts of the globe by virtue of cultural imperialism. The actual medium may be a formalized imperialism such as the British empire, or else in the modern era may be the global spread of a multinational such as Nike or the NBA spreading the basketball message around the world. Allen Guttmann has offered the clearest account of the process.[119] A model of ludic diffusion was offered in the groundbreaking work of J.A. Mangan[120] and is still to be found in recent work on imperial cricket.[121] Within the process of ludic diffusion the great championing of the national arrives when any given nation adopts the imported game to their own national style, a process that is completed when they defeat the relevant colonial force on the field of play. It is a model that has a great deal of value, yet clearly fails to work in Ireland. Rugby union is still played only in specific regions of Ireland, and soccer, as will be shown in the next chapter, only captured the public imagination in the 1960s, and yet has still failed to gain a credible domestic foothold in the Republic. The only mass sports in Ireland are the Gaelic games. Ireland has resisted the process of both British imperialism and general ludic diffusion. Gaelic games are traditional sports that have survived the twentieth century, have adapted to the various forces of modernity (sponsorship, media, paying spectators and so on), yet remain as a successful representation of an Irish sport.[122]

Allen Guttmann concluded his coverage of what he called 'resistance' to ludic diffusion by engaging with the work of Henning Eichberg. Eichberg is a supporter of the traditional ideal of games. Guttmann notes that Eichberg has predicted that modern sports that reinforce an age of Western colonial dominance will eventually come to an end, and that as people reject the circus-like mentality of modern sports they will return to their own 'festivals revealing their own patterns, their own traditions'.[123] One feels that Guttmann, while respecting Eichberg's intellectual abilities, is far from convinced. Yet surely the GAA's continued existence, their steady popularity and their ability to still be seen as a definition of Irish culture and traditions, proves Eichberg's point. While the GAA is in no way comparable to Eichberg's own example of the Inuit games of northern Canada, the force of traditionalism is still present. Guttmann argued that traditional games become modern games as they take on the characteristics of modernity. The religious significance of the game becomes residual, a bureaucratic machinery emerges to run the sport, performances are maximized and television takes over.[124] While many, if not all of these processes have taken place in the context of the GAA, they remain traditional games. The twin gods of the GAA at the time of its formation were nationalism and self-definition against Britain. Those gods still exist. As chapter six demonstrates, the GAA is dominated by nationalism to this day and self-definition is still enforced through the symbolism and rules of the Association such as rule 21. It is a game that is linked to the blood and soil of Ireland and to the force of Irish nationalism. To this day the names of Gaelic grounds across Ireland are remembrances of the traditional, of the Irish giants of politics and religion. 33 per cent of grounds are named after political figures (55 per cent of whom were active during the revolutionary period of 1916–22) while another 33 per cent have names related to religious figures.[125] Gaelic games have been used by the Irish state to create a sense of nationhood. In the days following independence the new state radio station, 2RN, used sport as a method of identifying a modern form of communication with traditional games.[126] The whole process of broadcasting to the nation linked the games of the GAA with a newly unified nation. As Raymond Boyle commented, 'the media played [a role] in constructing sport as part of the national psyche that ultimately reinforced the dominant political system'.[127] It is unthinkable that the newly founded Irish state could have used anything but a traditional form of recreation to connect sport with the ideals of the state.

To understand Gaelic games as a powerful force that resisted imperialism and ludic diffusion is to rationalize why they represent a vigorous form of nationalism, why they deserve the title of the national game. The next chapter will offer an assessment of the role of soccer in promoting and representing notions of Irish nationalism. It will be suggested that soccer does indeed form an important part of the definition of nationalism, but that it is a nationalism which is different to the nationalism presented by Gaelic games. Soccer is not the national game of Ireland. It is an imported game that is poorly supported within the domestic environment. Its resonance and importance is that it offers that image of the national on the international stage in a manner that Gaelic games cannot. The two sports have developed differently and have separate histories. While one sport, Gaelic games, has always been in a position of dominance in defining the national, both contribute to the idea of nationalism as nationalism itself, is, as defined in chapter two, a multifaceted and mobile force. With the growth of support for soccer in recent years the position of Gaelic games as the national game, although not seriously threatened, has, in some quarters, been questioned. The problem for Ireland is coping with the co-exisiting demands of the modern and the requirements of the traditional. James Riordan offers some salient advice that should be heeded in Gaelic games circles, 'Western sports and local games often provide an unstable mixture; and it is a long haul to revive folk games. The corrosive effect of Western sports and values is hard to withstand, especially as traditional games emerged from and reflected a pre-industrial, patriarchal and ritualistic pattern of life'.[128]

Gaelic games have a long history and have played a central role in definitions of Irish nationalism. It is a nationalism that is the product of an historical connection with the force of political nationalism and the demand for separation from Britain. It is not the nationalism that was projected by the original founders of the GAA, nor is it a nationalism that was projected successfully to the population by Irish means alone. It is a nationalism that has often been immobile over the decades, one that has been supported by writers and left unchallenged by academics. It is above all, however, a nationalism expressed through a sport which is highly exciting, immensely popular and one that should be seen as central to a large section of the Irish population.

5 / Soccer

In this new era of peace and reconciliation, in this year of righting wrongs, on the crest of this tidal wave of change, the only option for politically correct republicans is to be out there cheering for Glen Hoddle and his boys.[1]

Give it a lash Jack.[2]

His Excellency, the Lord Lieutenant was present and in arriving without any semblance of State was very heartily cheered. The band of the West Ridings played the National Anthem, Ireland's own bands apparently having some difficulty about the inclusion of God Save the King in their programme. This is another example of that spirit which cannot allow even sport to be uncontaminated by hostility to everything dear to the King's loyal subjects.[3]

Soccer in Ireland, especially amongst followers of the Gaelic games, has always been viewed, as the secondary game of the country, something that is inferior, yet has to be tolerated. As a domestic game, soccer has had far more importance in the north of Ireland, and it is there that the most extreme examples of the politics of nationalism impinging upon, and shaping, that particular sport can be found. These will be discussed in full in the next chapter. The focus here is international football, and most importantly the recent history of the Republic of Ireland squad, which has both contributed to and represented the rapidly changing ideas and multifaceted nature of Irish nationalism. The speed of recent change in Irish politics and the success of the peace process led the *Irish News* to suggest, tongue-in-cheek, that a good modern republican should cheer on England in the 1998 World Cup Finals as there was no Irish representation. Joking aside, it is unimaginable that a paper that is so representative of the force of Irish nationalism would have ever suggested such a thing prior to 1998. Supporting England, in anything, was tantamount to betrayal. In the same way that Irish Republicans have long suggested that England's danger is Ireland's opportunity, in sport, England's opponents were Ireland's heroes! The *Irish News* suggestion is indicative of the whole shift that has taken place in recent years with regard to the mobility of Irish nationalism and its retreat from dogma, especially amongst many Northern Irish nationalists.

The 1990 and 1994 World Cup Finals demonstrated the changing nature of Irish nationalism, in the Republic and amongst the Irish diaspora. They could all celebrate a successful Irish team drawn from the families of the diaspora, playing a non-traditional (even foreign) game on a world stage, and managed by an Englishman. Despite these anomalies, the Irish Republic's football team became representative of a new nationalism.

The mobile, forward-looking and inclusive versions of Irish nationalism presented through soccer in the 1990s, contrast sharply to the longer history of the game in the island. In 1913 (and on many other international occasions) the playing of the 'wrong' national anthem caused problems for Irish nationalists. They were expected, prior to 1921, to cheer on an Irish team that was representative of the Union and their place within it. With such problems, and the GAA's ban on foreign games, soccer had a difficult early life. On one hand it expressed all the nationalist fervour of any sporting or cultural institution, yet at the same time fellow sportsmen and Irishmen denounced it from within.

This chapter seeks to explore the history of soccer, its place within Irish life, and how it has contributed to the construction and representation of Irish nationalism. Such a process does pose difficulties. While the written history of the GAA is small, the written history of Irish soccer is minuscule by comparison. Those who have attempted to write any history of soccer in Ireland have either been enthusiasts or sporting journalists. There has been little, if any, academic treatment from an historical perspective either as a whole study of the sport or through a passing mention in a wider study. What has emerged in recent years is a strong strand of ethnographically driven sociological study of the impact of the Republic of Ireland's recent success and the supporters that have followed the team.[4] While using elements of the history of Irish soccer here to understand how the game has coloured Irish nationalism, the coverage is not intended to be, or designed as a history of the game. That work should form the wider agenda of a general sporting history of Ireland.

ORIGINS

Soccer has a long history in Ireland and writers such as Sugden and Bairner have located its origins in the game of Cad. This ball game, played across open countryside was common place in Ireland over 1000 years ago. The Statues of Kilkenny did not ban cad, nor was it listed in the 1527 laws that banned all games that diverted people from archery practice.[5] In the eighteenth century a ball game was widely played inside and beyond the Pale. In

Oxmantown, Kilmainham, Milltown and Drumcondra, Dublin tradesmen played each other frequently. While outside Dublin in 'Kerry, Antrim and Donegal entire villages engaged in massive football matches, driving a pig's bladder or bull's scrotum from one end of the parish to another'.[6] What is difficult to decide is whether Cad and the other large scale folk football games are the precursor of what we now understand as soccer, or whether they form the basis of Gaelic football. Following the J.A. Mangan and Allen Guttmann line of ludic diffusion through public school boys, many writers exploring the Irish situation have seized on the importance of Trinity College in the history of Irish soccer. Arguments are made such as

> during the nineteenth century this [the ball carrying version of football] was replaced in numerous English public schools by a kicking game. Irish pupils at these schools brought this latter form back to Ireland, either during vacations or on completion of their studies.[7]

Though neither seeking to dismiss the notion that such a process may have taken place or that Trinity College was an important centre for the diffusion of foreign tastes and cultures across Ireland, is it really possible that returning public school boys who belong to an elite stratum of Irish society could transfer a game so quickly and readily across Ireland?[8] A country that was so diverse geographically, relatively unmodernized and rife with political and social dislocation as a result of the famine, the ongoing land war and pressure for national reform. That a ball game existed in Ireland in the second half of the nineteenth century is beyond doubt, and partially explains, I would suggest, the success of the Gaelic Athletic Association. However, the GAA's initial growth was based around the success of athletic meetings. Gaelic football would prosper and take root more slowly. The evolution of soccer, also very slow, and far more geographically fragmented than that of Gaelic games, suggests that while a ball game did exist it was not instantaneously nor readily codified, nor did it become quickly and universally popular.

Peter Byrne suggests that the spread of soccer into Ireland had very specific origins, and relied on the ingenuity of one man. He lists John M. McAlery as the father of Irish soccer. McAlery watched soccer in Scotland on his honeymoon and arranged in 1878 for two Scottish teams, Queen's Park and Caledonians, to play an exhibition in Ballymafeigh at the Ulster cricket ground.[9] In 1879 McAlery founded the Cliftonville club, and a year later the Irish Football Association (IFA) was founded. McAlery, who was the honorary secretary of the new Association, wrote at the time of formation if the spirit which pervaded those present be acted upon the result will be a strong Association for promoting the game which we have espoused.[10]

That McAlery and his colleagues served a vital function in the history of Irish soccer is beyond doubt. By establishing a national body to formulate rules and organize competitions the early IFA played a central role in the spread of the game. It organized an annual competition, the Irish Cup from 1881, and the first international match in 1882. The first internationals provided a stark illustration of the relative prowess of Irish soccer. Although the English Football Association had only been formed in 1876, the earlier development, their strength and skill, meant that the 1882 inaugural international for the Irish led to a 13-0 drubbing. The first league championship took place in the 1890–91 season.

The establishment of the IFA is, within the context of the history of codified sport, unsurprising. Britain, only next door, and legally part of the same unit of Union, had led the world in establishing sporting associations and bringing order to various games and sports. An attempt had been made at forming a single Irish athletics body in 1873 with the foundation of the Irish Champion Athletic Club, the Irish Rugby Football Union had been formed in Dublin in 1874 and the GAA had come together in 1884. The establishment of a national soccer body in the centre of all these other developments seems quite unexceptional. What is different however, is that the IFA was the only national sporting body to establish its headquarters in Belfast. It seems clear from the location of the IFA in Belfast, the driving force of northern individuals such as McAlery and the fact that it took until 1883 before a southern team (Dublin Association FC) applied for membership of the IFA, that soccer in Ireland was, in its infant years, a northern-dominated sport.

The northern domination of Irish soccer would ultimately be challenged and broken down. However, the presence of such domination from the outset suggests two things. First, that the supposed role of elite educational institutions such as Trinity College in the spread of soccer in Ireland should be challenged. If Trinity, indeed the whole Anglo-Irish elite, was so important, why then did soccer initially establish itself in Belfast among the industrial and working classes? Why did it take three years for the game to spread, in its codified form, to Dublin? Second, that the location of soccer's headquarters, indeed the whole thrust to have the game established lay with the unionist population.

These two suggested ways of understanding and interpreting the origins of soccer are instrumental in recognising the development of links between soccer and nationalism. As the last years of the nineteenth century passed by,

Irish nationalism became an increasingly potent force. The GAA's use of the ban on foreign games had a huge effect on the growth of soccer, but the ban was essentially symbolic. For many nationalists, soccer, even if it was a game that they may have enjoyed or have had local access to, was a foreign game. As nationalists, the Irish were encouraged to reject all manifestations of West Britonism. Soccer was identifiable with the forces of unionism. In expressing their identity the Irish had to make a choice which sport would be the best vehicle, and in this soccer was unacceptable. All that said, soccer was popular despite appearing identifiable as the preserve of a specific sector of Irish society. As the 1890s progressed soccer became increasingly popular across wider areas of Ireland. The work of Neal Garnham has clearly demonstrated that soccer spread amongst both Catholics and Protestants during the 1890s and was played by a wide mix of social classes. Although geographically weak in many rural areas such as Munster, the game thrived in Belfast, eastern Ulster and Dublin. The most interesting figure offered by Garnham detail how the sports pitches at Phoenix Park in 1906 were dominated by soccer pitches (of 32 available, 29 were laid out for soccer).[11] Despite the steady growth of soccer, and its success in urban areas, it was not able to prosper in the long term. Under different circumstances soccer may well have challenged and even overtaken Gaelic games as the most popular sporting pastime in Ireland. However, Ireland's politics in the twentieth century divided soccer along the lines of partition. Institutionally soccer split and the Football Association of the Irish Free State (FAIFS), despite still being regarded as the organising body for a foreign sport, had to duplicate the process of state formation and stress its nationalism by achieving separation from Northern Ireland.

ALWAYS THE RUNNER-UP?

Soccer in Ireland, despite its growing popularity at the beginning of the twentieth century would be overtaken by events and circumstances which would seriously hinder its ability to organize as a major national sport, and would bring it directly into the sphere of the politics of nationalism.

As the First World War approached, to be followed so soon after by the period of revolution and Civil War in Ireland, soccer was beginning to divide. While many clubs had developed in the south, and Shelbourne and Bohemians had both managed to bring the Irish Cup away from the north, the game was still the preserve of people who identified themselves with the Union, the forces of the British administration and the army. Prompted by arguments regarding the northern bias in the selection of international squads, and in an attempt to encourage the further growth of southern soccer, the IFA sanctioned the creation of the Leinster Football Association on 27 October 1892. The creation of a southern body to govern soccer was a portent of the future. As the forces of nationalism took hold in Ireland, so the Leinster FA became increasingly single minded in its dealings with Belfast. In supporting what was effectively a banned game in the minds of GAA followers and many other political and cultural nationalists, the soccer authorities in southern Ireland had a problem. They did not have the same political and religious views as their counterparts in Belfast, indeed they shared the views of the majority of their countrymen, that Ireland should be free of British control. In the sporting arena this meant that the Leinster FA had to break from Belfast in an attempt to prove its nationalist credentials. If it failed to do this, and attempted to preserve the unity of soccer across the island of Ireland, it would be open to accusations that they were supporters of the garrison game and all the symbolism of West Britonism that entailed. As Byrne noted

> the IFA was still perceived by many as a puppet of the authorities of the FA in London and by extension, a symbol of British imperialism in Ireland. If Dublin could establish its independence football wise, a telling message would be delivered across the Irish Sea.[12]

In 1920 Belfast Celtic, seen by many in the Leinster FA, as the sole Catholic representatives of soccer based in the north, played in an Irish Cup semi-final. The game was played out against a break down in north-south relations in soccer and the ongoing War of Independence. The game ended in a riot, shots were fired above the heads of the crowd, and Belfast Celtic supporters waved Sinn Féin flags and sang nationalist songs such as *A Soldier's Song* and *A Nation Once Again*.[13] Belfast Celtic were suspended from the tournament, and by way of response Shelbourne, Bohemians and St James's Gate all withdrew from the league. A two-nation football association had become untenable. On 1 June 1922 the FAIFS was founded. Although the IFA attempted to have the new association blacklisted within international competition, the move failed. The FAIFS organized its own league and cup competitions for the 1921–2 season, but obviously needed the international recognition that had become such a part of soccer life by the 1920s. In 1923 the new association arranged for Bohemians and Pioneers to play as its representatives against Athletic Club Gallia from France. In August 1923 soccer's governing body, FIFA, admitted the FAIFS as a member, and recognized its right to organize the game within its borders. Despite the FIFA recognition, the four 'home' nations continued to refuse to recognize the FAIFS. The first full international of an Irish team selected by the FAIFS took place in Turin on 21 March 1926 against Italy. Despite a lively second half the Irish were convincingly defeated 3-0 by the home team. The first Irish victory had to wait until 12 February 1928, in Liege against Belgium, a match they won 4-2. The first symbolic home victory on the international stage took place on 20 April 1929, again against Belgium. A crowd of 15,000 at Dalymount Park saw the Irish win 4-0 with a hat-trick from the Shamrock Rovers player, John Joe Flood. It took until 1988 before the Irish qualified for the finals of a major championship, the European Championships in Germany, and a further two years before they made their first World Cup Finals.[14]

What then was the function of soccer in fermenting and realising an Irish nationalism? While the organisational progress of the newly formed FAIFS was complex and at times traumatic, the important fact was that FIFA, as an international body, had recognized it. The FAIFS would not gain sole control of Irish international players from the twenty six southern counties until 1950. Before that date the IFA refused to recognize the 1921 political settlement and continued to select its international teams on the basis of all thirty-two counties. It took until the late 1960s before there was a clear recognition that two international teams, Northern Ireland and the Republic of Ireland, existed. Before that date both associations had claimed the title, Ireland.[15] The FAIFS, later the Football Association of Ireland (FAI), had to fight for recognition as the symbolic representation of the nation within the international soccer scene. This is a central issue in understanding the value of soccer as a purveyor of Irish nationalism that is absent from the story of Gaelic games.

From its very inception, the GAA had opposed all British forces within Ireland and had fought for the creation of an Irish nation. Part of the GAA's function, was, as has been demonstrated, the political realisation of Irish nationalism. In carrying out such a function, the GAA, was self serving and self contained. The GAA was able to unilaterally declare itself as the sporting body and association that represented Ireland, and which regulated Gaelic games across the whole island. In this the GAA was not challenged. There was not an earlier sporting body that claimed the same territory and there was no international organisation that controlled the global network of Gaelic games associations. The GAA had the simpler task of establishing itself on its own terms, and rejecting everything that it felt the need to oppose. It did not have to justify itself to anyone but itself. The experience of soccer is the exact opposite.

Soccer had developed originally on an all-Ireland basis, but one that was governed from the north. The IFA saw Ireland as part of the Union, and a home international organisation that was no different from that of Scotland or Wales. It organized its own leagues and cup competitions, indeed had its own international team, but the IFA stressed a national identity, that while Irish, was constructed firmly within a unionist mindset of loyalty to the Crown and State of the mainland. As an all Ireland organisation playing a foreign game, and one that was so closely allied with the forces of occupation, soccer, or the garrison game, was opposed by many nationalists such as those in the GAA. This set up a problem for those who regarded themselves as nationalists, yet who wanted to play soccer. Was playing soccer a betrayal of national identity and nationalist aspirations? If the decision were taken to play soccer, would it lead to the rejection of the individual in wider nationalist circles as a result of the ban? As the period of nationalist agitation progressed and gathered pace in the lead up to, and after, the First World War, what did soccer represent?

I would argue that soccer had to work twice as hard as the GAA to prove its nationalist credentials. While being established and supported by many at the time of its origin as an apolitical and value-free game, soccer quickly became contentious as it was seen as the property of the outsider. Those Irish nationalists who wanted to play soccer had to fight an internal battle with forces such as the GAA so that they were not seen as traitors, while also seeking to wrest control of their game from Belfast. The soccer authorities based in Dublin at the Leinster FA, and the various clubs in the south, argued long and hard against the IFA in Belfast. At the practical level they were well aware that clubs that represented Catholic and nationalist areas in the north were suffering physical attacks from other supporters. At an ideological level they realized that they could not continue to be ruled from Belfast and function under the auspices of a northern-dominated structure in the period of revolution and later independence. In breaking from the IFA, southern soccer had a huge problem. It had effectively towed the nationalist line and by breaking with Belfast had come to represent independence. Alongside government, military forces and a host of other institutions, the soccer authorities in Dublin had formalized partition and independence. They were, once formed as the FAIFS, a physical and sporting manifestation of the Free State. However, while the FAIFS may have sat alongside the GAA in being an independent body, free from British control, it needed recognition. The GAA only had to appeal to its diaspora and retain its contacts with the north of Ireland to retain its nationalist credentials and to continue as a successful sporting body. The FAIFS needed foreign recognition. Soccer was not a game of glorious isolation, but a game of international organisation, fixtures and competition, a mobile labour market and national kudos. The FAIFS were the creation of a statist version of nationalism. It was a formal organisation that sought recognition for the nation that it represented and embodied, i.e., the Irish Free State. As a formalized organisation that had to seek external and international recognition to achieve the identification of the nation, the FAIFS built its identity around the nation state, and not, as with the GAA, a mythical ideal of the nation.

Bert Moorehouse has summed up the Irish situation as being complex. He identifies three main problems. First, that Ireland had existed as part of the UK until the 1920s and had been recognized by the international soccer authorities along those lines. This created the dilemma as to just 'what Ireland was in football terms, and which organisation was to control it'.[16] Second, that soccer was identified within southern Ireland as a game of the imperialist aggressor and did not receive great encouragement from state and moral authorities. In the north of Ireland there had been problems as soccer clubs are identified as either Catholic or Protestant. This led to inter-communal violence and a struggle for some teams to switch allegiance between governing bodies. Finally, soccer had developed slowly and had failed to become a mass professional sport anywhere in Ireland. As a result, allegiances amongst supporters often switch to 'foreign' clubs where Irish players are located.[17] The very complex nature of Irish soccer and its place, both domestically and internationally, has had a profound effect on the manner in which nationalism has been projected by the game. Moorehouse's first point which questioned what Ireland actually was in soccer terms, is of the utmost importance here.

At the time of independence Ireland sought recognition from a variety of international bodies, and set out to acquire the symbolism of a nation state. Ireland is in an unusual position in that it was a nation that achieved independence in the 1920s.Few new nations came into existence at this point in time. The fact that Ireland did emerge as a new nation was not uncontested. The British were highly concerned about the impact of a newly independent Ireland on Empire and Dominion relationships, and many factions within Northern Ireland either failed to recognize the Irish Free State, or else sought to undermine it. While Ireland was recognized by the League of Nations, established embassies around the globe, called a legislative parliament and had a national flag, it struggled to gain acceptance elsewhere. As it struggled to gain international acceptance, especially because of its intimate relationship with Britain, self definition in areas such as sport became hugely important.

The GAA sat proudly at the heart of the new state. It projected an image that placed it at the centre of the revolutionary struggle and as an organisation it sat secure with the knowledge that it ran the national game. Soccer did not have such a luxury. Internal recognition of the FAIFS was not enough, to secure its place a representative of the nation, FIFA recognition was vital. FIFA recognition gave soccer the ability to represent a physical manifestation of the nation. While Gaelic games could be representative of a national culture and of a national sport, they could never regularly field a team of players under the name Ireland. Soccer, while not a national culture, provided Ireland with a physical nation, a nationality that could be measured against other nations, which could be cheered and applauded. The effect of such a national squad and international recognition was hugely important for soccer. In 1946 Ireland played their first competitive international against an English team which they lost 1-0. On 21 September 1949 at Goodison Park, Liverpool, the Irish defeated the English 2-0. Not only was this hugely important for the Irish as the English were the old colonial enemy, and they had supported the Northern Irish in keeping the Irish out of home international football, but it was the first ever international defeat inflicted on the English at home. Clifford Webb of the *Daily Herald* wrote clearly what such a defeat meant to the English

> Football history, bleak black history was made. Let it be known that this was the first time that any country outside of the international championship has won here. Éire, small and weak by soccer standards, triumphed where the great European teams in their pre war hey-days failed. Before the gloom is too deep upon me, all praise to the boys in green ... they caught England fuddling and fiddling like a junior girls' hockey side, set about them with keen swift direct action and flayed the hides off them.[18]

International competition allowed the Irish to grasp victories that boosted moral and provided a common focus for the nation. Perversely, such international success as the 1949 match against England was borne out of a highly underdeveloped domestic league. Irish players have always sought their fortunes in England, Scotland and further afield, as neither the FAI or the IFA leagues are big enough nor attract enough finance to provide the rewards for quality players. As the domestic scene is so weak, Irish soccer supporters have always looked overseas for the big matches and the glamorous stars, a situation exacerbated by the advent of live television coverage. By choosing to follow Leeds, Manchester United or Celtic, it may appear that the Irish supporter is jettisoning their own national identity, and appear to follow a foreign game in a foreign land. It is clear, however, that the teams which have a large section of Irish support, are those clubs who have historic connections with Ireland, have regularly hired Irish players, or else are located in areas of high Irish emigration. Those who choose to support a foreign team are not merely following their game, but are specifically selecting an Irish connection and identity to pursue. The support for clubs outside of Ireland and the relative weakness of the domestic Irish league has had a profound effect on support for the international squad and its whole status. In most other countries that follow soccer, the domestic league is the most central competition. While either those club sides that enter wider tournaments such as the various European competitions, or the national squad at times of international competition will carry national prestige, soccer is more often than not the national game. As such, soccer fulfils an important function in forming identity throughout the year. In Ireland, soccer is such a small-scale sport compared with Gaelic games, that it relies solely on international competition to form notions of national identity. In soccer the focus of nationalism and national fortune is not the game per se, as it does not signify anything specifically national. Instead the focus of nationalism is the national squad. Why are international team sports such as soccer so important in creating a sense of national identity?

Notions of identity are formed at many different levels, and in sport one of the most important has been the creation of nation states competing against each other in an 'us and them' contest. This allows national prestige to be played out on the sports field with all the supporters of that nation investing their identity in the fortunes of their representatives. A victory against another nation produces a sense of elation, national pride and unites the individual behind the team and the accompanying symbolism of the national strip, the flag and the anthem. Solely domestic competition (such as Gaelic games) does not allow for this as all emotional attachments are invested in communal opposition or support, for or against the town or region rather than the unifying ideal of the nation. Although a particular sport may have a specific resonance for a particular nation (baseball for Americans), may encapsulate the spirit of a specific culture (sumo wrestling for the Japanese) or may, through the style which an international game is played exhibit national characteristics which are real or imagined (the natural flair of Brazilian soccer players), the real test of identity is in comparison with others. Any given ethnic, minority or national identity group, whether as willing (Lennox Lewis as a representative of Britain rather than Canada in World Boxing) or unwilling (Dynamo Kiev as representatives of the former Soviet Union rather than the Ukraine) members of the nation state, become the symbols of that nation on the sports ground when international competition is entered into. It is through successful comparison with the 'other' that a celebratory notion of 'ourselves' emerges. Although a culture or nation may have a sport which exists in splendid domestic isolation which is central to a definition of 'us', identity and notions of it, have always, either militarily or through sport, measured 'us' against 'them'. Gaelic games, by comparison, have remained the preserve of the Irish domestically and, to a lesser extent, of the Irish diaspora overseas.[19] Such exclusivity does not allow for internationalism and excludes players from representing their country. Gaelic games are an Irish sport without an Ireland to represent on a world platform. In discussing the appeal of rugby union to the Afrikaners Albert Grundligh noted

It has to be recognized that even if nationalist cultural entrepreneurs had hoped to establish a completely new and authentic all-Afrikaner culture, such a project was not always feasible or viable. To create a pure, hermetically sealed culture is not easily accomplished; it is often more practical to adapt, reshape and mould whatever promising material is at hand. In the case of rugby, Afrikaners had already proved that they could excel at the game, and therefore it made sense to proceed in Afrikanerising rugby.[20]

Whereas the Afrikaners had failed to produce an authentic native culture and had been forced to appropriate and adapt a sport (rugby) connected with the prestige of empire, the Irish had managed to hermetically seal themselves in the sporting arena by developing Gaelic games. The Afrikaners were able to use their Springbok team as a symbol of their identity and achieve global success (both prior to and after the apartheid sanctions) because rugby is an inclusive game in which nation states can compete in test matches and a world cup. The Irish have not developed a similar international outlet for their primary sport. Thus although the GAA have been successful cultural entrepreneurs they failed to play on an international platform in any sustained fashion and have thus robbed the Irish nation of moral-boosting and identity-forming national success. This is in stark contrast to the recent success of the Irish soccer team who have galvanized the nation behind them with their qualification for, and success at, the 1990 and 1994 World Cups. The importance of international competition and success was made clear by Michael Billig who wrote

> I read the sporting pages, turning to them more quickly than is appropriate, given the news of suffering on other pages. Regularly I answer the invitation to celebrate national sporting triumphs. If a citizen from the homeland runs quicker or jumps higher than foreigners, I feel pleasure. Why, I do not know. I want the national team to beat the teams of other countries, scoring more goals, runs or whatever. International matches seem so much more important than domestic ones: there is an extra thrill of competition, with something indefinable at stake.[21]

A sport needs international success. Without it the sport might prosper domestically in terms of spectator numbers or participants, but it cannot galvanize a nation and become representative of a successful competitive identity. International events allow 'the imagined community of millions [to] seem more real as a team of 11 named people. The individual, even the one who only cheers, becomes a symbol of his nation himself'.[22] Likewise Grant Jarvie

has argued that 'sport itself provides a uniquely effective medium for incul-
cating national feelings; it provides a form of symbolic action which states the
case for the nation itself ... sporting struggles, and international triumphs and
losses, are primary expressions of imagined communities'.[23]

The force of soccer as an international sport that can so easily represent a
nation and its nationalism has been demonstrated quite clearly in Ireland since
1986 and the arrival of Jack Charlton as the Republic's manager.

JACK CHARLTON AND THE NEW NATIONALISM

Since the foundation of the FAIFS in 1921 the Irish soccer team has had a
poor record. The Irish played their first World Cup match on 25 February
1934, a game they drew 4-4 with Belgium. Despite this steady start, they
finished bottom in their qualifying group. Since such an inauspicious start, the
Irish have taken a long time to improve in the World Cup qualifying events.
Although occasionally finishing as runner up in their group, as in 1954 and
1958, the Irish more regularly finished bottom. The European
Championships served Ireland little better. In the inaugural 1960 tournament,
the Irish lost in the preliminary round to Czechoslovakia 4-2 on aggregate,
and until the 1988 tournament always failed to progress past the qualifying
round.

The problem for Irish soccer at the international level, was that while the
team performed a function as the carrier of national prestige, they never
succeeded, and thus any victory or accomplishment could never be appropriated by the nation. As a result soccer at the international level never captured
the public imagination. It remained the preserve of a small handful of soccer
faithful. Crowds at either Dalymount Park, or at Lansdowne Road since it
started to be used as an international soccer venue in 1972, could never match
the crowds at major Gaelic games events or Rugby Union internationals.
Matti Goksøyr has suggested that soccer is vital for the creation of a national
identity because

> what football provides is an arena for identification with the chosen
> ones. In collective identification, which had now become closest to a
> global opportunity, lies football's potency and force as a spectator
> sport.[24]

The problem in the period prior to the 1980s was that Irish soccer players
were not the chosen ones, they were the also-rans. They did not inspire a
huge following in Ireland, nor did they break into the higher (or even the

mediocre) echelons of international soccer. The game could not compete with Gaelic games for popularity, was stifled prior to the late 1960s as it was not regularly shown on Irish television, and appeared representative only of an average collection of journeymen soccer players. Although the Irish squad had always included a large cohort of players who were practising their trade in England and Scotland, through the 1930s, 1940s and 1950s they had at least been drawn from club sides playing at the highest levels. By the 1960s and 1970s, it was clear that the Republic of Ireland squad was being selected from the lower levels of English and Scottish soccer, and yet even then only a few Irish League players could make the grade.[25] As the Irish Republic failed to make an impact on the international scene, more and more quality Irish players would use their usually multifaceted backgrounds, and choose to play for one of the other home nations. Without good results and a quality reputation the Republic could not get the players, without the players the Irish could not get the results, and without the results soccer could never become a popular carrier of Irish nationalism. By the early 1980s Irish soccer at the international level was locked into a vicious cycle it could not break.

Prior to the mid 1980s then, the Irish were possibly worse at soccer than they were at any other team sport. With the exception of reaching the quarter-final stage in the 1924 Olympics, the soccer team of the Irish Republic was, to put it bluntly, awful. They had never qualified for an international final and their playing record was seemingly getting worse. Eoin Hand, the Republic's team manager from 1980 until 1985, fielded an Irish team in forty games, won only eleven and lost twenty. Irish soccer was definitely the runner up in the nation's affections. While many would follow the television exploits of Irish-born players overseas, the international squad was little more than a joke. Irish soccer, while supporting the statist version of nationalism as it was a formalized sporting body with international recognition, did not engender a sense of national pride nor feed the force of nationalism. Matti Goksøyr has argued that

> sport is a suitable stage for displaying, provoking and asserting national sentiment. Although this may be no more than '90 minute nationalism', it is an expression of an underlying reality which still exists ... short lived moments can live a long time in the nation's collective memory.[26]

As has been argued throughout this book, sport is a vehicle for nationalism. Goksøyr is absolutely correct in his assertion that such sporting nationalism will often only capture the imagination for ninety minutes (or whatever the duration of any given game may be). Such nationalism, which I would term evanescent nationalism, is especially relevant to modern international soccer within the western developed world. Games are broadcast direct into homes, pubs and clubs, and those watching will be brought together for a short period to cheer on their national heroes against the 'other'. Once the game is finished (especially when the team is defeated), the feelings of commonality and the euphoria attached to soccer will disappear. The problem for Ireland prior to the late 1980s was, that no matter how evanescent the nationalism that accompanied soccer, it was usually the nationalism of defeat. The period before the late 1980s witnessed an Ireland that was simplistically labelled throughout the world as the home of terrorism, which had recently been through the traumatic period of the late 1970s prison protests and the 1981 Hunger Strikes, and a nation that had not yet shook off its links with the past. Ireland was economically struggling, the links between Church and state had yet to be challenged and it was still in many ways culturally isolated. A soccer team that was as bad as that of the Republic's did little to inspire any kind of national fervour or sentiment. In the face of a nation that was struggling to find a confident place in a rapidly changing world, Ireland's soccer team reflected the general fortunes of the country, a couple of paces too slow to get to the ball first and claim the prize! Soccer was not, prior to the late 1980s, a medium for the representation or translation of nationalism.

Jack Charlton was appointed as the manager of the Republic of Ireland in February 1986. He arrived at a time of deep malaise within the game. The problems for Irish soccer were numerous and complex. Firstly, soccer had always played second fiddle to Gaelic games. Soccer was the English game, and in the context of the pre-1970s had very little media attention. It was not until the 1970s and the genesis of Ireland's modernisation in the context of a wider Europe that its media opened up, and crucially started screening domestic English soccer – for the youth of that period their heroes suddenly came from Manchester United and Liverpool rather than the Gaelic squads of Dublin or Cork. With heroes to adulate, the youngsters of Ireland wanted to play soccer for the first time. The next major problem was that while soccer came second to Gaelic games, any Irish players had to look across the water to England and Scotland if they wanted to play at a higher level. The domestic Irish league has still never developed beyond the semi-professional level. Without a thriving league, domestic talent would always be difficult to generate. The absence of such a league further compounded the problems of creating a successful international team – where would the managers and coaches come from? Finally, and most crucially, there was the diaspora problem. While there were countless numbers of professional players in the UK who could lay claim to Irish parentage and thus qualification for the national squad, many would chose not to play for the Republic. Why play for such a desperate outfit as the Irish, when it was possible to use one's Scottish, Welsh, English or even Northern Irish background to enter the international arena, thereby playing for a team which at least managed to qualify for a major final?

Jack Charlton, was an Englishman, a member of England's 1966 winning World Cup Squad and someone with a steady, but not glittering, career in soccer management.[27] Despite his credentials within soccer, Charlton's job was a massive undertaking. The FAI was estimated to be £30,000 in debt, the Republic was in the doldrums of international soccer and the FAI's international structure was in a state of disarray.[28] His reaction to being appointed was honest and revealed much about his motivations.

> I like Ireland. I like the Irish people, I like a pint of Guinness, I like the crack. I like the fishing in Ireland ... And I wanted to be an international team manager.[29]

Charlton was not interested in constructing a successful notion of Irish nationalism. He was solely interested in managing an international squad and achieving success with his squad on the international stage (and one would suggest that he was driven by a personal desire to beat England who had overlooked him as a national team manager). His very presence, and what he would eventually achieve, did mean however, that Charlton was instrumental in the creation of a new nationalism.

Charlton was more or less immediately able to smash many of the problems that had held back Irish soccer. He created a great deal of media and public interest in the national squad, as he was such a well-known figure. As he was well respected in the game he was able to convince players who would had previously snubbed Ireland to don the shirt of the Republic. He also ruthlessly exploited the rules of soccer's international body FIFA which allowed a player who could claim grandparentage in any given nation to play for that country. Popular mythology has even claimed that the Irish football authorities appointed a genealogist who traced the family trees of every player in the major UK leagues. Whether true or not, the simple fact is that overnight Charlton increased his potential squad sixfold. The Charlton story is a lot more complex and involves much more than this, but suffice to say it created an atmosphere where soccer could become the national game, if, and it was a big if, Charlton could bring success. Charlton brought success more or less immediately. In May 1986 the Irish squad travelled to Iceland to compete in a triangular tournament to celebrate the 300th anniversary of the foundation of Iceland. Ireland won the tournament, and thereby placed the first championship cup in the FAI trophy cabinet in 65 years. Success though it was,

Ireland's following was meagre. 'Only a handful travelled to witness the break-through, the roll-call of fans shorter than the slogans on their T-shirts: "Seven Irish geezers go to Rec-the-Kip, Iceland 300 years".'[30] As the years progressed Charlton would galvanize the following of soccer in Ireland and amongst the diaspora. Within two years of his arrival, Charlton qualified for a major championship and transformed the Republic of Ireland soccer team from second raters with a small following, into national heroes and signifiers of the nation.

The success Charlton brought was staggering and surpassed everyone's wildest expectations. The team qualified for the European Championship finals for the first time ever in 1988. In 1990 they went to their first World Cup Finals and reached the last eight and in 1994 they again qualified for the Finals, this time in the US. Charlton's Republic completely changed the perception of, and enthusiasm for, soccer in Ireland, and, as I will attempt to demonstrate through the rest of the chapter, created a new idea of what Irish nationalism and national identity was about. It is a nationalism and an identity which is located in eleven men wearing green who have been talked about, written about, filmed, interviewed and celebrated in a way that no other Irishmen have ever been.

The success of the Jack Charlton years and the Republic's squad has to be located within the wider context of Irish nationalism that was discussed in chapter two. The 1990 and 1994 World Cup Finals coincided with several catalytic events in Ireland. These included: the arrival of Mary Robinson as president of Ireland who transformed the place of women within the state; the referendums on divorce and abortion which liberalized Ireland in a way unimaginable only a decade before; the creation of Ireland's first non-agricultural and non-rural economic success now encapsulated in the expression 'the Celtic Tiger'; and, possibly most importantly, the beginnings of sustained moves towards peace in Northern Ireland.

The first event that the Republic qualified for under Charlton was the 1988 European Championship. The Irish qualified at the head of a testing group that included teams such as Scotland and Bulgaria, and were thus able to travel to Germany. They did not progress beyond the group stage of the tournament, but only lost one game in a hard group that comprized England, the Soviet Union and Holland. Most valuable of all was a 1-0 victory over the English, a match described on RTE as 'a great historic moment for Irish football'.[31] Charlton has commented, quite perceptively why this result mattered more than anything else at the Championships,

> over the years, I had seen how easily the Scots were motivated at the thought of beating England. And I'm certain that the same was equally true for Wales and Northern Ireland. The Republic of Ireland didn't

play in the home championship, of course, and because of that, any meeting with the English was special, very special ... but for a couple of marvellous saves by Packie Bonner, we might well have lost the game. But we didn't, we won it. We'd done what we'd set out to do, and given Ireland the win the country demanded.[32]

By giving the Irish the win they demanded, not only a win against the English, but a win on an international platform at a major championship, Charlton and his team transformed Irish sport. Ireland had never achieved on the international platform in such a fashion in any sport, let alone one that attracted such a big following as soccer did in the summer of 1988. The success was so appealing as it was a success that could not be channelled through a solely domestic sport such as Gaelic games. It was a success that was achieved on a European platform in front of a huge media audience and thereby placed Ireland in front of millions of expectant eyes. The huge relief for the Irish, the cause of celebration, was that they did not fail in front of such an audience. Stereotypical images of the self-defeating Irish were banished, and instead the victory over England allowed for a self-confident glorification of being Irish, an Irishness that stretched beyond the boundaries of the Irish Republic and captured the hearts of the Irish diaspora. Soccer provided a global outlet for an expression of Irishness that had not existed before. Dermot Bolger's now famous and regularly referred to play, *In High Germany*, used the 1988 Championships as its background. The play explored how members of the diaspora found an Ireland that they could relate to in a soccer team, in a way that they had been unable to through any other medium or vision of the nation. Bolger wrote of the final match in the championships against the Dutch

> And then they were gone, solid to a man and woman, thirteen thousand of us, cheering, applauding, chanting out the players' names, letting them know how proud we felt. I thought of my father's battered travel light bag, Molloy drilling us behind the 1798 pike, the wasters who came after him hammering *Peig* into us, the masked men blowing limbs off passers by in my name. You know, all my life it seems, somebody somewhere has always been trying to tell me what Ireland I belong in. But I only belonged there. I raised my hands and applauded, having finally found the only Ireland whose name I can sing, given to me by eleven men dressed in green. And the only Ireland I can pass onto my son who will carry my name in a foreign land.
>
> I thought of my uncles and my aunts scattered through England and the States, of every generation culled and shipped off like beef on

the hoof. And suddenly it seemed that they had found a voice at last, that the Houghtons and McCarthys, the Morrises were playing for my children to come too who would grow with foreign accents and Irish faces, bewildered by their father's lives.[33]

Bolger signals what the Republic's soccer team would come to signify in the 1990s. In the same way that the GAA has come to represent a defensive form of nationalism, so soccer in the 1990s became representative of a forward-looking nationalism. A nationalism, which, in the same way Mary Robinson questioned what Ireland was, and what it had come to mean, signified an ease with a history of emigration and defeat. Soccer allowed Ireland to revel in its identity on a world stage, confident that the nation had survived a long and difficult history, and presenting a modern inclusive celebratory nationalism through its soccer team.

After the heady successes at the European Championships, the Republic then qualified for the 1990 World Cup Finals. The whole trip to Italy would be a celebration for Ireland, and it did not matter if the team were not successful, as being there was the important part. Ireland progressed through the first round stage, and then beat Romania on penalties to progress into the last eight where they played the hosts Italy and lost 1-0. It is the game against Romania, and the all-important penalty shoot-out, which is the centre of most writing on the World Cup experience and what it meant to Ireland.

Roddy Doyle, in his fictional work, *The Van*,[34] wrote about the penalty shoot-out through the medium of his main character, Jimmy Rabbite Snr

> They watched Packie setting himself up in his goal for the fifth time.
> – Go on Packie!
> – ONE PACKIE BONNER –
> – Shut up; wait.
> – He has rosary beads in his bag, yeh know, said some wanker.
> – They'll be round his fuckin' neck if he misses this one, said Jimmy Snr.
> No one laughed. No one did anything.
> Packie dived to the left; he dived and he saved the fuckin' thing.
> The screen disappeared as the whole pub jumped. All Jimmy Snr. could see was backs and flags and dunphies.
> Someone had to take the last penalty for Ireland.
> – Who's tha?
> – O'Leary.
> David O'Leary put it way like he was playing with his kids at the beach.

> – YESSS!
> It was the best day of Jimmy Snr's life. He went home and Veronica
> was in the kitchen and she did a fry for him, and he cried again when
> he was telling her about the pub and the match. And she called him an
> eejit. It was the best day of his life.[35]

The fictional character of Jimmy Snr represents, in the same fashion as
Dermot Bolger's main character, the celebration of the victor. An Ireland that
had, at long last, achieved success on a world stage. It was an Ireland that was
free of terrorism, poverty, drunkenness, famine, violence or any of the other
cliched stereotypes applied to the Irish. It replicates in many ways the true
experience of the Irish that night. No one stirred in Ireland while the TV
relayed the pictures from Italy. Mick Jagger and the Rolling Stones cancelled
their gig in Dublin that night due to lack of interest and the European Heads
of State in Dublin Castle at a European Union Council meeting all commented with bemusement at the sight of 500 assorted Irish government ministers
and civil servants dancing on the committee tables.[36] The true story of the
penalty shoot out is best relayed by Eamon Dunphy.

> Back home, the nation fell silent: cars pulled over to the road, the occu-
> pants unable to drive and listen to their radio; watching big screens in
> pubs, village halls and offices, people urged hush, as if the noise might
> break the concentration of the heroes in Genoa.
> O'Leary struck with calm conviction, the ball curled with the inside
> of his right boot, hit the top of the net, a yard wide of the Romanian
> keeper's desperate left arm. Those at home, and the millions scattered
> round the world, the Diaspora which had embraced this team with
> particular fervour because so many of the players are sons of exiles,
> symbols of the comforting thought that Irishness survives the sorrow
> of exile, for them the O'Leary goal is a moment that will never be
> forgotten.[37]

Italia '90 was central in the creation of a new nationalism in Ireland. It gave
the nation a collection of heroes that were representative of both the history of
Ireland and the contemporary changes which it was undergoing. To be able to
rally around a foreign game and to celebrate the deeds of an English manager
demonstrated the transferability of national culture. Nationalism does not have
to be conveyed solely by vehicles of culture that are native. The culture of the
outsider and of the global can be used to project the spirit of the nation. Italia
'90 was a huge success for the Irish and created a debate in Ireland that sought
to understand its meaning. I would argue that Italia '90, although being unique

as it was Ireland's first World Cup Finals, were part of the general evanescent nationalism that accompanies sport. It is clear that the Irish nation lost itself in soccer for three weeks, and all sectors of society developed an appetite for the television images from Italy that transmitted Big Jack and his band of heroes back home to Ireland. In amongst the enjoyment there was an awareness that Charlton and his squad represented a profound moment in Irish history and the ways of thinking about Irish nationality, identity and nationalism.

If Italia '90 offered the Irish a new sets of heroes, drawn from the diaspora and representing Irish success on a world stage, the qualification for USA '94, the key home of Irish emigration, was even more profoundly important.

The 1994 World Cup Finals, although an equally amazing celebration, were tempered by the bloodshed of the north of Ireland. Ireland had qualified to go to the US by drawing with Northern Ireland in the final qualifying match. It was a game played in Belfast's Windsor Park in front of an crowd that was 100 per cent Northern Irish. In cross-border games no away fans are allowed for security reasons. The political backdrop of the game was the highest monthly death rate in the Northern troubles in fourteen years. In the four weeks before the game the IRA had exploded a bomb on the Loyalist Shankill Road killing ten and wounding fifty-seven, and in response the Ulster Freedom Fighters had entered the Catholic Rising Sun Bar in Greysteel, fired randomly into the packed bar, and left seven dead and thirteen wounded. Mary Hunt, in her diary of the Republic's qualification for the 1994 World Cup Finals, explored the effect of the events in Greysteel and how its ramifications might have posed a threat to the Republic versus Northern Ireland match.

> The whole country was shocked, horrified as day after day heartbreaking scenes of anguish and devastation were relayed by every form of media ... Windsor Park is in a loyalist part of Belfast and the presence of Irish fans, with or without tickets, would pose a major security headache, while those with access to the ground, would inevitably end up in a part of it they wouldn't want to be – separated from the main Irish party ... 'Maybe my number's up anyway', some of them remarked with great bravado – until the week's atrocities. Then fear crept into their gung-ho attitude.[38]

The desperate need for peace which stemmed from this period of violence was signalled by the Irish and British governments publication of the Downing Street Declaration of December 1993, and it is here that we find another context of the Irish soccer story.

Whereas qualification was played out against a backdrop of recent violence, the first match in the finals at USA '94, was played against a backdrop of actual violence. The Irish team's first match was against Italy in New

York. The challenge was fantastic – an opportunity to revenge the Italian defeat which had taken the Irish out of Italia '90 and a setting in one of the world's most famous cities with its huge Irish population.

The Irish had one of their greatest days ever.[39] In front of a sea of green in the stadium, outnumbering the Italians three to one, the Irish, through Ray Houghton's goal, banished the memory of 1990 and defeated the favourites for the World Cup 1-0. Joseph O'Connor wrote in his World Cup diary,

> Saturday 18 June: We play Italy. The rest is a bit of a blank.
>
> Sunday 19 June: On the morning after the Italy game I wake up about seven. I am still wearing my clothes – at least, I think they are my clothes, although they don't seem to fit too well. My head is pounding like the Kilfernora Ceilidh band on ecstasy. My throat is sore. My mouth feels like Oliver Reed died in it. The sheets when I roll over, are full of loose change, crumpled beermats and segments of soggy luke-warm pepperoni pizza.[40]

At home Roddy Doyle was slightly more sober and certainly more profound,

> The second half. Schillachi hit the bar. Schillachi scored but was offside. But the Irish kept at it, kept running and bullying. They were great and I loved them.
>
> Then it was over.
>
> We said nothing.
>
> The fans in Rome were still waving the flags, still singing. People in the pub were doing the same. I told Belinda that I loved her.
>
> It was over.
>
> It was one of the great times of my life, when I loved being from Dublin and I loved being Irish. Three years later it still fills me. The joy and the fun and the pride. Adults behaving like children. Packie gritting his teeth. Being able to cry in public. Getting drunk in daylight. The t-shirts, the colour. The excitement and the madness and love. It's all still in me and I'm starting to cry again.[41]

The final scoreboard read IRELAND 1 ITALY 0. As Don Watson rightly pointed out it was a sight that 'the photo-processing labs in Dublin will be sick of that scoreboard in a couple of weeks'.[42] The importance of USA '94, which was similar to Italia '90, was that it offered success, an Ireland on a global platform, and an Ireland that was universally recognisable, yet at the same time deeply personal. It was an Ireland, at long last, of successful emigration. None of the team in 1994 lived in Ireland, all of them had Irish roots, they worked overseas – their absence from Ireland was a measure of successful Irishness in a competitive sport and a mark of a nation's long history of famine, emigration and exile. By being able to cheer their eleven men in green, the Irish, native or exiled, new born or fourth generation, could claim something for themselves. Success in terms which were wider than success in Gaelic games, success in an environment where the competitors were England, Brazil, Italy and the US, and success which everyone could identify with. You could now, in the new Ireland of the 1990s, cheer a game which, although not a native game, a game without nationalist credentials, Ireland excelled at. The very location of the 1994 World Cup Finals, the US, was of huge significance. The US had strong links with Ireland, and had been the promised land for generations of Irish emigrants. As Eoghan Corry noted with respect of US '94

> Irish football has a little further to go. Going to America serves as a starting point; Ireland's physical and spiritual arrival on the far side of the Atlantic is merely a departure of another type. Thus was it ever in the history of Irish people, Irish culture and a wider world. People who are always kicking. Always putting them under pressure.[43]

It created the highest levels of pregnancy fear that Ireland had ever seen, and the first mass wave of morning after pill consumption which was itself a by-product of modern secular Ireland. Unfortunately, when Ireland were knocked out of the tournament Ireland's Women's Aid reported a sharp upswing in domestic violence – modern Ireland may have been a developing reality, but the warrior king male was still alive and well.[44]

For the final context of the Irish soccer team, I return to the troubles in the North. As TV's across the island of Ireland relayed the magical game against Ireland, two gunmen from the Loyalist Ulster Volunteer Force (UVF) force entered a bar in the Catholic village of Loughinisland. They fired into the bar full of people glued to the game. In seconds six men were killed. The UVF claimed that the people in the bar were not watching a soccer match, but instead 'these scum who carried out this deed are saying that there was some sort of republican meeting going on'.[45] An editorial in the *Independent* summed up the two stark images offered by the 1994 World Cup Finals for the Irish; on the one hand the victory over Italy, on the other the murders in Loughinisland.

> The Republic of Ireland's World Cup victory over Italy and the simultaneous loyalist massacre of six men in an Ulster pub might seem to be worlds apart. Yet these are the faces of Ireland today, one a modern aspect offering hope, the other a savage impression that continues to haunt that island. In the United States, the world sees a team that symbolizes the breadth of Irish nationhood and the self confidence and

competence of Irish culture ... Yet the killings in Loughinisland are a reminder that an identity crisis is occurring within Northern Ireland.[46]

In the same vein, Matthew Engel wrote,

It was utterly in keeping with the whole of Ireland's history and experiences that, on the morning after what was probably the nation's greatest sporting triumph, everyone should have to come to terms with the tragedy of Loughinisland... [the supporters in the Giants stadium] represented a harder edged, more modern Ireland – a place where it is easier to find a karaoke bar than a pub with a decent fiddler – than is recognized in the myths, somewhere that has moved on a long, long way from the senselessness that produced the North's latest horror ... As someone said after John Kennedy was shot, there is no point in being Irish if you don't realize your heart is going to be broken eventually.[47]

The division between the new nationalism of soccer and the old nationalism which belongs in the chaos of Northern Ireland's troubles was never more starkly illustrated. On one hand a nation rejoiced as they were Irish and proud and successful and victorious. In a small village six men lay dead for their religion, their nationality and the team they chose to watch on televison.

Within two months the IRA called their cease-fire and the current peace process became an urgent political necessity. Most commentators agree that the message of Loughinisalnd was that Ireland, a nation that had arrived on the global stage in New York that night could not be allowed to pursue a nineteenth century struggle into the twenty-first century. The new nationalism personified by soccer, which stresses a nation at ease with itself, its history of emigration, one which can compete with other nations at the highest levels, and one which can celebrate its nationality without recourse to violence, intolerance and dogma is an Ireland profoundly changed from the Ireland of a backward looking and politically-dominated sporting body such as the GAA.

A more sober Joseph O'Connor was able to conclude, after the Dutch had knocked Ireland out of USA '94,

the sound of Philip Lynott and Thin Lizzy comes blaring down from the loudspeakers. There is a tumultuous roar of recognition from the Irish fans ... the sound! I don't know if you've ever heard 'Dancing in the Moonlight' sung by ten thousand Irish soccer fans, but for some reason I can't really figure out it is unforgettably moving ... It was a wonderful moment. Somehow, it lifts the whole night. Fans are embracing each other, hugging the Dutch fans, hugging the waitresses, the policemen, hugging the police horses for God's sake, and signing 'Dancing in the Moonlight'. The laughing voice of Phil Lynott, reminding us in some weird intangible way that being Irish always has its consolations. So we lost. Big swinging deal. We lost. It's not the end of the world.[48]

O'Conner's acknowledgement that the cohesion of experience, the celebratory nationalism of the World Cup was dented by defeat, but did not necessarily signal an end to the commonality of Irishness, forms a perfect juxtaposition to the thoughts of Joe Joyce. Writing after the Loughinisland killings and having watched the Italy match in Dublin, he noted,

> the morning after Jack Charlton tried to bring the euphoria back to earth. Talk of winning the World Cup was nonsense, he said in his interview: 'We're not a big enough nation for that, we've not got the depth of people'. As for the massacre, what is there to say? W.B. Yeats said it all a long time ago:
>
> > 'Out of Ireland have we come.
> > Great hatred, little room,
> > Maimed us at the start.
> > I carry from my mother's womb
> > A fanatic's heart'.[49]

What soccer in 1990 and 1994 allowed the Irish to create was a new celebratory nationalism where it was acceptable and gracious to lose, something that they had not been willing to do throughout the first ninety years of the twentieth century. The new nationalism connected with the World Cup and symbolized by Jack Charlton was something that was championed and celebrated by the media and various literary figures, yet was an idea that was always thrown into stark relief by events in Northern Ireland. The work of Michael Holmes (and to a lesser extent that Richard Giulianotti)[50] concurs with many of the arguments that have been made here.[51] Holmes argued that 'soccer represents an Ireland that cannot be symbolized by Gaelic games as they are not international; that the team Charlton played was ethnically diverse and thus accommodating of a wider cultural agenda; and that the presence of Charlton at the head of the team and a large number of UK based players led to a more mature attitude to the British'.[52] Alan Bairner offered a challenge to the conclusions of Holmes and argued that the success of the Irish soccer team had not led to a wholesale shift in the nature of Irish nationalism. Bairner suggested that while there had been some shifts in Irish culture, it was difficult to speak of a transformation in identity until the issues of the troubles and partition had been settled.[53] While understanding the thrust of

Bairner's argument, it is possible to suggest that as 1998 has witnessed the breaking down of so many barriers within the Northern Ireland situation, so the new nationalism personified by the Irish soccer team can be seen as real and to some extent, permanent. The actual support for a soccer team at the international level, is, as has been shown here, an evanescent nationalism. However, as the success of Jack Charlton's team was located in a period of such profound change within all areas of Irish life, so the evanescent nationalism became representative of a larger picture. While the euphoria connected with the national team in the 1988–94 period has passed away (especially as the Republic failed to qualify for France '98), the inclusiveness that the team symbolized has lived on within the general shifts that have taken place across Irish national culture. Soccer is representative, at the international level, of one particular kind of nationalism. It is statist at the administrative level, and symbolic on the pitch. It is a nationalism that is very different from that of the GAA, but is not one that should be dismissed as unimportant because of its apparently transient nature.

6 / Northern Ireland and the Troubles

On Tuesday night hurlers trying to get to their training sessions were prevented from arriving at their destinations by roadblocks, burning vehicles and other obstacles... Hurlers, with their distinctive playing equipment and jerseys in cars, decided not to risk being searched by vigilantes who would immediately be in a position to identify them.[1]

UUP MP Mr Jeffrey Donaldson said his party was not seeking to demonize the Gaelic culture or the GAA. He said, however, there were some features of Gaelic culture which were offensive.[2]

The Greeks recognized that there was something sacrosanct about the athletic ideal and regarded any violence during the period of the games as sacrilegious. Athletics and drama, two of the great civilising activities of Greece, were two of the activities which Sean Brown promoted.[3]

All aspects of what might be called 'normal' life in Northern Ireland have been dislocated during the period of the modern troubles. The death toll over the years has been horrific, people have been forced from their homes, while many others have chosen to emigrate. There is not an aspect of Northern Ireland's society that has not been affected in the past thirty years. There are signs in 1998 that all sections of society in the Province are making the decision to move away from violence and to pursue only democratic means within the political arena. While the moves towards peace in Northern Ireland are laudable, they are well overdue. The cost to the people of Northern Ireland has been devastating, and while they may live in an environment without arms or bombs in the future, the efforts needed to heal the wounds will take far longer. The atmosphere of violence that has existed in Northern Ireland over recent decades would, in many people's eyes, make sport seem irrelevant. Why should sport matter when men, women and children have been killed? Sport matters because it is, as with many other aspects of Northern Irish life, a mirror for the troubles that lead to the killing. To understand the deaths in Northern Ireland as a battle between two identities on opposing sides of a sectarian divide is to understand sport.[4] The plethora of forces and groups within society that line up behind the generic identities of nationalist and unionist, separate along the same lines in sport. Put simply, the game that the men and women of Northern Ireland play, or the team that they watch, will distinguish which side of the ideological line that they stand on. This despite the fact that 'sport is often proclaimed as being above politics and communal conflict', this is a 'claim that needs substantial revision'.[5] The quotes at the head of the chapter demonstrate the idea. They are randomly selected extracts from recent years, and there is a multitude of others to choose from. They illustrate how identity is entwined with sport. The hurlers are seen by the extremist supporters of the Orange Order's right to march the Queen's high-way as a valid target, easily identifiable because of their sporting equipment. An Ulster Unionist Party MP can dismiss the culture of the GAA as offensive as it is not part of what he would see as the official culture of Northern Ireland, which, to his mind, is British not Irish. Finally, there is Sean Brown, who was killed by loyalist gunmen as he locked up the local GAA clubhouse. In each of these cases sport is seen as the agency through which nationalist aspirations are transmitted. The GAA is understood by large sections of the unionist community, not as a sporting body, but as an instrument for the advancement of nationalism within Northern Ireland against the wishes of what they see as the majority. For supporting the GAA or playing Gaelic games, people have been intimidated, attacked and murdered. For the same reasons the followers of Derry City, Cliftonville, Donegal Celtic and other soccer clubs in Northern Ireland have also been attacked. Sport in Northern Ireland says who and what you are. To try and suggest that sport could, in such an environment, be a neutral pastime to unite the opposing communi-ties, is to deny the experience of history.[6]

The aim of this chapter is to examine the reasons why sport has been such an important signifier of identity in Northern Ireland during the troubles. It will assess how nationalism has both showed itself, and been portrayed in the sporting arena. It will once more deal briefly with the value of studying sport as a way of understanding the question of identity and then move onto two specific examples, one from Gaelic games and one from soccer. One of the most contentious rules of the GAA is rule 21, that which excludes members of the security forces from the Association. The chapter will explore the historic rationale behind the GAA's Northern policy generally, and that of rule 21 specifically, and examine what it has signified for the nationalist community and why, in the recent spirit of peace and reconciliation, the GAA has not been able to jettison rule 21. The example from soccer is the fall and rise of Derry City football club. By examining how sport has been directly affected by the troubles it is possible to assess why a local identity, that of Derry, can be transformed into representing the national. The two examples will demon-strate how nationalism has functioned within Northern Ireland's sport, and the wider ramifications that this had for an understanding of Irish national-ism.

SPORT AND IDENTITY IN NORTHERN IRELAND

In a recent book Vic Duke and Liz Crolley explored the linkages between soccer, nationality and the state.[7] They argued that soccer is deeply linked with the identities of either the state, the region or the nation. Feeding off Benedict Anderson they stated, 'Football captures the notion of an imagined community perfectly. It is much easier to imagine the nation and confirm national identity, when eleven players are representing the nation in a match against another nation ... when football support and nationalism are combined, the brew is particularly strong'.[8] That sport generally is a vehicle for national identity is an idea which has already been explored, has been well developed by a host of writers[9] and is not contested here. What is at issue here are the links between sport and identity when the whole notion of identity is a contested one. For the majority of English or Italian players and fans of soccer their notion of what constitutes their identity is unquestioned. They may have disagreements over regional identities, for example north versus south, during the domestic season, but once the national team is the centre of attention it becomes quite simply 'us and them'. This simple equation is not allowed for when the nature of the nation is questioned. Northern Ireland is not alone is provoking such questions of identity. Barcelona is a classic example of a team, which while playing in the national Spanish league, is a focus for Catalonian nationalism and therefore promotes a minority notion of national identity in the face of a formalized nation state. The same was true for many regional teams during the days of the former USSR where Dynamo Kiev were a prime example of a regional identity, in their case that of Ukrainian national prestige, competing against the official political nationalism of the larger Soviet nation.

Northern Ireland is officially part of the United Kingdom. As such the majority of the population professes itself to be British and these people are to be found in the Protestant and unionist sections of society. However, a minority of the population, Catholic and nationalist, which views itself as Irish, contests this sense of belonging to Britain. Both the majority and minority identities are expressed in Northern Ireland through constitutional politics with the Official Unionist and Democratic Unionist parties (plus other smaller fringe groups) representing Protestants and unionists, and the Social Democratic and Labour Party (SDLP) and Sinn Féin representing Catholics and nationalists. The two identities have also been represented on occassions in a non-constitutional manner by a host of paramilitary forces. Many other aspects of Northern Irish life are equally divided such as urban geography (e.g. East Belfast as Protestant and West Belfast as Catholic), schooling, and, to a lesser extent, job provision.

Before examining the specific course of events in Northern Irish sport this chapter has to revisit what is meant by a contested identity. Put simply Northern Ireland is a battle ground, both in the real and political/cultural sense, between those who want to remain within the United Kingdom and those who do not. There is obviously a mass of intricate detail which actually separates and distinguishes the different groupings and their exact vision of what they will settle for, but that is not at issue here. The Protestant/unionist population stresses an official and existent nation state version of nationalism, while the Catholic/nationalist population stresses an unofficial and aspirational version of nationalism which demands separation from Britain and independence as part of the Irish Republic. Within Northern Ireland both groups can support their claims in terms of historical precedent, ethnocentricity and nationalist ideology. Essentially what exists is two versions of national identity, one British and one Irish, which are diametrically opposed to each other. For both groups the comments of Kellas on nationalism ring true. He stated

> Nationalists are clearly idealists, since they propound the idea of the nation and the ideology of nationalism. They are also people with interests of their own to promote, whether it be feudal power in relation to a monarchy, or a material or psychic advantage as individuals or members of a group. So nationalist ideology is a justification for the pursuit of self-interest.[10]

There is however a dividing line between the two groups which does exist. Although Jenkins and Sofos have contended (quite rightly in respect of nationalism as an ideology) that 'a starting point for the study of nationalism is not whether nation exists; it is rather how the category operates in practice, that is, how nationalist logics and frames of reference are formulated and deployed',[11] the Northern Irish state as part of the United Kingdom is a reality. The two nationalisms do exist, but one has the weight of a nation behind it while the other is disenfranchized and is therefore contesting the legitimacy of the former.

The Catholic/nationalist population of Northern Ireland posses all the elements listed on the modern check list of nationalism – language, history, culture, religion, territorial aspirations, and ethnic distinctiveness – but it does not posses the nation state. Instead it contests the legitimacy of the nation state which it finds itself belonging to. In this sense the Catholic/nationalist population of Northern Ireland fits into Guibernau's definition of nations without a state. As he notes, 'the common feature lying behind any minority's nationalist movement calling for greater autonomy or independence is dissatisfaction with its current situation. The feeling that they could benefit from distancing themselves from the state'.[12] This brand of nationalism is in direct competition with the nation state and is thus 'likely to be perceived as a threat to the state's integrity'.[13] With this direct competition between the two brands of nationalism present in Northern Ireland all aspects of life, including sport, become an arena for conflict between the official and contested versions of nationalism. As a result of the ambiguity of how nationalism functions as an ideology it is relatively easy for its violent and divisive manifestations to encroach on the cultural or sporting sphere. As Breuilly has argued, 'the identity of the nation is provided in arbitrary ways. The leap from culture to politics is made by portraying the nation at one moment as cultural community and at another as political community whilst insisting that in an ideal state the national community will not be split into cultural and political spheres'.[14] For insurgent nationalism there is no need to paper over the cracks and promote the ideal state as unionists may have to do. Catholic/nationalists have no intrinsic investment in Northern Ireland as it exists at present (although this situation may change if the deal struck in the 1998 Good Friday Agreement succeeds in a way that other attempts at crisis resolution have not). This allows for the manifestations of their contested nationalism to be poorly defined and to operate in a variety of different ways. At times they will operate politically, militarily or culturally and the different modes of operation need not be coherent.

One of the problems in contextualising Irish nationalism is that the majority of work has, as previously demonstrated, concentrated either on the historical basis of political nationalism and the creation of the Irish Republic,[15] the nature of political nationalism in the context of the troubles[16] or the impact of cultural nationalism. It is the work on cultural nationalism which is most problematic in the context of this chapter on Northern Ireland. Work such as that of John Hutchinson[17] has concentrated specifically on the impact of 'high' culture, that is, intellectual and literary, on the emergence of official state nationalism in the south. What is lacking is any sustained attempt to understand how 'low' culture, the populist leisure pursuits, have formulated an idea and practice of what nationalism in Northern Ireland is.[18] Hutchinson argued that cultural nationalism is distinct from political nationalism with its aim 'the moral regeneration of the national community rather than the achievement of an autonomous state'.[19] Two groups promote cultural nationalism: humanist intellectuals and a secular intelligentsia. The former formulates the 'historicist ideology of cultural nationalism and establish its first cultural institutions' while the latter form 'the cadres of cultural nationalist movements that seek to build in antagonism to the existing state a regenerated national community'.[20]

That cultural nationalism as described by Hutchinson existed in late nineteenth- and early twentieth-century Ireland is beyond doubt. Cultural nationalists were highly successful in mobilising behind the nationalist dream and were influential in the process of state building after 1922. However it can be argued that Hutchinson's views need to be refined both in the context of the Irish revolutionary period and the modern North. In the late nineteenth century it was possible, as Hutchinson contends, to separate high cultural nationalism from political nationalism but this needs qualifying in respect of the Gaelic Athletic Association (GAA).

The GAA promoted native Irish sports across Ireland from its foundation in 1884 and played a key role in the pursuit of political independence. However it was neither a specifically political nationalist organisation nor can it fit into Hutchinson's concept of cultural nationalism as its appeal is to 'low' culture not the 'high' culture of the intellectual. The GAA allowed for the interchange of nationalist ideas and aspirations as championed by the Association's hierarchy, dominated in the first four decades by members of the radical IRB, and the tens of thousands of sportsmen across the nation. While these men were undoubtedly nationalist, they expressed themselves through sport as 'low' cultural nationalists rather than as political nationalists. To play and support an Irish game in the context of the revolutionary period was to stress oneself as Irish and a nationalist. Membership of the GAA did not directly involve political activism but rather afforded members the opportunity for expression of national identity and characteristics which were an inherent part of a game which by its nature encapsulated an historic ideal of Gaelic manhood. This mass of sportsmen drives a wedge between the political or cultural nationalism as proposed by Hutchinson. Such a mass movement, which encapsulated a populist expression of Irishness, cannot be ignored in the context of academic categorisation. The same is even truer for the period of the modern troubles. There has not, and does not exist in modern Northern Ireland, a viable group of cultural nationalists which can be compared to Hutchinson's cultural nationalists of the turn of the century. There have been no humanist intellectuals or secular intelligentsia who have any impact on the course of events. The majority of nationalist activity has been in the variety of different political nationalisms as was explained earlier but these have been accompanied by a whole group of 'low' cultural nationalists. The GAA still functions in Northern Ireland as a mass sporting body promoting sport and the accompanying nationalist message. GAA clubs serve as an important focus for the Catholic/nationalist population. Due to the failure of the GAA to attract any support from the Protestant/unionist population it has served an exclusive function for its own constituency group. As the only mass-membership Catholic/nationalist grouping in Northern Ireland which functions legally and is not directly connected to politics, the GAA allows for the promotion and celebration of a Catholic/nationalist culture and identity. Although this is a contested identity, the GAA's isolation from the majority identity in Northern Ireland allows it to function largely unmolested.[21]

Those following soccer teams identified as Catholic/nationalist are part of the same 'low' cultural nationalist grouping as those who follow the GAA. This is not to deny that followers of Catholic/nationalist soccer teams in Northern Ireland are political nationalists as well. Kellas has argued, 'the most popular form of nationalist behaviour in many countries is sport, where masses of people become highly emotional in support of their national team. But the same people may display no obvious nationalism in politics, such as supporting a nationalist party or demanding home rule or national independence'.[22] Contrary to what Kellas rightly states about most sports followers, the supporters of Catholic/nationalist teams in Northern Ireland probably do support a nationalist party and demand a change to the territorial status of the Province. Where there is a distinction to be made is that most Catholic/nationalist soccer followers in Northern Ireland, while having political nationalist sympathies, will expresses those views primarily through the ballot box only. The day-to-day sense of identity will be expressed through a variety of mediums, be that the Church, the school they went to or where they live. Soccer fits into this sense of identity and expresses the notion of 'low' cultural nationalism as advanced earlier. An afternoon on the terraces allows for a communal expression of a geographical place which will be identified with Catholicism/nationalism, will present the opportunity of displaying Irish symbols such as the tricolour or the Irish Republic's soccer shirt, and will hopefully, in their eyes, present the opportunity for defeating a symbol of the Protestant/unionist majority such as Linfield. This communal expression, while symbolic of many of the aspirations of political nationalism, is fundamentally driven by the collective need of those excluded from the hierarchies of political or culturally elite nationalism to express who and what they are.

If it is thus possible to see the support of Catholic/nationalist sport and sporting teams as indicative of 'low' cultural nationalism, how does this actually show itself? Kellas outlined three ways in which nationalism manifests itself in sport. These he listed as

> nationalist behaviour (perhaps biologically and psychologically derived
> – the 'animal behaviour' of the 'Soccer Tribe'); a strong national
> consciousness (the 'imagined community' – the 'tribe' is now the nation
> and its object of emotion the national team); and an ideology of nation-

alism (the 'learned' sentiments of the national anthem with its patriotism and occasional xenophobia).[23]

It is arguable that Northern Irish sport has exhibited all three of Kellas' manifestations of nationalism. As will be shown later Northern Irish soccer has been inflicted, along with other nations, by the animal behaviour of the soccer tribe. This is different from violence attached to English soccer that is either driven by identification with a local club or attaches itself to the national team. In Northern Ireland violence has been attached to local clubs but this is in itself a manifestation of nationalist behaviour as the clubs, although local, are representative of nationalist groupings, Linfield as Protestant/unionist and Belfast Celtic as Catholic/nationalist. This distinction in the type of violence informs Kellas' second category of a strong national consciousness as any game between Protestant/unionist and Catholic/nationalist clubs is necessarily a national clash and thus representative of the imagined community. The same is true for Gaelic games in Northern Ireland as they allow for a 'real' statement of a thirty-two county Ireland as the GAA does not recognize, not organize around the border. This, again, feeds into the third category of the ideology of nationalism. Although not official or learned, games between the two competing identities are conducted against a backdrop of identifying symbols, patriotism and xenophobia. National flags, paramilitary ensignia and the singing of nationally defined songs or unofficial anthems dominate soccer terraces, while Gaelic games are played under the tricolour of the Irish Republic. This use of symbols is highly important as it is far advanced from the mere use of club colours as is usual in many other domestic sports. As Guibernau states, 'the consciousness of forming a community is created through the use of symbols and the repetition of rituals that give strength to the individual members of the nation ... they provide a revealing device to distinguish between members and outsiders and heighten people's awareness of, and sensitivity to, their community'.[24] For members of the Catholic/nationalist community attending soccer matches, their use of symbols such as the tricolour, GAA county jerseys or the national colours of the Irish Republic's soccer squad contests the identities on the opposing terraces which are evidenced by Union flags, the red hand of Ulster and the colours of the Northern Irish team. To invert Smith who argued, 'the fangs of nationalism are thereby drawn [after international recognition of the nation-state] and a benign and healthy national identity or patriotism with its replicated symbolism of flags, anthems, and ceremonial parades is de rigeur',[25] nationalist identity in Northern Irish soccer can be seen to show itself through the use of symbols. Although the 'fangs of nationalism' are still drawn through the use of such symbols in the low culture nationalism of the soccer ground, those symbols, rather than celebrating a benign nationalism present after acceptance of an uncontested nation state, demonstrate that the contested unrecognized Irish nationalism is still alive and well. It offers succour to those who display such symbols while provoking opposition from those on the other side.

What I have proposed thus far is a contextualisation of Irish nationalism in Northern Irish sport that is the practical embodiment of 'low' cultural nationalism. This nationalism, while having links to the political nationalism present in Northern Ireland, in practice promotes the cultural identity of a contested nationalism in an arena, the soccer ground or the Gaelic park, where the 'enemy' is either present on an opposite terrace or completely excluded. The tribal nature of soccer support in particular, adds to the divisions created by the sport which results in the emergence of an 'us and them' mentality which is further exaggerated by the use of symbols and the apparent Protestant/unionist domination of the game and the direction of security surrounding such. As Sugden has argued 'if there is one single sport which does most to emphasize the polarity of Northern Irish society it is association football'.[26] To put the 'low' cultural nationalism and contested nationalism ideas into an historical context the experiences of the GAA and Northern Irish soccer teams are worthy of closer scrutiny.

THE GAELIC ATHLETIC ASSOCIATION AND THE NORTH

The Joint Framework Document, published in February 1995, stated that 'a climate of peace enables the process of healing to begin. It transforms the prospects for political progress, building on that already made in the talks process. Everyone now has a role to play in moving irreversibly beyond the failures of the past and creating new relationships capable of perpetuating peace with freedom and justice'.[27] The aim here is to explore the history of the GAA in Northern Ireland, to build on the GAA's self-perceived belief that it forms a central part of the force of Irish nationalism, and show how it has operated both North and South of the border along these lines. This belief in its own importance has meant that the GAA has been unable to move forward in the general spirit of the peace process. Instead it has clung onto old dogmas and past history and has not attempted to create the new relationships needed to perpetuate peace.

During 1987, over a hundred years after the founding of the Gaelic Athletic Association, a new magazine title appeared in newsagents across Ireland which dealt exclusively with the Irish sports of Hurling and Gaelic football. In itself, the arrival of the *Gaelic Review* on the newstands was nothing extraordinary; as the editor Martin Breheny pointed out 'the [All-Ireland] finals are watched annually by a live audience of 140,000 and on television by over two million'. Gaelic games are mass participation and mass spectator sports – in an age of leisure such a magazine supplies an uncontroversial and popular demand. The GAA is not, however, uncontroversial. During the hundred odd years of its existence the Association has attempted to place itself at the centre of Irish life. The image that it projects is not solely that of a sporting body, but that of an organisation which feeds off historical myth to create a central definition of nationalism. In the editorial of the first *Gaelic Review*,[28] Martin Breheny criticized the higher echelons of the Association. He was completely aware of the dangers of such criticism, and was able to conclude that 'criticize the GAA and you are immediately labelled as unpatriotic. A big and influential core of officials confuses criticism with ill will. It is a childish outlook, yet it continues to be prevalent.'

Since the 1993 Downing Street Declaration, the peace process, despite many set backs, has stayed on course. It appears, in the wake of the Good Friday Agreement, that there is a chance that the issues of Irish nationality and self-determination might finally be resolved so that the different societies within Northern Ireland can reach a point of compromize and accommodation. Ultimately this process has been influenced by the political expediency of the main players; but this has also been accompanied by a wholesale questioning of the respective historical positions of ideology. Sinn Féin and the Irish government have made certain concessions; the former moving away from the position of armed struggle, the latter holding the referendum on the continued place of articles two and three of the constitution. A general overview of the whole process sees the understanding and definition of nationalist politics and rhetoric in an apparent state of transition. How then can the modern, mobile and 'realistic' vision of nationalism, which is currently presented in the peace process, be reconciled with the seemingly outdated view of the GAA and its dogged determination to keep rule 21? As part of the current process Gerry Adams has demanded 'the equality of treatment for the Irish culture (… scores of traditions, maybe hundreds, all equally valid) and identity',[29] and the Joint Framework Document instituted the 'protection of common specified … cultural rights'.[30] It has to be seen that while the rest of the world has moved forward politically, attempting to accommodate the different traditions in Northern Ireland, and historians have attempted to revise our notion of the mythic nationalist past, the GAA has blindly clung onto a self-created and self-preserved image of Ireland. Although their organisation is concerned with sport, their message is centred on nationalism; the self-styled defenders of the nation. In the current climate of change the GAA has failed to move forward and accept the opening out of the different cultural traditions which exist in the island of Ireland.

A common view of Gaelic games from outside Ireland was echoed by Nicholas Woodsworth who noted as he travelled round the west of Ireland that 'by Letterfrack I stopped in a thin Irish mist to watch two local teams savage each other in the game of Gaelic football. It is such an odd, exotic sport I found it hard to believe I was still in Europe'.[31] This cosy view of a game somehow divorced from the realities of the modern world ignores the reality of the situation in the North since 1968 and the GAA's role in the troubles. Its agenda, although still centrally concerned with promoting an Irish game on an amateur basis, has been driven by its political role at the centre of the nationalist community. As Sugden and Bairner noted 'as the oppositional political dimension of the GAA in the Republic disappeared, north of the border its controversial political profile has remained high. At no time has Northern Ireland, as a political entity, achieved total acceptance from the minority Irish Catholic population and, in continued support for the cause of Irish unity, the GAA has gone on playing a political role'.[32]

In the North the GAA has been able to play out the role it apparently believes it played in the South up to 1922. It has been able to position itself as one of the few legally functioning national-based bodies in the North, and from that position play a central role in defining nationalist identity and fermenting nationalist agitation. It has consistently stressed a separate Irish identity and has pursued the cause of Irish unity and the destruction of the Northern State with its Protestant, British-backed hegemony. Throughout the years of the troubles the GAA has used its history to promote its own standing amongst the nationalist community. It has constantly referred to the nationalist heroes of the past and used the language of romantic nationalism by stressing the fourth green field ideal. The correlation between the Irish revolution of 1912-22 and the Northern situation is problematic. The GAA has pursued in its rhetoric ideals which belong alongside the language of physical force Republicanism rather than the more realistic constitutional nationalism of the SDLP. A common revisionist critique of the IRA and Sinn Féin is that their view of history has become warped in the pursuit of a contemporary political agenda. The same is true of the GAA, not only in the thrust of its own beliefs, but probably more importantly in view of the dynamics of the North, in the way the Association's aims have been perceived by their opponents. Mc Garry and O'Leary have summed up the GAA's position by stating

the GAA has been the most successful cultural nationalist organisation in Ireland, and has undoubtedly revived and strengthened traditional native sports – and on a wholly amateur basis. However, it success has been at a price. Ulster Protestants and the security forces have viewed the GAA with suspicion, as a nursery school for republicans – Padraig Pearse was one of its most famous graduates, and numerous convicted IRA prisoners have followed in his footsteps. It is not therefore surprising that GAA games and members have been subject to harassment.[33]

The GAA's position as nationalist flagbearers has been transferred to the North, not only in their own minds, but also and problematically, in the minds of their opponents. This position has resulted in the GAA taking a central role in the politics of the North whilst 'operating a very narrow definition of politics'.[34]

The tradition of the ban has taken on a new significance in the North, now covered by rule 21, which allows for members of the RUC and the Army to be excluded from the Association. While all other county boards now conduct their business in English, the Ulster board continues to use the Irish language. As with Bloody Sunday and the attack on Croke Park, elements within the security forces and the loyalist community identify GAA clubs with nationalism, and clubs have become the targets for attacks of violence and arson. In October 1991 the Ulster Defence Association added the GAA to its lists of legitimate targets because of its 'continual sectarianism and support for the republican movement'.[35] This was reinforced by a further press release which declared that targets are 'those associated with the republican war machine ... and identified at least a dozen members of the Gaelic Athletic Association as being involved'.[36] The reality of this threat has resulted in the deaths of individuals associated with or present at GAA-owned premises, and attacks on GAA clubhouses. In 1992 a man was shot dead at the Sean Martin GAA club in east Belfast, and the landmark 3000th victim of the troubles was killed while outside the Lámh Dhearg GAA club in Hannahstown West Belfast. The attitude of the British Army has added to the feeling of siege amongst members of the GAA. As Gaelic games were organized on a thirty-two county basis there has always been constant traffic across the border made up of supporters, officials and players of the different teams. These have been stopped and searched by the army, and in 1988 Aiden McAnespie was shot by the army at a checkpoint while travelling to play Gaelic football in the South. The Army has also been criticized for its occupation of Belfast's Casement Park in the early 1970s, and its use of the Crossmaglen Rangers' ground in South Armagh as a helicopter base. The place of the GAA at the centre of the nationalist community, whilst existing primarily as a sporting organisation, has thus led to heightened levels of animosity towards it.

The British government has funded the GAA in ground building, promotion of the sports and so on through the Sports Council and the Department of Education, yet the GAA maintains its ban on British Army and RUC personnel under rule 21. This has led to opposition from Unionist politicians who object to what they perceive as a front organisation for terrorism receiving funding. In this there is an obvious dichotomy. While on one hand the British state funds the GAA, the other sees its elected officials in the Unionist parties, the army and the RUC remaining deeply suspicious.[37] Problematically this has led at times to increased surveillance of the GAA by the security forces and a heightened sense of animosity from loyalist paramilitaries because they view both the GAA, its clubs and its members as inseparable from the cause of republican terrorism. This cycle of mutual suspicion and conflicting political ideologies cannot be broken until the GAA removes its political message from its sporting agenda, an idea that was unthinkable until the start of the peace process.

The practicalities of mutual suspicion has not been helped by the official pronouncements of the GAA. In 1972 when the GAA constitution was re-written it included a firm commitment to the creation of a united Ireland, and the language used by GAA personnel has constantly stressed the need for action on the whole question of the North's sovereignty. As the president of the GAA in 1973, Pat Fanning stated

> Our charter proclaims the determination of the GAA to work for a 32 county Ireland. Our very rules exclude from membership the British Army, undisciplined elements of which are now mounting a fresh reign of terror in our Northern land. Our games even in the torn North are still played in GAA fields and under Ireland's flag.[38]

In the North during the troubles the GAA has been a central focus for the nationalist community under its cover as a sporting association. It has espoused the broad republican and nationalist cause and in doing so has cemented its support amongst the nationalist community whilst bringing about the wrath of Unionists politicians, loyalists paramilitaries, the RUC and the British Army. Institutionally and socially the GAA has backed the creation of a thirty-two county Ireland in direct contradiction to the wishes of Ulster's other tradition.

RULE 21

With the onset of the peace process all members of Northern Irish society were encouraged to examine their beliefs and decide if their own political standpoint was compatible to the spirit of change and whether they had a place in the new Ireland. As we have witnessed, the paramilitaries of both sides, accompanied by politicians of all shades have, albeit with certain reservations, attempted to move forward, away from violence and towards constitutionalism. The spirit of reconciliation has had a direct impact on the society and economy of the North as the days of the killings became part of a collective memory. Increasingly, different bodies are questioning their allegiances and their adherence to different forms of symbolism and accepting that in the new Ireland all the different religions, cultures, political loyalties and traditions have to be embraced. Members of the GAA were as hopeful of change as everyone else. After the announcement of the 1994 cease-fire Michael Walker attempted to assess how practical changes resulting from the peace process would affect the business of the GAA. He wrote

> the GAA have always been organized on a 32-county basis and have always been anti-British; their banning of security force personnel legitimized the organisation as a target in the eyes of Loyalist terrorists. If the cease-fire holds, and if the loyalists join it, then the British Army's role would decline and their checkpoints decrease. Last year there were complaints that people going to Gaelic football's Ulster final, and other games, were unnecessarily delayed at checkpoints. The GAA's Ulster Secretary, Micky Feeney is 'delighted' with the cease-fire and hopes to see demilitarisation quickly. 'Just in certain areas' he said 'checkpoints were holding people up, border checkpoints especially. We'd hope very shortly that all that would go'.[39]

Feeney could see the obvious benefits from peace, but during the peace process of the 1990s it has become apparent that while welcoming the whole process of reconciliation, the GAA has, it seems, contributed very little to that process.

Rule 21 is, as with previous bans, a symbol. It stands for the purity of Gaelic games, and prevents the acceptance into the Association of those perceived as the enemy. While others involved in Irish life have moved away from symbolism, or at least questioned such, the GAA has remained immobile. By doing so they have clung to their own peculiar notion of nationalism, their own place in and version of nationalist history, and their over-inflated sense of importance as a national organisation. The GAA's belief in the ban has admittedly been reinforced by the practical lessons of the troubles: harassment by the security forces; the occupation of grounds by the army; attacks by loyalist paramilitaries and a need to give a voice to the nationalist community. These beliefs have been backed up by a general interpretation of the GAA's aims which stress: the need to halt the incursion of foreign games; to oppose the dilution of Irish culture and to protect the historical legacy of the GAA. As understandable as these beliefs and aims might be in the light of the GAA's support for the nationalist community in the North, does rule 21 belong to the spirit of reconciliation? As the editorial of the *Irish Times* stated

> the GAA has still to rid itself of a damaging piece of historical baggage [rule 21] which has no place in the new Ireland ... Croke Park often appears content to speak to only one tradition on this island. Its refusal even to contemplate sharing its sporting facilities with soccer, the so-called garrison game in some GAA circles, is symptomatic of this inward looking approach.[40]

Yet on the same day the Gaelic games correspondent of the same paper, Sean Moran, was able to conclude that the question of rule 21 could not be addressed by the GAA as abolition would be to 'betray the nationalist community'.[41] Herein lies the GAA's problem. After building up its nationalist credentials, and by presenting themselves as defenders of the nation, can the GAA move in tandem with the peace process without completely revising their own understanding and interpretation of their past, thereby destroying their radical nationalist roots, and, it could be argued, betraying their self-constructed version of Irish nationalism? Another difficulty for the GAA was that those members from the Republic of Ireland often 'exist untouched by many of the considerations which endure in Northern Ireland'.[42] In this the GAA does not exist as a single entity and has to, as with all sporting bodies in the island, cope with different experiences, opinions and beliefs.

In April 1995, six months into the first cease-fire, the county boards of Carlow, Down, Dublin and Sligo put forward a motion calling for the deletion of rule 21 at the GAA Annual Congress. In the event this motion was withdrawn from the order paper without discussion. The reasons given centred around the procedural rules of the Congress which state that unless a motion received the backing of two-thirds of delegates it could not then be debated for a further three years. A compromise was reached. Rather than losing the motion for three years the issue would be discussed at a special congress to be fixed at a future date. This would allow for events to overtake the GAA and hopefully make the rule obsolete before the Association had to take the initiative itself. With the return to violence in February 1996 the Association may have been vindicated in their decision not to move to hastily.

However, the decision not to debate rule 21 in 1995 was seen by many commentators as the GAA missing a golden opportunity to show good faith in keeping with the spirit of the peace process. As the *Irish Times* leader concluded 'at a time of peace and reconciliation it [the GAA] should climb out of the trenches and cast aside some of its baggage'.[43] The GAA clung on to its perceived historical agenda and failed to move forward. The decision received widespread condemnation. Father Denis Faul stated 'the ban is the essence of vindictiveness and pettiness. It should be lifted immediately, especially in these days of peace. Nationalist politicians are asking us to draw a line over the past'. Mark Durkan, SDLP chairman echoed similar sentiments, 'the ban is not appropriate in such a fine sporting body with such high achievements. The peace process can help remove some of the sensitivities surrounding the issue. This is a time when our society should be inclusive'. There were however others who supported the GAA's decision, most notably Gerry Adams, 'I would be opposed to the ending of rule 21. The GAA is more than just a sporting body. It seeks to promote our sense of Irishness. This is clearly at odds with the role and function of the RUC and the British Army which seek to deny us this right'. Jack Bootham, then president of the GAA was opposed to the removal of the ban, yet seems aware of the changing political situation in Northern Ireland. A week before the 1995 Congress he stated, 'that following the cease-fires and the commencement of the peace process the GAA would not be found wanting in the pursuit of reconciliation'.[44] On the same page of the *Evening Herald* the Gaelic games correspondent tries to unravel this contradiction. He argued

> being in favour of the retention of rule 21 is surely adopting an ambivalent approach towards the pursuit of reconciliation … the abolition of this controversial rule would be a magnanimous and real reconciliatory gesture on the Association's part which would almost certainly help to improve relations between the two communities.

The twists and turns of the peace process, the failed ceasefires and the agreements of 1998 that have brought so much hope to Northern Ireland, are far to complex to assess here. However, it has to be argued that the Good Friday Agreement and the ensuing referendums in Ireland, north and south, demonstrated that the overwhelming majority of people backed the moves towards peace. Especially important were the Irish Republic's alterations to its constitution that removed its territorial claim over Northern Ireland, and the failure of the Drumcree march to go ahead in July 1998. These two incidents are central as they represented the removal of two of the most high profile symbols within nationalism and unionism respectively. The Irish state jettisoned its historic claim to Northern Ireland, something that had long been argued was vital to any prospective peace process as it would reassure the unionist community, while the Orange Order complied with the Parades Commission decision that the most contentious of marches could not go ahead. As part of the peace process generally, but in 1998 specifically, all groups involved in the Northern Irish troubles have been forced to question their central ideology, and the vast majority demonstrated a clear commitment towards peace. Such commitment has demanded that many jettison long and firmly held ideas, and that they deal with a wealth of contentious issues. The peace process has profoundly altered the historic and ideological foundation of the nature of Irish nationalism within Northern Ireland. To seemingly reject, in the short to medium term at least, the idea of a united Ireland, parties such as Sinn Féin and groups such as the IRA, have transformed the definition of what it is that they demand as nationalists.

It is the specific issue of sport that concerns us here, and more centrally the GAA. Having built up the nationalist credentials that it projects, and having been so careful at the time of the first ceasefire of the modern peace process, how would the GAA respond to the rapidly changing political scene in 1998? Would they, as a 'mere' sporting body, question their central ideology, their historical mission? Would they be prepared to jettison rule 21 as a concession to the peace process, even if that might force a redefining of their nationalism?

The speed of change in Northern Ireland meant that the 1995 refusal to debate the issue, although condemned as not in keeping with the spirit of the peace process, can be understood as a pragmatic move by the GAA. While not prepared to become persuaders for peace by acting unilaterally, the GAA demonstrated a sensitivity towards its supporters in Northern Ireland. The GAA's nationalism is a function of its own historical image and serves, first and foremost, the needs of its followers. The 1995 Congress allowed the GAA to call as Special Congress to deal with rule 21, 'should circumstances in the Six Counties call for such action'.[45] The ruling on how the Special Congress would be called, allowed the GAA and its policies, to be dependent on the developments within an external, rather than be forged from within.

The manner in which the rule 21 debate is shaped by external forces is clear by following press coverage of the issue from the time of the 1995 Congress. In January 1996 the *Irish Times* noted that 'for the time being, the question [abolition of rule 21] doesn't really arise as greater pessimism about the political situation in the North has slowed what momentum existed a year ago for the repeal of rule 21.'[46] One of the constant difficulties for the GAA and the whole rule 21 debate is that the Northern Counties are seen as being the driving force for any decision. There is an air of opinion that exists around the GAA that appears to argue that while all agreed on their common goal of a thirty-two county Ireland and the rejection of the British military presence in Ulster, it is the Northern GAA who must take the lead. They are the ones at the cutting edge, they are the people who suffer for their belief in an Irish nationalism, and they must decide whether rule 21 stays or goes. The Central Committee of the GAA and the Southern Counties, no matter what agendas or beliefs they may have, do not have the right to shape the policy over rule 21. Some in the northern counties find this approach problematic, as there is such a wide range of views even within the counties there. In 1995 Down was the first northern county to back the annulment of rule 21. The proposer of that motion argued in 1996 at a time when the politics of Northern Ireland were far less hopeful than they had been in 1995, that

> debating it [in 1995 at the Annual Congress] might have caused diffi-culties because my perspective would be very different to the perspec-tives in East Tyrone, Fermanagh or South Armagh. When you look at the situation, at the end of the day we need leadership from the centre. Leaving it to northern counties would be an abrogation of responsibil-ity.[47]

In 1996 the GAA did not debate rule 21. This was a product of the stalled peace process and the fact that there was no significant demand for such a debate. In his address to the Congress, the GAA President, Jack Boothman, argued that the Association was committed to playing a role in the peace process while it remained an attainable objective. In his speech Boothman reiterated a constant mantra of not only the GAA, but any sporting body which is by its very nature political, by stating

> we are not a political body ... What restrictions we place on membership of the GAA are a reaction to political circumstances. In the context of an acceptable political settlement in which the national and cultural tradi-tions of the people of all Ireland are equally recognized and respected, the concept of an exclusion rule will not have any relevance to us.[48]

The GAA is clearly a political body, and to say otherwise is contradictory. The contradiction is clear in Boothman's speech. While stressing the Association's apolitical nature he is concomitantly stating the future of rule 21 depends on a political settlement that is acceptable to the GAA and its supporters.

The 1997 Congress again failed to deal with the issue of rule 21 in any considered manner as the political situation, although more hopeful than it had been a year previously was still slow and any headway that had been made in the earlier part of the year had dried up as all parties awaited the outcome of the British general election. The only reference made to rule 21 by Jack Boothman in his last speech as President placed the whole story of the rule in the context of the peace process.

> My Presidency was a time of great hope and fierce disappointment in Northern Ireland. I am sad to say that as regards rule 21 which excludes British soldiers and policemen from GAA membership, we did not make the strides that might have been expected in changing circumstances.[49]

The situation in Northern Ireland changed rapidly throughout the second half of 1997 and 1998. The political will to solve the problem was heightened by the arrival of the Blair administration in Downing Street, while the political parties in Northern Ireland made increased headway in the round table talks at Stormont. In the context of the gathering momentum towards peace, a situation akin to that which existed in 1995, pressure was placed on the GAA to make concessions over rule 21 in keeping with the spirit of the wider peace process. In response to a question by Proinsias De Rossa, leader of the Democratic Left in the Dáil, asking if the GAA should remove rule 21 as a confidence-building measure, Bertie Ahern, the Fianna Fáil Taoiseach stated, 'I would certainly welcome it in the future ... I do think, in the passage of time, that it is a move the GAA should make'.[50] The following weekend a sporting editorial in the *Irish Times*, written by Sean Kilfeather added to the pressure. Kilfeather argued that while the GAA was in such great shape as a sporting body that was representative of Irish life, it should also be courageous with regard to rule 21. Kilfeather argued, quite rightly, that rule 21 and the other bans had appeared from a history of suppression by British forces, intimidation of GAA members and their activities by opponents and a need to underpin the feelings of nationalists in the North. The thrust of his case was that the political landscape was so changed that it was possible for a British prime minister to have met with the leader of Sinn Féin without too hostile a reaction. In such changed circumstances the GAA 'could capture the high moral ground by outlining the reasons for the rule in the first place and the decision now to remove it as archaic and unhelpful in the context of the future'.[51] The newly elected president of Ireland, Mary McAleese, added the weight of her opinion to the debate by revealing that she had called for the deletion of rule 21 back in 1995.[52]

In 1998 the pace of change in Northern Ireland became, it appeared, unstoppable. After much behind the scenes jockeying for position, hard bargaining and no doubt some political bullying, the parties of Northern Ireland signed up to the Good Friday Agreement, that, it was argued signalled the end of the modern troubles. While people have continued to be killed in Northern Ireland during 1998 on the back of situations such as the Drumcree standoff and as a result of Real IRA activities in Omagh, the majority of parties have remained committed to the spirit and frameworks of the Agreement. While some issues seem resolved, other such as that of decommissioning of terrorist weapons still have to be addressed. These problems, as real as they are, can however be settled within the confines of democratic discussion. At the time of writing only one terrorist force, the Continuity IRA, has failed to declare a complete and total ceasefire. The politicians are in session, and Northern Ireland appears, despite all its wounds and divisions, to be moving steadily towards a lasting and commonly agreed peaceful society.

Three days after the Good Friday Agreement, one of the leading press-based GAA commentators, Tom Humphries, penned a long piece for his newspaper entitled, 'Time for the GAA to become a persuader'.[53] Humphries returned in his piece to the problem of who should call time on rule 21: the North or the South? Humphries summed up what is a battle between an emotive nationalism born of the North that supports rule 21, and the a more pragmatic nationalism of the South that demands its abolition.

> As one who has stood with defiant club secretaries in the charred rubble of burned out clubhouses, who has seen murdered GAA men buried in coffins with jerseys draped over them, who has heard the stories of intimidation and harassment that GAA people in the north have been subjected to, this column has always been a little reluctant to issue oracular statements on the status of rule 21.
>
> From the warm comfort of a Dublin newspaper office it is easy to talk tough about rule 21. It is a marketing disaster surely, an old anachronism which has survived because of historical circumstance and fear. An organisation whose member were once exhorted to 'join the volunteers to learn how to shoot straight' was always going to have difficulty sloughing off its past.[54]

Humphries, while understanding and rationalising why rule 21 existed, encouraged the GAA to build on the spirit of the Good Friday Agreement and become a cultural persuader for reconciliation. Sport, he argued, was the ideal medium for the joining together of the two cultures in Ireland.

The timing of the Good Friday Agreement was unfortunate for the GAA as it came one week before their Annual Congress. Rule 21 was not even on the order paper for discussion at the Congress, a realistic stance considering that many commentators doubted that a document such as the Good Friday Agreement would ever emerge from the talks at Stormont. Once the Agreement had been signed however, the GAA, were in a problematic situation. In the spirit of the moment, everyone appeared to be making major concessions with regard to historical positions. The GAA, were not in a position where it could realistically debate rule 21 only a week after such an important document had been signed, and at a time when no one knew what the Agreement would actually achieve. There was however, a realisation that if the GAA was seen to do nothing, then 'the wait and see attitude of the past three years is becoming embarrassingly inadequate'.[55]

At the Annual Congress, the GAA President, Joe McDonagh, took the step that had been open to the GAA since 1995, and called the Special Congress to debate rule 21 on 30 May. McDonagh's argument for debating the possible deletion of rule 21 centred on the spirit of Good Friday Agreement, specific articles contained within the agreement that would review policing in Northern Ireland and the view that sport generally, and the GAA specifically, should be playing a broader role in fostering good community relations. It is clear that McDonagh's move was made in close consultation with the Taoiseach and that a two-way offering was being made by the politicians; if the GAA gave up rule 21, the British government would end the British Army's occupation of the Crossmaglen GAA grounds.[56] The deletion of rule 21 could not take place that weekend as the northern counties wanted to consult their members. In returning home for such debates the counties were reminded by McDonagh of what was demanded, that the GAA should take 'a leap of faith in support of the Peace Process'.[57] He also warned the Congress that 'as the largest organisation in this country [we cannot] shirk our responsibility or role in achieving and contributing to peace … we must play our part in the evolution of peace and equity, even if it means some risk'.[58]

In the lead up to the Special Congress debate was intense, and both newspaper and political opinion flowed freely in advising the GAA which way to go. Many commentators agreed that rule 21 was a symbolic statement rather than practical act. If rule 21 were deleted there would not be a long queue of Army or RUC personnel waiting to join the Association. One writer, building on this aspect of rule 21, noted like many things in the six counties, it is a label, in the same way as an Orange sash is a label or a Lambeg drum, and people are reluctant to shed these badges of identity for fear of being seen to be weak. In this respect rule 21 fits snugly beside Articles Two and Three of the Constitution which are aspirational and have never had any positive effect on what is seen as the national question, at least not as far as most of us are concerned.[59]

Symbolism is central to the construction of nationalism and national identities. Within the rule 21 debate there appeared a double-headed nationalism that is so indicative of contemporary Irish nationalism generally. One looks towards the forces of modernity, communality and commonality within a functioning democracy as the values of nationalism (the Southern Irish experience), while the other looks towards self defence and definition against the other, in this case, Britain (the Northern Irish experience). Both nationalisms are contained within the GAA, and while a traditionalist body with a strongly nationalist and unrevized history, not a unitary one with single values.

That the decision to call the Special Congress came days after the Good Friday Agreement was a result, many argued, of a hasty desire by GAA President, Joe McDonagh, to fit in with the spirit of reconciliation. A product of the Good Friday Agreement was the simultaneous referendums held in Northern Ireland and the Republic on 22 May 1998. They were held a week before the Special Congress and both returned massive yes votes. In Northern Ireland the yes vote supported the Good Friday Agreement, in the Republic it backed the deletion of articles two and three from the Constitution. Such votes threw the GAA's debate over rule 21 into stark relief. Could a mere sporting body go against the general feeling in Ireland and do anything but vote for the deletion of rule 21? Albert Fallon, former chairman of the Leinster GAA Council, while accepting that rule 21 had performed a vital function in supporting the northern GAA community, argued, 'in view of the massive yes vote, north and south in support of the Good Friday Agreement ... how can we claim that the time and climate is not right? What purpose does the rule now serve?'[60]

Around the period of the referendum, as it became clear that there would be a huge yes vote, and in the wake of the actual vote, criticism of those campaigning for the retention of rule 21 became more intense. There was an increasing public acceptance that rule 21 had been a necessity for the Northern GAA, as it was a defiant rule that defined their nationalism against the British. Increasingly however, the yes vote in the referendums was seen as a signal that the troubles and any accompanying sectarianism or symbolism had disappeared, whereas rule 21 was viewed as a backward-looking relic of a sectarian struggle. One commentator stated quite clearly that 'rule 21 is a log on the bonfire of sectarianism in Northern Ireland. Regardless of what happens in the weeks ahead, the rule should go'.[61] The nearer the vote came, the clearer it was that the vote for deletion would not be a formality.[62] The Ulster counties were expressing open hostility to Joe McDonagh's tactics and they vocalized a feeling that the GAA was being forced into debating and possibly deleting rule 21 as part of the general peace process, rather than on the basis of a consideration of the rule itself. The Ulster argument was that the peace process, while laudable, had not solved all the problems of Northern Ireland. One of the remits of the Good Friday Agreement was to examine the role of policing within the Province, and deal with the problematic relationship between the RUC and the nationalist community. Ulster's GAA boards argued that rule 21 excluded the RUC and the Army as they were instruments of oppression and abuse. Until the various committees ordered by the Good Friday Agreement had come together and reported on the issue of policing, the GAA should not delete rule 21. The RUC was seen as a body that had colluded with Loyalist terror groups, a collusion that has led to the deaths of, and systematic discrimination against GAA members. As one GAA member offered by way of the defence of rule 21

> how's this for a scenario? On the twelfth of July, you go to the Garvaghy Road and the GAA has rescinded rule 21. And you get the same scenario you got a year ago, where people are not allowed to go to their Mass. Where they're batoned off the streets by the British army and the RUC. How do you square that? Do you put the thumbs up to the fella who's beating you across the head and say 'See you at the match tomorrow, pal'? I don't think so.[63]

I would argue that the whole rule 21 debate, during 1998, became a debate that went to the heart of nationalism. It was not a debate that considered the merits of the peace process. All those included in the GAA had lined up full-square behind the Good Friday Agreement, and most recognized that the Association had a role to play in the push for peace. The debate was about whether the men and women of Northern Ireland were free to express their nationalism and their national identity through their sport, free from molestation and oppression. It was a nationalism unrecognized by the southern GAA as they never suffered such harassment, and who had to, as members of a modernized state, believe that political processes would heal all wounds. The peace process though, is not merely a political process played out between ministers and civil servants. It is a process that must deal with the difficult issues of contested and

166 / Sport and nationalism in Ireland

competing identities, and attempt to forge a situation where such can exist peacefully. The northern GAA does not, and most would recognize the good reasons why, believe that an unreformed RUC or British Army, even if they are functioning within a 'new' Northern Ireland, will respect their nationalism. As Vincent Hogan wrote

> GAA life in Ulster is about much more than kicking footballs and whipping sliothars. It has a political dimension perhaps not fully appreciated in the south. For a Six Counties man, the playing of Gaelic games is an expression of culture, identity and in some cases, defiance.[64]

The problem for the GAA is that outsiders see rule 21 as a blatantly aggressive act of sectarian exclusion. The sister of the murdered GAA player, Aidean McAnespie, who was shot dead by a British soldier at a border checkpoint in 1988, realized that rule 21 would be used by the opponents of the GAA as 'a stick to beat it with because the Association aspires to a 32-county national identity'.[65] The views expressed by certain members of the Unionist community were extreme. In seeking to apply pressure on the GAA to delete rule 21, some commentators returned to the age-old method of identity based abuse and scathing asides against the force of nationalism. David Christopher, the head of the Independent Unionist Society at Trinity College Dublin, provided an excellent example of the dismissive attack that sought to place the GAA and its adherence to rule 21 in the context of a blatantly sectarian struggle. He wrote

> I have a slight problem understanding the nationalism of the GAA. Why for instance do the gaels indulge themselves in what is inherently a pathetic sport only played by paddies? Why do you not all go and play lovely gentlemanly games like cricket and bowls? I fear for this country and her people who are unable to accept that Ireland is eternally part of the British Isles.[66]

For many within the unionist community the support by Sinn Féin for those who sought to preserve rule 21, would have served as concrete evidence that despite any moves in the peace process, the GAA was a sectarian body motivated solely by a republican agenda. The week before the vote on rule 21 Sinn Féin's newspaper, *An Phoblacht*, advised delegates attending the Special Congress that they retain rather than delete the rule. *An Phoblacht* located the need for preservation within the context of the lack of any concrete settlement of the policing issue, and continued concerns that despite the Good Friday

Agreement, the 1998 marching season would still see the Orange Order on roads marching through nationalist areas. The newspaper included a call from Breadan MacCionaith of the Garvaghy Road residents group for the GAA to retain rule 21. He argued that until issues such as the Drumcree march had been settled and the nationalist community of the Garvaghy Road were free from intimidation and attack in and around 12 July, then the GAA should not accept the forces of the crown into the Association. To do so, would show those forces respect they did not deserve. An editorial in the same issue said that those who wanted to scrap the rule as part of the goodwill of the peace process were 'seriously misguided'.[67] Other notable voices of the nationalist community were equally clear in their calls for the retention of the rule, claiming that Joe McDonagh and the GAA had become political pawns in a wider game.[68] By the time the of the Special Congress two facts were clear. First that all the Ulster delegates would vote against deletion, thereby placing the two-thirds majority needed to secure the abolition of rule 21 in jeopardy. Second, that mainstream opinion in Dublin media circles was appalled at the idea that the GAA could fail to do anything but abolish the rule in the context of the Good Friday Agreement and the yes vote in the referendum.[69]

The actual vote on 30 May to consider rule 21 never took place. During the Special Congress it became clear that the votes for and against keeping rule 21 were fairly evenly matched (slightly favouring abolition), and the two-thirds majority needed for abolition could not be reached. The conference backed a motion tabled by delegates from Cork which framed an amendment that suggested rule 21 be suspended, but not deleted until the envisaged reforms in policing Northern Ireland had taken force. The GAA was widely condemned for its decision, but one can see little else that they could do. Irish organisations, especially those with a history as long as the GAA, are terrified of division, a terror that stems directly from the Civil War. It was better for the GAA to preserve unity rather than face a split between north and south.

The decision met with widespread condemnation and the GAA was labelled as an organisation out of step with the general move towards peace and reconciliation. Tom Humphries suggested in the *Irish Times* that the GAA had misunderstood the modern idea of Irishness which is big and inclusive, and adopted instead for a move that was narrow and small minded. He argued that if

> mainstream republicanism has stopped holding up its dead and its wounded as justification for eternal war, why should the GAA be persisting? From Hume to Adams, the nationalist strain in the North has been in the business of taking the first step. Not the GAA ... For

a great and unique sports body with so much to offer, it was a sad day.[70]

The *Belfast Telegraph* condemned the GAA for not entering into the spirit of the peace process, while the *Irish Independent* expressed disappointment that the Association could not make a gesture when Ireland stood on the brink of peace.[71] The *Irish News* pointed to the emotive statements made by speakers favouring retention and the manner in which the whole debate had been tied in with the issue of police reform. As with other newspapers the *Irish News* made clear that they saw the GAA as out of step with the 85 per cent of people who had voted yes in the referendum days previously.[72] The *Irish Echo* was more sympathetic towards those who supported the retention of rule 21 admitting that while there had been a great momentum of change in Northern Ireland, the GAA was not yet ready to line up behind such change.[73] Newspapers such as the *Andersontown News* and the *Irish Post* applauded the decision of the GAA as supportive of northern nationalists.[74] The most blatant criticism of the GAA's decision came from what may have appeared a surprising source. The GAA's own patron, Archbishop Dermot Clifford, argued that the Association had missed a glorious opportunity and that the delegates at the Special Congress who he had addressed should forget the past and make a central contribution to peace. His comments were widely reported and backed up by a host of other key figures.[75] In the letter columns of the press, the decision of the GAA was both applauded and condemned. Some writers demanded that the GAA's public funding be withdrawn until rule 21 was abolished,[76] while others made clear that they felt the policing issue was a real concern of nationalists in the north, and until this was addressed the rule should stay.[77]

At the time of writing it is unclear which way the GAA will go with regard to rule 21 and when it will next be debated. What is evident is that the GAA serves to define a variety of forms of nationalism in Ireland through its sport and organisation. It is my contention that while it may appear that the GAA is existing in an historical backwater and is not prepared to deal with the current realties of the changing situation in Northern Ireland, the broad nature of its appeal to different manifestations of Irish nationalism has to be appreciated. That the Association has successfully promoted Gaelic games across Ireland in the last hundred years, and continues to do so, is not at issue here. What I have argued throughout my coverage of the GAA is that the Association has had a problematic relationship with its own history, its function during the Irish revolutionary period and in the modern troubles of Northern Ireland. As such it has placed itself in a position where it finds it difficult to cope with modern realities. To go in step with the current peace process the GAA would have to confront its own history, the political and cultural role it has played and what it now represents. The nationalist credentials it has built for itself after the manipulation of the history of the Irish revolution and its centrality in the Northern situation has meant that the GAA is seen by many as the defender and definer of Irish nationalism. As such it could not move forward without questioning the whole historical basis of its sporting and political mission. It could not be seen to desert the ethos of its founders or its community in the north. This problematic haunted the entire rule 21 debate. How to square a confident, self assured nationalism that exists in the southern GAA, with a nationalism that still considers itself under attack in the north, irrespective of the huge steps made in the peace process? At the time of the 1995 debate the following advice was offered to the GAA

> the time has come to move on. The nationalist community in the North, from which the GAA draws its members and its goodwill, no longer needs any advice about making the first move towards reconciliation. They have the high ground there. Rule 21 has served its purpose and has now outlived its purpose. The GAA has reached the stage where there is far more to be gained from dropping rule 21 than there is to be gained from keeping it. Rule 21 persist in a climate where the nationalist community north of the border ask justly for the reform of a despised police force, and yet play their games in an association which is unable to make a symmetrical reform.[78]

In 1998 the GAA appeared out of step once more with the spirit of reconciliation. It is possible to argue that while such sweeping judgements are understandable, they are only valid if the GAA is seen as an outdated organisation representing only one version of Irish nationalism. I would argue that while having a difficult and detailed history that is intertwined with nationalism, the GAA is not merely an organisation that promotes an old fashioned republican ideal of the nation. It is a body that is hugely popular across Ireland and which dominates the domestic sporting scene. It would be ridiculous to pretend that the GAA could stay out of politics. The Association is struggling to deal with the aspirations of Irish nationalism, its history and most importantly for the north, its fears. To understand rule 21, its background and current place in the peace process debate, is to understand how potent a force sport can be in constructing and defining nationalism. To understand such in the context of Northern Irish soccer as well, is to show how extreme the position of sport in Northern Ireland has become.

DERRY CITY, SOCCER AND SECTARIANISM

As a result of the troubles, sectarianism has permeated most aspects of life in Northern Ireland in a way it did not prior to 1968. The Province has to be seen as a land divided between two mutually opposed political and cultural ideologies. Sport, although it may be considered a trivial matter by compari-son to the real human cost of the troubles, provides countless examples of how the struggle in Northern Ireland can polarize society and lead to the destruc-tion of day-to-day activity within the community. The experience of Derry City, which is the central focus here, shows all too clearly how destructive the troubles and the accompanying sectarianism can be.

After the partition of Ireland, as a result of the Anglo-Irish Treaty of 1921, two separate bodies emerged to govern football in the island of Ireland. In the Irish Free State, what is now the Irish Republic, the Football Association of Ireland (FAI) took control. In Northern Ireland the Irish Football Association (IFA) held sway. In the North teams such as Linfield and Belfast Celtic contin-ued to dominate the soccer scene in the Province's first city, while 1929 saw the foundation of Derry City in the second city. Soccer was hugely popular and the rivalry intense. Not only were Linfield, Belfast Celtic and Derry City the three leading teams from the two most important cities, but the rivalry was given an extra dimension by the very nature of Northern Irish society. Teams such as Linfield were identified as Protestant and unionist, while Belfast Celtic and Derry City were identified as Catholic and nationalist. Violence between fans, and at times on the pitch, was part-and-parcel of the match-day experience when these teams met. Although this violence may have the normal sporting rivalry as its basis, it was always played out against a backdrop of sectarian hatred. This was, and still is, a problem endemic in Northern Irish society. As Dominic Murray noted 'the more obvious manifestations of cultural life in Northern Ireland are inextricably built into the separated communities. The normal avenues of communication and contact between people which would provide a tendency towards the creation of a single shared culture are closed'.[79] Within the framework which Murray suggests we can see the base root of all Derry City's problems. Although soccer should be a leisure pursuit, a common language and an experience which unites elements within a society, in Northern Ireland this has not been the case. John Sugden and Scott Harvie were able to conclude 'the vast majority of clubs currently operating at senior level are associated to a greater or lesser degree with the Protestant communi-ty and are, by and large, administered and supported by people from such backgrounds'.[80] So despite the fact that soccer has always been a game which provides a common language for everyone in Northern Ireland (interest in the English and Scottish Leagues is high and cross community, as is participation in the sport at grass-roots level), the actual operation of senior soccer in the Province has not reflected this common interest. As the game is predominantly Protestant (and can thus be seen as tendentially unionist) individuals on the terraces, in the boardrooms, and on the pitch, have always brought their own preconceived notions of what they, and their opponents, represent into the soccer arena. It doesn't matter that Derry City has always pursued an open policy in the recruitment of players and committee men from both sides of the sectarian divide and was traditionally supported by fans from the Catholic Bogside and the Protestant Waterside, what mattered was that the followers of teams such as Linfield, the representatives of Protestantism and unionism, perceived Derry City as a bastion of Catholicism and nationalism. This is the central idea here, that soccer (and indeed most aspects of cultural and leisure life) in Northern Ireland acts not as an arena which unifies competing traditions within the community, but instead acts as another forum in which division, mutual suspicion and sectarian hatred can be reinforced by both traditions present within the community.[81]

Before moving onto discuss the experience of Derry City in the post-1968 period it is worth exploring the events surrounding Belfast Celtic in the late 1940s. This will demonstrate that soccer in Northern Ireland, even in a period prior to the modern troubles, was rife with the destructive sectarian tensions which led to the demise of Derry City some twenty years later.

Belfast Celtic was founded in 1891. It was based in Catholic West Belfast and took the inspiration for its name from the famous Glasgow Celtic. As a junior team Belfast Celtic had beaten Linfield 1-0 and a great rivalry began. After their admittance to the senior league in 1896 Belfast Celtic became locked into a constant struggle for footballing dominance with Linfield with the league championship and the cup doing a constant shuttle across the city between the two teams. As a result of the intense competition between the two teams, the religious and political nature of their respective support bases and because of the huge political upheavals in Ireland up to the mid 1920s, Belfast Celtic withdrew from the league from 1915 to 1918 and again from 1920 to 1924. This was in response to club fears over the safety of their staff and supporters while games were being played out against the monumental political changes of these years. The last game of the 1919 to 1920 season illustrates how real these fears were. At a Belfast Celtic–Glentoran game violence between sections of the crowd led to an abandonment of the match. The response to the abandonment was for an individual in the Belfast Celtic section of the crowd to fire a revolver at the Glentoran crowd.[82] It was difficult for sporting normality to exist in such a climate. Although Belfast Celtic rejoined the league in the 1924-5 season their games against traditional enemies such as Linfield and Glentoran were often marred by violence. In

1948 the final straw came. On Boxing Day Belfast Celtic played Linfield at the latter's Windsor Park ground. The game ended in a 1-1 draw, but the final whistle was the signal for a riot in which the Linfield crowd attacked the Belfast Celtic players. Most of the team and many officials received serious injuries, the worst being Jimmy Jones, the Belfast Celtic striker, who suffered a broken leg. As a result of his injuries Jones never played again. The supreme irony of this blatantly sectarian fuelled riot was that Jones, although a Belfast Celtic player, and thus identified with Catholicism and nationalism, was actually a Protestant.[83] The response of the Belfast Celtic board to the events of Boxing Day was swift and absolute. They announced that at the end of the season they would withdraw from senior football as they could no longer play soccer in such a climate. Despite their inter-war record of 14 league championships and their undoubted pedigree as one of the finest and best supported teams in Northern Irish football, Belfast Celtic left the league and never returned. The forces of sectarianism had claimed its first soccer victim.

As previously stated, Derry City, although based in a predominantly Catholic city, had historically operated an open policy which encouraged cross-community involvement in the club. This stretched as far as having equal representation of both sides of the community on the club's board of directors. If a Catholic member of the board left, he would be replaced by a Catholic, and vice versa for the Protestant members.[84] In a similar vein Derry City recruited players who were both Catholic and Protestant, unlike Linfield who only began to question their unofficial bar on Catholic players in 1992. As a result of this identification with both sections of the city's communities, and the historic strength of soccer as the primary game in Derry (Gaelic games have always struggled to become established in the city), the club was always well, and enthusiastically supported. This is not to say that the club did not encounter problems on its trips to Linfield and Glentoran, but the scale of the problem never reached the proportions of the Belfast Celtic experience. The start of the modern troubles in 1968 changed all this, led to the departure of Derry City from the league and nearly brought about their complete extinction.

The modern troubles erupted in Northern Ireland in 1968, and many of the first important stages of the conflict were played out in Derry. 1967 had witnessed the formation of the Northern Ireland Civil Rights Association (NICRA) which aimed to end the widespread anti-Catholic discrimination which existed within Northern Irish society. NICRA quickly built up a solid base of support amongst the Catholic and nationalist population, while their activities produced an increased level of intransigence amongst many in the Protestant community, most notably from unionist politicians, loyalist paramilitary groups, and elements within the Royal Ulster Constabulary (RUC).

Before explaining the fall of Derry City during the period 1968 to 1972, the major political events need brief explanation. October 1968 saw a major Civil Rights march in Derry which ended in violent confrontation between marchers and the RUC. This led to weeks of inter-communal rioting in the city, and a sharpening of grievances on both sides of the sectarian divide. In January 1969 a People's Democracy march was attacked by a loyalist mob outside Derry and again was followed by weeks of rioting in the Catholic Bogside area of the city. The marching season of the summer of 1969 followed this pattern of communal violence. The Catholic community of the Bogside, assisted by the IRA, declared the area as 'Free Derry' in an attempt to exclude elements of the unionist community and RUC who were attacking Catholics and their homes. In response to the near total collapse of civil order in Northern Ireland British troops were sent to the Province on 14 August. Although initially seen as the defenders of the Catholic community the army was quickly demonized as another facet of the British/unionist machine which oppressed Catholics. Rioting, communal violence, sectarian murder and IRA attacks on the army quickly became part of the day-to-day experience of life in Northern Ireland. 'Free Derry' remained unbroken and from 1969 to 1972 the army and RUC had to treat Derry's Bogside as a no-go area. In August 1971, in an attempt to restore order and reduce the death toll the government introduced internment. On the first day alone 452 Catholics were interned. The Catholic/nationalist community saw the whole process as another direct attack on them by the corrupt British-sponsored Stormont regime. In response to internment NICRA again gathered momentum, and they organized a major demonstration in Derry in January 1972 to oppose the policy. The day entered legend as Bloody Sunday when the Parachute Regiment murdered thirteen demonstrators. Community relations, and more specifically relations between the Catholic community, the RUC and army, completely broke down in the aftermath. In another attempt to seize the initiative the British mounted the biggest landforce gathered since Suez, named Operation Motorman to break 'Free Derry' in July 1972. Unsurprisingly another bout of rioting ensued.

Obviously there is far more to say in relation to the troubles, the high levels of inter-communal violence and the depth of suspicion and alienation amongst the Catholic community in Derry, but a brief trawl through the major events of these four years should illustrate well the climate in which Derry City were supposed to be playing football. A key point to remember throughout any coverage of Derry City during this period is that their ground, the Brandywell, is in the heart of Derry's Catholic Bogside – the centre of 'Free Derry'.

By examining the record of Derry City in the season 1969–70 it quickly becomes apparent the cost which the troubles had on the club. The season began on 9 August with an Ulster Cup match against Ards at the Brandywell. Derry City were roundly beaten 3-0 and booed off the pitch – a sure sign of footballing normality! Due to the troubles however, it took until 4 September before Derry City kicked another ball. Their home matches against Cliftonville and Crusaders in August were postponed because of rioting in Derry, and two away matches in Belfast were postponed as a result of disorder there. All Derry's 'home' matches during September were played away because the Brandywell was inaccessible for visiting teams because of the barricades and their refusal to enter 'Free Derry'. The first game played at the Brandywell in the League did not take place until October 18, some ten weeks after a ball had last been kicked at home. The pattern continued throughout the season, with games regularly postponed or played elsewhere. The matches against Linfield were as difficult as ever. The match in Belfast in March was disrupted by violence in the stands, and the match in Derry was never played as the RUC feared a breach of the peace if the game went ahead.

The 1970–71 season was somewhat more peaceful, and access to the Brandywell far easier. A sign of the relative calm was the visit by Wolverhampton Wanderers to Brandywell to play a Texaco Cup match in December. Despite these signs of hope, some games, such as the visits of Linfield, had to be played at the Coleraine ground, some thirty miles away from Derry, in an attempt to avoid trouble. This tactic did not work as both the League game at the end of January and the Cup match of March were both marred by serious fighting between supporters. The most poignant sign of the increasing toll of the troubles on Derry City was the 1971 Irish Cup Final. The match was to be played against Distillery, one of the most uncontroversial teams in terms of sectarian identity, but was to be staged, as all Cup Finals are, at Windsor Park, the home of Linfield. Windsor Park is in the heart of a fiercely Loyalist area, and Derry City fans had obvious concerns over their safety in such an area. As a result only 180 Derry fans travelled to watch their team in the final, a final they lost 3-0.[85]

The 1971-2 season was Derry City's last full season, and the last season in which Northern Irish League soccer was played at the Brandywell. The start of the season was backdropped by an increasing escalation of the troubles in Derry in response to the introduction of internment and an increasing sense of alienation amongst the Catholic population from the British Army who were supposed to be their protectors. The first three games of the season were postponed or played elsewhere because of the trouble. The cancellation of games is instructive in how Derry City was increasingly rejected by the rest of the Irish League. At this stage of the troubles violence was a norm in most towns and cities across Northern Ireland, yet the predominant Protestant and unionist ranks of senior soccer would always construct violence in Derry, and hence the postponement of games as something different – that violence was political, nationalist and anti the Unionist establishment. These notions were reinforced on 19 August 1971 when the game against Crusaders at the Brandywell was postponed because of the barricades around the ground. On that Saturday afternoon the ground was used by the SDLP and NICRA to hold a rally to encourage a campaign of civil disobedience amongst the Catholic and nationalist population to overthrow the Stormont Parliament. A crowd of 7000 packed the ground to hear the various speakers. John Hume stated 'we have pledged ourselves to lead you in a campaign of civil disobedience and passive resistance to bring the system that has governed you for fifty years to an end'.[86] The use of the Brandywell for such a meeting is understandable as it is the only large venue in the Bogside and shows the willingness of the club to support its community. However, the meeting has to be seen from the standpoint of the opposing tradition in Northern Ireland – what message does the use of a soccer stadium for a political meeting which aimed at bringing down the government give to the rest of the teams in the league, the majority of whom believe in that government? The message from the Brandywell that day, at the heart of 'Free Derry', removed Derry City from the realm of a mere soccer club and into something which could be demonized, hated and attacked by Protestant/unionist soccer supporters and the Protestant-dominated soccer establishment.

The first actual game of the 1971–2 season to be played at Brandywell against Cliftonville was watched by a crowd of only 200. This contrasts with crowds which regularly reached 5,000 in the years before the troubles. This game, and two others in late August and early September were played behind the barricades of 'Free Derry'. The local paper describes the scene on the day of the Cliftonville game, 'Cliftonville had second thoughts about accepting the security forces clearance for Brandywell. Even after a trouble-free week there were still the remains of barricades on four roads outside the ground, with single-lane motor traffic through three of them, and a pedestrian passage in another'.[87]

In the second week of September two events occurred which brought an end to soccer at the Brandywell and made Derry City's long-term survival in the Irish League unlikely. On 10 September there was widespread rioting around the Brandywell after a seven-year-old boy had been killed when run over by a British Army Land Rover. During the riot the following occurred, 'after being under almost constant attack with stones, bottles and petrol bombs, a gunman fired shots at the soldiers from the Brandywell stadium. The fire was returned by soldiers'.[88] A few weeks earlier Derry City's ground had housed a political meeting much to the disgust of the Protestant/unionist tradition, now it was housing republican gunmen. For those opposing

Catholic/nationalist aspirations this spoke volumes about Derry City and the perceived nature of its political and sectarian colouring.

Saturday 11 September 1971 is a key date in the Derry City story. The opposition that day was Ballymena United. Despite the reservations of the visiting team, the Security forces and the Irish League had ordered the game to go ahead. The Brandywell was surrounded by barricades or the remains of barricades on the day of the match. The start of the game witnessed rioting outside the Brandywell and 'spectators in the ground could hear rubber bullets being fired and see CS gas being used to disperse the rioters'.[89] While the match was still in the first half 'a mob of youths, most of them wearing hand-kerchiefs over their faces invaded the Brandywell ground and seized the bus [belonging to the Ballymena team]. The driver refused to part with the keys and the youths started the bus in gear and pushed it through the showground and out by another gate and set fire to it'.[90] In the aftermath of these events Derry City were forbidden to use their ground for any further matches by the Security forces and the Irish League. This was a mere formality as most clubs (even those with a predominantly Catholic support base) had been vocalising doubts over travelling into 'Free Derry' to play a soccer match. In the wake of Ballymena's experience all the clubs unanimously refused to play at the Brandywell. The local newspaper stated a widespread opinion in the aftermath of the Ballymena game

> Derry City seem to live in a world of their own. They persisted in their plan for opening the season at Brandywell in a completely no-go area and ignored a riot a couple of hundred yards away on the eve of their third match behind the barricades. It took the burning of a visitors bus to make them realise that they were asking too much of other clubs and the public to expect them to take the chance of getting to Brandywell under present conditions.[91]

For the rest of the season Derry City played their 'home' matches at the Coleraine ground – this in itself was bad enough, but the continuing high levels of violence across Northern Ireland cast a long shadow over soccer. Increasingly this was having a devastating effect on the finances of the club. At an Ulster Cup game against Crusaders the crowd was so low that gate receipts totalled only £33. By the end of the 1971–2 season Derry City was facing financial collapse. The club was attempting to play soccer thirty miles away from home, while most of its supporters were having to deal with the realities of the huge political upheavals taking place in Derry at the time. Revenue was falling and the ravages of the situation was forcing star players such as Rowland to leave the club and go back to England. The end was coming closer.

At the start of the 1972–3 season Derry City received security clearance to return to Brandywell. The Irish League, after hearing the continued objections from majority of other clubs in the League, refused to sanction Derry City's move home. The club dug in their heels and insisted that they be allowed to play at home. They forfeited their first three home games of the season as a result of their insistence of playing at the Brandywell and their refusal to play at Coleraine. On Saturday 14 October Portadown were due to play Derry. Derry City once more demanded that the game be played at the Brandywell, the Irish League again refused their application to do so. On 13 October, and citing the Irish League's intransigence over the issue of Brandywell, Derry City withdrew from Irish League football. A club statement noted

> the Board have considered all relevant matters and, in particular the fact that the Management Committee of the Irish League have not seen fit to accept the recommendations and indeed the encouragements of the security forces that a return to Brandywell was feasible. At a considerable cost to the club, Derry City, for the past three years have kept senior football alive in the interests of the Irish League and indeed of the community at large in what can only be described as the most difficult of circumstances. Over the past three years attendance's at Brandywell dwindled from 5000 to a few hundred and reached almost vanishing point when City had to move out of Brandywell to Coleraine. A resolution was unanimously passed by the Board of Directors that membership of the Irish League be withdrawn as from October 13'.[92]

Within the club and across the city there was a view that Derry City was allowed to die because the Irish League and the majority of clubs did not want to deal with the realities of playing soccer in such a Catholic/nationalist stronghold. An editorial from the nationalist *Irish News* echoed this view

> Derry City found little camaraderie in the Irish League when the crunch came … Did Derry City deserve such a fate? Can Irish League soccer face the dreary future in the knowledge that a former stronghold of the sport is no longer functioning? All the hocus pocus about security, lack of it, too much of it and so on makes for unpalatable memories. Derry City is dead – officially – and I suppose it is only right that the last will and testament of an isolated unit bound for the gas chamber is disclosed. At a risk of being over critical there is a broad view in Derry that the team has been sent down the drain due to territorial rules. Unless they set up camp in Buncrana Derry City cannot gain entry to the League. I suppose that the lack of real feeling for Derry City is but a final phase of a long and rather irritating problem that is no longer.[93]

A club with forty-three years of senior soccer behind them, with one League championship, three Irish Cups, and a record as the only Northern Irish team ever to reach the second round of the European Cup, bowed out – a victim of the troubles. In many ways their hardest battle was still ahead of them, that of attempting to bring senior soccer back to Derry. In 1972 the signs were bleak. It was increasingly obvious that the Irish League was not prepared to invest any time and effort in helping Derry City back into the League while the club insisted that the Brandywell remained their chosen ground. The other option, a move to the Southern League was dismissed as 'impossible' by the sports editor of the Dublin *Irish Times*.[94]

From 1972 until the early 1980s the Derry City story would emerge on the back pages of the newspapers every summer to compete with the other stories of the media's silly season. The story was always the same – that some director, local businessman or ex-player was gathering together a group of people who would bring senior soccer back to Derry. These stories were as futile as those other silly season tales of crop circles and little green men. A return of Derry City was an impossibility as nobody in Northern Irish soccer wanted them back.

The spring of 1984 saw the first real and sustained moves to solve the problem of Derry City. A new board was attempting to find a new ground for the Club in conjunction with the City Council and other interested parties. The rationale behind this attempt was to avoid the territorial symbolism of the Brandywell and its connections with the Bogside, 'Free Derry' and the Catholic/nationalist struggle. The Club suggested five new sites for the ground, two on the banks of the River Foyle on the Catholic side of the city, and three others in the Protestant Waterside district. Despite these genuine attempts to find a solution to the territorial problem the security forces rejected all the proposed locations. The chairman of the club, Robert Ferris stated with resignation,

> we seem to have come to the end of the tunnel without achieving anything. We feel that the police's decision has far reaching implications not only for Derry City, but also for potential investors in the club. If the police feel they cannot provide security for senior soccer in the city then what will industrialists think when they are weighing up the possibilities of investing here?[95]

The line being taken by the police reinforced the view that Derry City were being excluded from senior soccer for political and sectarian reasons. The lack of support from the Irish League contributed to a further strengthening of the belief that the issue was not just about soccer. Robert Ferris was quite clear about this in stating the city is the second city in the Province and it is known as a football city. It seems that our hurdle now is the intransigence of the RUC. Many people in the Londonderry area believe that the League Committee is discriminating against the club under the pretence of security. The police should not have the power to dictate who should be admitted to the Irish League.[96]

The pressure for readmittance gathered pace throughout the first months of 1984. The City Council sent a deputation to the Secretary of State for Northern Ireland, James Prior, and had a meeting with Nicholas Scott, a junior Minister. The Northern Ireland Office line was clear, although they sympathized they would not involve themselves with the operational decisions of the RUC. In late March the Derry Chamber of Commerce carried a unanimous vote in support of the club stating, 'The Chamber would be pleased to give Derry City any support which might help it to influence the Irish League and police authorities on the matter and we fully back the effort to bring senior soccer back to Londonderry'.[97] Despite the campaign the Annual General Meeting of the Irish League rejected Derry City's application to rejoin the League on 11 May 1984. They cited, as they had done previously, the objections of the security forces as the reason for rejecting the application.

With all avenues to readmission to the Irish League blocked by the RUC and the IFA Derry City looked south to the League of Ireland and the FAI. The club had warned the Irish League Management Committee in February that if their application for readmittance to the League was turned down at the May AGM they would approach the FAI. True to their word the board of Derry City contacted the FAI on 11 May with a view to joining the League of Ireland. The FAI Executive Committee noted the letter from Derry City on 11 May and referred it to the Council.[98] At an FAI Council meeting in June the Derry City application was considered. The members of the Council were clear in their support of Derry City's attempts to bring senior soccer back to Derry, but as Mr D. Casey warned the Council, until the Irish League and the IFA had granted permission for Derry City to leave the auspices of their federation, the FAI could take no firm action.[99] As the summer of 1984 approached there seemed to be a general sense that Derry City should be encouraged to join the southern league, but that all the soccer bodies involved, including FIFA, would have to be consulted before the FAI could take definite action. Derry City would not be starting senior soccer in the 1984–5 season. The real hope for Derry City came in July 1984. The problem for the club, the FAI and the League of Ireland was that any admission of Derry City to the southern league would involve an expansion of the league. In 1984 the league consisted of only one division. If Derry were admitted the claims of smaller southern clubs to be admitted to the league would have to be overridden. Derry City would be seen as having leap-frogged their way in and that would breed resentment and possibly create problems for the League of Ireland. At the League of Ireland AGM in July 1984 a long-standing plan was activated – the restructuring of the league into a Premier Division of twelve clubs, and a new First Division of ten clubs – four clubs relegated from the old First Division and six newly admitted clubs. This new system would begin in the 1985–6 season. Derry City could now hopefully gain admittance to the League of Ireland without upsetting the claims of any of the south's junior teams.

Despite the general hopefulness of a new channel for Derry City events once more confirmed the real difficulties which the club faced in re-establishing soccer in the city. Throughout the marching season of summer 1984 rioting was widespread in Derry. Even Robert Ferris had to admit that 'violence is destroying our chances. Rioting is turning into a nightly event with property and businesses being destroyed. I must be realistic about the issue – we will never get back into senior soccer while the destruction continues'.[100]

With the new League structure in place for the 1985–6 season Derry City pushed ahead with their application. There were three strands involved. First being freed from the auspices of the IFA. This was never going to pose problems as the IFA had made clear ever since 1972 that they were unlikely to readmit Derry to the Irish League – Derry City moving south would allow the IFA to have a problem solved without having to confront many difficult issues. The dispensation for Derry City to seek membership in the southern league was granted by the IFA in October 1984. The second strand was the most problematic. Derry City had to present a case to FIFA which would allow the international governing body to sanction the movement of a team from its natural national federation into the federation of another nation. This move was also granted in October 1984 on the understanding it was a one-off. FIFA accepted that Derry City's membership of the IFA had become untenable and that the situation was unlikely to change. It also recognized that the geographical location of the Brandywell near the border would not pose logistical or security problems for visiting teams. A spokesmen for Derry City outlined the FIFA ruling by stating

> Derry City alone have been given permission to apply for League of Ireland membership. We are affiliated to the Irish League and the League has made it clear that the no other Northern club will receive the same dispensation. FIFA rules say that unless this dispensation is given, no club can play outside their geographical jurisdiction.[101]

The third and final strand was to seek admittance to the League of Ireland. This process was begun in November 1984 with an official application to the FAI for membership. At various IFA meetings during November the submissions of FIFA and the IFA were taken into account and the process of vetting Derry City's application begun. It was agreed at both General Council and Executive Committee level that there was no legal impediment blocking Derry City's application at either the FIFA or IFA level.[102] The League of Ireland Management Committee met on 23 November and approved the Derry application. All the representatives at the meeting supported Derry with the exception of Limerick, Shelbourne and St Patrick's Athletic whose opposition centred on the extra expenditure that they would encounter by having to travel to Derry. The meeting received agreement from the RUC that Derry City's involvement in the southern league would pose them no security problems.[103] On 1 February 1985 the final stages of Derry's move to the League of Ireland were completed when the new members of the first division were formally elected. James McAuley, the chairman of Derry City responded to the news by saying, 'we are absolutely delighted and we can promise that we will play a full and active role in ensuring the success of the new division'.[104]

Training for the new season began within a week of the announcement from FAI headquarters and a team was built around local talent and some ageing stars from England. The spirit of reconciliation after the ravages of their exile became apparent in press releases from the club during the run up to the new season. Eddie Mahon, the club's PR spokesman made it clear

> that we will not be asking people where they go on Sunday or for whom they vote. We are purely and simply a football team – nothing else. We are not in the business of attracting people from any specific side of the fence. We want to see football supporters and nothing else. Politics should be kept outside the ground. As a club we want no involvement with politics. In fact we are doing our best to avoid the topic at all times'.[105]

The first game of the 1985–6 season and Derry City's first senior game in fifteen years was played at the Brandywell against Home Farm in front of a crowd of 7000.

> Those of us who made our way to Brandywell early on Sunday will have witnessed the most amazing scenes. Craigavon Bridge resembled Wembley Way as red and white bedecked fans walked towards Abercon Road en route to their personal mecca. Driving into the car park made the heart beat pound that bit faster. The PA system was blaring out the commemorative record called 'Derry are back'. Only the hard hearted

or Home Farm supporters could have failed to get caught up in the atmosphere of the occasion.[106]

For the record Derry City won the game 1-0.

Since 1985 Derry City have prospered on the pitch. They won promotion to the League of Ireland Premier League after two seasons and have never left. In the 1990–1 season they won the League and Cup double and have represented Ireland in European competitions on a regular basis, the high point being a 1991 home fixture against Real Madrid. Off the pitch life has not been easy. Derry's home crowds have dwindled ever since that first game against Home Farm. Expensive English players cost too much and produced little in return revenue. The board has been replaced on numerous occasions and financial crisis is a state of normality. With the beginning of the cease-fire in 1994 there was talk that Derry City might return to the Irish League. This has only ever been talk. No formal discussions have ever taken place between the club and the IFA and despite the cease-fire, sectarianism and the accompanying violence have remained part and parcel of Northern Irish soccer. In this respect the fundamental problems which led to the demise of Belfast Celtic and Derry have not gone away, and City are as unwelcome in the Irish League as ever they were.

In essence that is the basic Derry City story, a club which emerged at the heart of a city which loved soccer, yet because of the sectarianism present in Northern Irish society and the ravages of the troubles which hit Derry hard, had to leave the Irish League. To their credit they reformed and found a place in the League of Ireland where they could pursue soccer glory without having to play against a backdrop of impending or actual violence. During the Derry City story I have alluded to many of the currents present in Northern Irish society and in its soccer. To place Derry City's experience in its wider context I will now explore some of the currents further.

It is clear from the experience of Belfast Celtic and Derry City that soccer in Northern Ireland could never be played without the forces of sectarianism encroaching into sport. Since the departure of Derry City there have only been two clubs clearly identified with the Catholic and nationalist traditions left in the League: Cliftonville and Donegal Celtic. There are endless examples of matches featuring Cliftonville ending in violence, but I will use the example of Donegal Celtic to demonstrate that the forces which led to the demise of Derry City are still present in Northern Irish soccer. In 1990 Donegal Celtic had been drawn at home in the Cup to play Linfield. Donegal are an Intermediate League team from the fiercely nationalist Andersonstown area. The RUC, acting as they had done with Derry City, advised the IFA that the game could not go ahead safely at the Donegal ground, and advised it be moved to Linfield's Windsor Park. Despite seeking a High Court judgement to overrule this move, Donegal were forced to visit Linfield. The game, despite the RUC's fears over playing the match at Andersonstown, ended in a riot, with fifty plus injured and the firing of plastic bullets. The nationalist press attacked both the RUC and the IFA for failing to ensure crowd safety and cast doubts on the political and sectarian neutrality of the IFA in making such decisions, that is that the IFA, based at Windsor Park, would always favour Protestant and unionist teams over Catholic and nationalist ones.[107] The experience of Donegal Celtic demonstrates that the problems of the early 1970s which plagued Derry City and the way in which members of the Catholic and nationalist tradition would view such problems had not been resolved some twenty years later.

It was my contention early in this section that soccer in Northern Ireland is dominated by one tradition over the other. That is not to argue that soccer is solely a Protestant and unionist concern in the way that Gaelic games are the sole preserve of the Catholic and nationalist tradition, but rather the senior levels of soccer in terms of team loyalty and administration are dominated by one tradition. The actions of FIFA and the FAI reinforce this domination.

To illustrate this point I return to Donegal Celtic. In 1991 another Irish Cup game, this time against Ards, was moved by the RUC again citing public order fears as the motivation. In response Donegal Celtic withdrew from the competition and applied to the FAI to join the Southern League. Both the FAI and FIFA rejected the proposed move, despite the precedent set by Derry City, and the similarity of Donegal's plight. By 1972 it had become clear that Derry City could not function in Northern Irish soccer because of the prejudices involved and the violence attached, in 1991 the situation for Donegal Celtic was identical as no one would ensure the safe conduct of soccer matches in Andersonstown. The reasons behind the FAI and FIFA rejection was the geographical situation of Donegal Celtic – no one could ensure the safety of southern teams travelling across the border into the heart of Belfast.[108]

Northern Irish soccer has reached a position where it cannot, and some would say will not, deal with teams coming from predominantly Catholic and nationalist areas. By seeing the Derry City situation as a one off – which evidently it is not – the FAI and FIFA essentially wash their hands of any responsibility to teams from Northern Ireland's second tradition. The result, as Sugden and Bairner were able to conclude, is that 'the integrative potential of football is increasingly difficult to realize'.[109] In a similar vein Arthur Aughey in his submission to the Forum for Peace and Reconciliation pointed out that 'In Northern Ireland association football has emerged during the troubles to become the symbol of Ulster Loyalist identity'.[110] Finally Alan Bairner was able to write that 'the impression created is of a Protestant community seeking to maintain control over a sport in a manner which could be said to reflect Unionist political efforts to maintain the Union in the face of growing encroachment by Irish Nationalists'.[111] In this I see few signs of hope for Northern Irish soccer. Even if the current peace process is an ongoing success, can sectarianism and its accompanying violence be removed from soccer in the Province? In fact, is it not more likely that with the removal of terrorist violence from the political scene as an outlet for sectarianism, that other venues and spaces such as football grounds will become the focus for those with an axe to grind?

In 1985 when Derry City joined the League of Ireland the club looked forward to welcoming all elements of Derry society back to the Brandywell. They were going to play soccer in a League devoid of Linfield matches, security forces and all the connected problems. Despite these best hopes sectarianism, or the fear of its effects continue to pervade the Derry experience. In 1985 a Protestant from the Waterside was able to tell a local reporter that he would not, despite being a lifelong supporter, be returning to the Brandywell. 'Look at the game against Shamrock Rovers last year [1984]. The majority of the crowd were only intent on annoying those people who were not of their own religious persuasion. They seem to me to have found a vehicle for their bigotry which they have searched for years to get. I want no part of that scene'.[112] In 1995 the veteran Derry sports writer Frank Curran maintained that Protestant from the Waterside would still not attend the Brandywell.[113] In a similar vein Sugden and Bairner wrote, 'Most of them [Protestants] express their feelings simply by staying away from the Brandywell. The hooligans among them, however, lie in wait ready to throw missiles at busloads of Derry City supporters as they return from games in the Irish Republic.[114] This is in many ways the saddest aspect of the Derry City story and the context within which soccer has to exist in Northern Ireland. After being forced out of the Irish League and having to reinvent itself in a foreign league, Derry City did not rid themselves of the accompanying sectarianism. The Protestant and unionist supporters chose to either stay away or else attack Derry City as a symbol of Catholicism and nationalism – now made all the worse after their entry into the southern league.

Derry City, like Belfast Celtic and Donegal Celtic, were victims of violent tendencies present in their society which could not be contained. Despite deserving credit for reforming, their rise from the ashes was a one off and offers nothing to clubs in a similar position. Once they had reformed Derry City were as much a victim of the old forces, albeit to a much lesser degree, as they had been in the early 1970s. If anything this demonstrates that sport in

Northern Ireland will always struggle to be removed from its political and social context.

On 19 October 1996 an Irish League match between Portadown and Cliftonville was abandoned after Cliftonville supporters and their buses had been attacked by a stone throwing mob before kick-off. These supporters never made it into the ground and once the team were aware of what had happened they refused to play the second half. In response to the violence one supporter, Gary Arthurs, vowed never to watch his beloved Cliftonville again. He said, 'It's only a matter of time before somebody is killed and no football match is worth that'.[115] The problem for Arthurs and his fellow Cliftonville supporters is that they are identified by their Protestant/unionist opponents as Catholics and nationalists. In Northern Ireland symbols of allegiance are centrally important to everyday life, and which soccer team you choose to follow defines, rightly or wrongly, who and what you are. This is not a new problem and pre-dates the emergence of the modern troubles. In Northern Ireland, sport rather than being a common unifying theme in a troubled environment, is too often another excuse for division and antagonism.

Sport is seen as a signifier of identity. These identities are the constructs of history, as well as realities of the present. Nationalism is foremost of the identities connected with sport in Northern Ireland. The GAA has constructed its own version of nationalism. This is a nationalism that has become distinct to that presented by the GAA in the South, and is one that is now wrapped up with the defence of rule 21. It is a nationalism, that, while self constructed, is reinforced externally as a result of pressure on the GAA from the security forces and elements within the loyalist community. In Northern Irish soccer, the nationalism is less obvious, and certainly less political. It is however clearly present. Derry City could not be removed from the context of the troubles and thus became the signifier of nationalism within soccer. Their presence since 1985 in the 'wrong' league links the club with a nation state that is, for the dominant Protestant/unionist community that follows soccer, representative of an oppositional 'other'. Both Gaelic games and soccer in Northern Ireland have become, in very different ways, representative of, and allied with, the force of nationalism. It is a complex and varied nationalism, but one that is opposed by others within Northern Ireland, and one that has recently become unrecognisable to the nationalists of the Irish Republic. While the peace process continues and politics become 'normalized', sport will become increasingly politicized. It will, I would argue, become the focus for those who feel disenfranchised by the peace process if they see that process as having sold them out. The labels that can be provided by Irish sport, be they a result of the history of Ireland's games and the easy recognition of one or other game with either tradition, or the demography that has produced a divided sporting map, will be used by those who need something tribal and easily identifiable to cling to. The mythical nationalism offered by sportsmen in coloured shirts will offer great succour and a direct enemy to those who no longer identify with the new Northern Ireland.

Conclusions: Sport and the ever-changing sense of Irishness

The match between Boherbue from Cork and Holy Trinity from Cookstown was decided in the final moments when Boherbue gained decisive scores. The referee, Joe Woods from Dublin, was immediately set upon, was kicked, punched and spat upon … Vicious sectarian and quasi-political comments were made. One observer remembers one comment in particular which was hurled at Woods: 'Where we come from, you f…, you would be shot!' A lone member of the Garda Siochana arrived to try and calm the scene. Again a taunt from the crowd came: 'You abandoned us in 1922 and you are at it again'.[1]

It is now well over a century since the different sporting bodies and associations were founded in Ireland, and nearly eighty since the partition of Ireland altered the organisational structure of some sports. It is clear from the reporting of a recent All Ireland under-16 Vocational Schools semi-final match, that the politics of nationalism and identity are alive and well at the sports ground. There is a huge amount of sporting detail and history involved in the last hundred years, but such a history is made more complex as a result of Ireland's long and complicated past. This book has not attempted to write the history of sport in Ireland. That is a task that needs undertaking and will take some considerable time to complete. What has been tackled here are the development and practice of the links between the two major team sports in Ireland and the ideology of nationalism.

What I have attempted to demonstrate is that sport is a centrally important vehicle for the transmission of ideology and identity to a huge proportion of the population in Ireland. The ideology, that of nationalism, and the identity, that of Irishness, which are projected through sport are complex and multifaceted. In the same way that there is no single conception of political nationalism that is universally projected by the different political parties across Ireland, there is no single sporting nationalism.

The nationalism that is afforded to the followers of Gaelic games is different to that which is offered to the supporters of soccer. The former is steeped in history, is exclusive and offers the rejection of a foreign culture and the embrace of the native. The latter is international, is played out in front of a global media and appears more representative of what has been called

187

'modern Ireland'. Despite this apparently straightforward distinction, there are further complexities that have been uncovered here. There is an ongoing (and some would argue growing) schism that exists between the followers of Gaelic games in the Republic of Ireland and those in Northern Ireland. Over the rule 21 issue in particular, the former group are seen as inclusive and attempting to move along with the spirit of the peace process, while the latter is often painted as being backward looking and intransigent. Likewise in soccer there are distinctions to be made. The nationalism that is offered by success at the World Cup is easily accessible, evanescent and could even be seen as trendy or glamorous. It is completely at odds with the experiences of exclusion, violence and rebuttal that has led many nationalists in Northern Ireland to identify Derry City as 'their' team. The real sporting experience within Northern Ireland, and its ready identification and involvement with the politics of nationalism was starkly illustrated in November 1998 when Donegal Celtic qualified for the semi-finals of the Steel and Sons Cup. Donegal Celtic were due to play the RUC team, a police force which, at that time, was still to be reformed under the Good Friday Agreement. Many nationalists, and most notably those in Sinn Féin, argued along those lines that they also use in the rule 21 debate. Until such time as the RUC is radically reformed or disbanded, there should be no contacts with a force which treated the nationalist community so harshly during the thirty years of the troubles. Many argued that to cancel the game would be a blatantly political move and not in keeping with the moves towards peace. The game was eventually cancelled as the Donegal Celtic players voted not to play. In response to the cancellation, many commentators accused elements within Sinn Féin and the IRA of bullying tactics.[2] Whatever the exact reasons behind the cancellation of the game, the intense debate that a 'mere' soccer game prompted suggests that sport in Northern Ireland will never be 'value free'. Notions of identity and connotations of ideology are hugely important and strongly rooted.

Sport should, in future, be used as a serious vehicle for understanding the issues that surround the history of Irish nationalism and identity. A main theme throughout this book was the failure of historians, political scientists and others who have explored the complexities of Ireland to give sport anything but a fleeting glance. Sport is not a minority pastime. The various examples from across the globe that have been used here, especially at the international level, demonstrate that sport is inextricably linked to the formation, maintenance and promotion of the ideal of nationalism in its many forms. Those who study Ireland have to ask themselves why the GAA has had such a profound impact on Irish society, both political and civic, across the decades. Why is it important that Michael Collins, that doyen of nationalism, was often seen with a hurley at hand or throwing the ball in at Croke Park? Can we continue to ignore an organisation that claims more members than any other body in Ireland with the exception of the Catholic Church? Equally, soccer must be explored as a body that responded to the force, both political and legal, of partition, and has come to represent the modern nation. In using sport as a way of understanding and illustrating the different forms of Irish nationalism, this book has reinforced an idea that has been demonstrated elsewhere, but needs pursuing further. Irish nationalism is a complex animal. It is not the specific preserve of politicians, gunmen or poets, but is something real that all members of Irish society share, and continue to express through a variety of vehicles, of which sport is but one. To appreciate the many different ways that nationalism has been expressed through sport over the years, we have to develop an understanding and appreciation of what nationalism is. This should be done at the theoretical level, but also by appraising the particular lived circumstances that shape and then allow for the expression of either nationalism or identity.

The nationalism that is connected with sport, and the identities expressed through such, have to be understood in the widest possible context. They are the product and culmination of a myriad of forces. At the broadest level there exists the general social and political context of any given moment of Irish history. Did the GAA prosper, and soccer struggle in the early twentieth century, because 'good' nationalists who supported the nationalist forces during the revolutionary period felt duty-bound to rally to the native game? Likewise, has international soccer been a great focus of expression recently because it reflects the modernising trends that are so apparent within wider society? Beyond that general context, consideration should be made of what a particular sport or its organising body represents. An acknowledgment has to be made that distinguishes the post-1968 experiences of a nationalist in Crossmaglen compared to one in Cork. They are both shaped by different local forces. Finally, we have to understand how either particular sport allows for the actual display of nationalism and identity. At Croke Park, while the mood is celebratory, the setting and the annual routine are commonly understood to be a monument to the GAA and the nation state. In soccer, internationally at least, the setting is always changing, Lithuania one week, the US weeks later, but the atmosphere is more informal and expressive of an inclusive and less structured Irishness.

As the end of the twentieth century approaches the complexities of Irish nationalism do not lessen. This is equally true of its relationship with sport. In soccer we witness Ireland winning two international tournaments within a year at the under-16 and under-18 level. A comment at the time expressed bright hopes for the future of Irish soccer on the international stage as 'we're really getting the hang of it'.[3] In soccer at least, the future is bright. There are great hopes that Mick McCarthy can repeat the success of the Charlton years, but with a squad of players that is somehow more 'home grown' than those players of the early 1990s. A soccer match between Cliftonville and Linfield was allowed to be played at Cliftonville's Solitude ground for the first time in 28 years in 1998. The RUC's decision to allow such a contentious match to go ahead in Catholic north Belfast was, for many commentators, a sign that sport had finally put the ravages of Northern Ireland's troubles behind it.[4] In Gaelic games, the schism between progress, inclusiveness and the embrace of the peace process is still counterbalanced by an adherence to a purist rule book that rejects the non-native. In the wake of the Omagh bombing of August 1998 in which 29 people died, the local soccer team, Omagh Town, organized a charity match against Manchester United to raise funds for the victims. Demand for tickets was such that Omagh Town, with a home ground that holds only 5000, asked St Enda's GAA club in Omagh, ground capacity 20,000, if the match could be played there. The GAA refused the request as the playing of non-Gaelic games on GAA pitches is forbidden under rule 42. The GAA had donated £100,000 of its own money to the Omagh fund, and expected clubs around the country to raise a further £1 million, yet it was condemned in the press for not relinquishing rule 42 for this particular match.[5] Both the main spectator sports in Ireland are prisoners of either expectation or history. It is difficult to assess whether or not Irish nationalism has reached a mature state of consensus and contentment where it is no longer the product of either a suppressed nationalism or of an emergent nation. It is clear that while many would be pleased to see the force of Irish nationalism reduced to the status of the 'ninety minute patriot' interacting only with major sporting events, others are still fighting a larger political battle in which sport is a weapon, rather than a medium, of expression.[6]

Until there is only one idea of Irish nationalism, and a singular and commonly shared expression of identity, then sport will continue to reflect the multifaceted and ever changing nature of Irishness. As that day will never come, Gaelic games and soccer will continue to be, as they have been throughout their histories, mirrors of the nationalisms and identities that exist within wider Irish society. As such, all those who seek to understand or map the nature of nationalism and identity should explore the sporting history of Ireland.

Notes

1 / INTRODUCTION

1 The Saw Doctors, 'Broke My Heart' (Warner Music 1992).
2 R. Holt, *Sport and the British* (Oxford 1989).
3 For example see D.G. Boyce, *Nationalism in Ireland* (London 1995, 3rd edn).
4 For example see R. Kearney, *Postnationalist Ireland. Politics, Culture, Philosophy* (London 1997), R. Kirkland, *Literature and Culture in Northern Ireland Since 1965: Moments of Danger* (London 1996), D. Kiberd, *Inventing Ireland* (London 1995) and R.F. Foster, 'Storylines: Narratives and Nationality in Nineteenth Century Ireland' in G. Cubitt (ed.), *Imagining Nations* (Manchester 1998), pp 38-56.
5 See D. Fitzpatrick, 'The Geography of Irish Nationalism 1910-21' in *Past and Present*, 78, 1978.
6 For example on Pearse see R. Dudley Edwards, *Patrick Pearse: The Triumph of Failure* (London 1977) and S.F. Moran, *Patrick Pearse and the Politics of Redemption: The Mind of the Easter Rising 1916* (Washington 1994) and on de Valera see T. Ryle Dwyer, *De Valera. The Man and the Myths* (Swords 1991) or T.P. Coogan *De Valera. Long Fellow Long Shadow* (London 1993).
7 See J. Hutchinson, *The Dynamics of Cultural Nationalism. The Gaelic Revival and the Creation of the Irish Nation State* (London 1987).
8 See T. Garvin, *1922. The Birth of Irish Democracy* (Dublin 1996), p. vi.
9 For work on women and nationalism see for example M. Ward, *Unmanageable Revolutionaries* (London 1995), and B. Aretxaga, *Shattering Silence. Women, Nationalism and Political Subjectivity in Northern Ireland* (Princeton 1997).
10 R.F. Foster, *Modern Ireland 1600-1972* (London 1989), J.J. Lee, *Ireland 1912-85: Politics and Society* (Cambridge 1989) and D. Keogh, *Twentieth Century Ireland: Nation and State* (Dublin 1994).
11 See E. Malcolm, 'Popular Recreation in Nineteenth Century Ireland' in O. MacDonagh, W.F. Mandle and P. Travers, *Irish Culture and Nationalism 1750-1950* (London 1983).
12 An excellent overview of the emergence of modern sport can be found in Holt, *Sport and the British*.
13 Examples of the many available works would be G.P.T. Finn, 'Sporting Symbols, Sporting Identities: Soccer and Intergroup Conflict in Scotland and Northern Ireland' in I.S. Wood (ed.), *Scotland and Ulster* (Edinburgh 1994), pp 33-56, or T. Hennessey, 'Ulster Unionist Territorial and National Identities 1886-1893: Province, Island,

Kingdom and Empire' in *Irish Political Studies*, 8, 1993, pp 21-36.
14 L. Colley, *Britons* (London 1996), K. Robbins, *Great Britain: Identities, Institutions, and the Idea of Britishness* (London 1998) and J. Paxman, *The English. A Portrait of a People* (London 1998).
15 See M. Cronin 'Which Nation, Which Flag? Boxing and National Identities in Ireland' in *International Review for the Sociology of Sport*, 32/2 1997, pp 131-46.
16 For a fuller discussion of some of these themes see J. Maguire and J. Tuck, 'Global Sports and Patriot Games: Rugby Union and National Identity in a United Sporting Kingdom Since 1945' in M. Cronin and D. Mayall (eds), *Sporting Nationalisms: Identity, Ethnicity, Immigration and Assimilation* (London 1998), pp 103-126, and Van Esbeck, E. *The Story of Irish Rugby* (London 1986).
17 For a history of camogie see, Padraig Puirseal, *Scéal na Camógaíochta* (Kilkenny 1984).

2 / NATIONALISM

1 J. Hutchinson and A. Smith, (eds), *Nationalism. A Reader* (Oxford 1994), pp 3-4.
2 F. Halliday, 'The Siren of Nationalism' in C. Hartman and P. Vilanova (eds), *Paradigms Lost. The Post Cold War Era* (London 1992), p. 34.
3 Throughout the text I am aware of the distinction between nationalism and patriotism. However, I see patriotism as an integral part of nationalism and nationalist expression. While accepting that there are clear differences and these should be acknowledged, to make distinctions within this text would become too burdensome. I would also suggest that patriotism is very much linked in with American ideals of the flag and the nation and signal a more civic concept of the nation. In Ireland there is a tradition of patriotism only in the context of nationalism. For a general discussion of the issues and a counterweight to my own argument here see M. Viroli, *For Love of Country. An Essay on Patriotism and Nationalism* (Oxford 1995).
4 See for example, P.F. Sugar, 'Nationalism the Victorious Ideology' in P.F. Sugar (ed.), *Eastern European Nationalism in the Twentieth Century* (Washington 1995), pp 413-30.
5 I would suggest that the best general coverage of this question can be found in D. Miller, *On Nationality* (Oxford 1995), and a fascinating variant on ways of studying nationalism in D. Heater, *The Theory of Nationhood. A Platonic Symposium* (London 1998).
6 P. Hall, 'Nationalism and Historicity' in *Nations and Nationalism*, 3, 1, 1997, pp 3-23, has argued

that the whole idea of the nation is now an historical construct.

7 For details of the battles within the different Yugoslav nationalisms and a useful coverage of the nationalism and ethnicity debate see V. Volkan, *Bloodlines. From Ethnic Pride to Ethnic Terrorism* (New York 1997).

8 As nationalism is often measured by academics, the whole discussion surrounding nationalism and nations has quite rightly spurned the question whether nations are real, and if so, whether some nations are more real than others. See for example C. Calhoun, *Nationalism* (Buckingham 1997), pp 98-103 and A.D. Smith and E. Gellner, 'The Nation: Real or Imagined? The Warwick Debates on Nationalism' in *Nations and Nationalism*, 2, 3, 1996, pp 357-70.

9 A. Hastings, *The Construction of Nationhood. Ethnicity, Religion and Nationalism* (Cambridge 1997), p. 4.

10 There are several excellent explanations of these different theories, but one of the clearest and most recent can be found in the conclusion of R. Eatwell (ed.), *European Political Cultures. Conflict or Convergence?* (Routledge 1997), pp 236-45 which has been used for the basis of discussion here.

11 Examples of primordialists include H. Seton-Watson, *Nations and States* (London 1977) and D. Hooson (ed.), *Geography and National Identity* (Oxford 1994).

12 Examples of modernists include E. Gellner, *Nations and Nationalism* (Oxford 1983), E. Gellner, *Encounters with Nationalism* (Oxford 1994) and L. Greenfield, *Nationalism. Five Roads to Modernity* (Harvard 1992).

13 One of the key elements in the view of B. Anderson, *Imagined Communities. Reflection on the Origin and Spread of Nationalism* (London 1991, revised edition).

14 An recent and fascinating exploration of some of these themes can be found in S. Chai, 'A Theory of Ethnic Group Boundaries' in *Nations and Nationalism*, 2, 2, 1996, pp 281-307.

15 Examples of statists include J. Breuilly, *Nationalism and the State* (Manchester 1982) and B. Moore, *The Social Origins of Democracy and Totalitarianism* (London 1967).

16 E. Hobsbawm and T. Ranger, *The Invention of Tradition* (Cambridge 1983).

17 Examples of political mythologists include Anderson, *Imagined Communities* and E. Kedourie, *Nationalism* (London 1963).

18 For details on commemoration and the construction of common or shared identities see P. Connerton, *How Societies Remember* (Cambridge 1989), and D. Lowenthal, 'Identity, Heritage and History' in J.R. Gillis (ed.), *Commemorations. The Politics of National Identity* (Princeton 1994), pp 41-57.

19 Gellner, *Nations and Nationalism*, p. 1.

20 W.J. Moses (ed.), *Classical Black Nationalism. From the American Revolution to Marcus Garvey* (New York 1996), p. 4.

21 I. Berlin, *Against the Current. Essays in the History of Ideas* (London 1979), p. 345.

22 P. Alter, *Nationalism* (London 1985), p. 2.

23 W. Connor, *Ethnonationalism. The Quest for Understanding* (Princeton 1994), p. 77.

24 See S. Hall, 'The Local and the Global: Globalization and Ethnicity' in A. McClintock, A. Mufti and E. Shohat (eds), *Dangerous Liaisons. Gender, Nation and Postcolonial Perspectives* (Minneapolis 1997), p. 177.

25 J. Bodnar, *Remaking America. Public Memory, Commemoration and Patriotism in the Twentieth Century* (Princeton 1992).

26 M. Billig, *Banal Nationalism* (London 1995).

27 An example would be a 1996 advert for Caffrey's, an Irish beer. The advert depicted red haired women, the rural west of Ireland, village priests and sweating hurling teams as a way of representing the imagined Irish nation.

28 J. Hutchinson, 'Irish Nationalism' in D.G. Boyce and A. O'Day (eds) *The Making of Modern Irish History. Revisionism and the Revisionist Controversy* (London 1996), pp 100-19.

29 Ibid., p. 117.

30 See for example the works of M. Dillon, *Twenty Five Years of Terror* (London 1996) or *God and the Gun: the Church and Irish Terrorism* (London 1997), and K. Toolis, *Rebel Hearts* (London 1995).

31 Boyce, *Nationalism in Ireland*, S. Cronin, *Irish Nationalism. A History of its Roots and Ideology* (Dublin 1980).

32 Boyce, *Nationalism in Ireland*, p. 9.

33 See T. Garvin's *The Evolution of Irish Nationalist Politics* (Dublin 1981) and his *Nationalist Revolutionaries in Ireland 1858-1928* (Oxford 1987).

34 Garvin, *1922: The Birth of Irish Democracy*.

35 Kearney, *Postnationalist Ireland*, p. 121.

36 Dudley Edwards, *Patrick Pearse*.

37 T. Dunne, *Theobold Wolfe Tone: Colonial Outsider* (Cork 1982).

38 J. O'Connor, *The Secret World of the Irish Male* (Dublin 1994) pp 147-8.

39 Boyce, *Irish Nationalism*, p. 17.

40 The journal, *Irish Economic and Social History*, continues to produce excellent work in this field, and in book form Joanna Bourke's, *Husbandry to Housewifery* (Oxford 1993) is a fine example of high quality social history.

41 P. Maume, 'nationalism' in S.J. Connolly (ed.), *The Oxford Companion to Irish History* (Oxford 1998), pp 378-9.

42 For full details of the different models that he suggests see J.R. Llobera, *The God of Modernity. The Development of Nationalism in Western Europe* (Oxford 1994), pp 194-209.

43 Ibid., p. 201.

44 For a discussion of famine literature see M. Daly, 'Revisionism and Irish History. The Great Famine' in Boyce and O'Day, *The Making of Modern Irish History*, pp 71-89.

45 Llobera, *The God of Modernity*, p. 202.

46 To understand how the past is mobilised within the literary and political movements in the late nineteenth and early twentieth century see C.C. O'Brien, *Ancestral Voices. Religion and Nationalism in Ireland* (Dublin 1994), pp 53-151. For a theoretical discussion of how culture impinges on nationalist movements see J. Penrose, 'Essential

Constructions? The Cultural Bases of Nationalist Movements' in *Nations and Nationalism*, 1, 3, 1995, pp 391-417.

47 For examples see D. Fitzpatrick, *Oceans of Consolation: Personal Accounts of Irish Migration to Australia*, (Oxford 1995) or in a more light hearted vein, J. O'Connor, *Sweet Liberty: Travels in Irish America* (London 1996).

48 F.W. Knight, *The Caribbean. The Genesis of a Fragmented Nationalism* (New York 1978), p. 178.

49 Hutchinson, 'Irish Nationalism', p. 110.

50 Fitzpatrick, 'The Geography of Irish Nationalism'.

51 P. Hart, *The IRA and its Enemies* (Oxford 1998).

52 See M. Orr, 'The National Question and the Struggle against British Imperialism in Northern Ireland' in B. Berberoglu (ed.), *The National Question. Nationalism, Ethnic Conflict and Self Determination in the 20th Century* (Philadelphia 1995), pp 158-79 and M. Ignatieff, *Blood and Belonging. Journeys into the New Nationalism* (London 1993), pp 162-190

53 For a good exploration of Northern Ireland within the context of the British state and the debate surrounding nationalism see T. Nairn, *The Break Up of Britain. Crisis and Neo-Colonialism* (London 1981), and by way of evolution, T. Nairn, *Faces of Nationalism. Janus Revisited* (London 1997).

54 For a general coverage of many of the themes here see, T. Garvin, 'Hibernian Endgame? Nationalism in a Divided Ireland' in R. Caplan and J. Feffer (eds), *Europe's New Nationalism. States and Minorities in Conflict* (Oxford 1996), pp 184-94, and for documents see W. Harvey Cox, 'Conflict in Northern Ireland' in M. Guibernau and J. Rex (eds), *The Ethnicity Reader. Nationalism, Multiculturalism and Migration* (Cambridge 1997), pp 100-19.

55 For an excellent recent coverage of many of the issues connected with the disapora and Irish identity see, J. MacLaughlin (ed.), *Location and Dislocation in Contemporary Irish Society. Emigration and Irish Identities* (Cork 1997).

56 For a discussion of the possible effects of European integration on Irish and other cultural concerns and identities see Y. Tamir, *Liberal Nationalism* (Princeton 1993), pp 150-67. This should be compared to the similar experiences of other nations with divided identities within a larger unit such as that of Canada, covered by I. Angus, *A Border Within. National Identity, Cultural Plurality and Wilderness* (Montreal 1997).

57 For a good general, although theoretical discussion of globalisation see R. Axtmann, 'Collective Identity and the Democratic Nation State in the Age of Globalisation' in A. Cvetkovich and D. Kellner (eds), *Articulating the Global and the Local. Globalisation and Cultural Studies* (Oxford 1997), pp 33-54, and A. McGrew, 'A Global Society?' in S. Hall, D. Held and T. McGrew (eds), *Modernity and its Futures* (Oxford 1992), pp 61-116.

58 For a general coverage of the Robinson years see G. Hussey, *Ireland Today. Anatomy of a Changing State* (London 1993) and J. Waters, *Jiving at the Crossroads* (Belfast 1991).

59 See for example J. Waters, *An Intelligent Person's Guide to Modern Ireland* (London 1997).

60 To understand how these forces work in a more general sense, and how universal they are see J. Jacobson, 'Perceptions of Britishness' in *Nations and Nationalism*, 3, 2, 1997, pp 181-99.

61 See J. O'Connor, *The Irish Male at Home and Abroad* (Dublin 1996), pp 150-59.

62 K.A. Manzo, *Creating Boundaries. The Politics of Race and Nation* (London 1996), p. 151.

3 / SPORT

1 C. Tobin, 'Ireland's War on Eamon Dunphy' in G. Williams (ed.), *The Esquire Book of Sports Writing* (London 1995), p. 138.

2 R. Butlin, 'Every Four Years We Become a Nation' in N. Royle (ed.), *The Agony and the Ecstasy. New Writing for the World Cup* (London 1998), p. 139.

3 M. Dyreson, *Making the American Team. Sport, Culture and the Olympic Experience* (Urbana 1998), p. 1.

4 G. Caldwell, 'International Sport and National Identity' in *International Social Science Journal*, 34, 2, 1982, p. 176.

5 For a general discussion of themes within the media see P. Drummond, R. Paterson and J. Willis (eds), *National Identity and Europe. The Television Revolution* (London 1993) and more specifically on sport and the media see N. Blain, R. Boyle and H. O'Donnell, *Sport and National Identity in the European Media* (Leicester 1993).

6 C. Tatz, 'The Corruption of Sport' in *Current Affairs Bulletin*, 59, 4, 1982, p. 4.

7 See J. Bale, 'Sport and National Identity: A Geographical View' in *British Journal of Sports History*, 3, 1, 1986, p. 18.

8 E. Hobsbawm, 'Mass Producing Traditions: Europe, 1870-1914' in Hobsbawm and Ranger, *The Invention of Tradition*, p. 28.

9 See K. Heinila, 'Sport and International Understanding – A Contradiction in Terms?' in *Sociology of Sport Journal*, 2, 3, 1985, p. 246.

10 For a useful discussion of the links between governments, their use of sport and identity, see B. Houlihan, 'Sport, National Identity and Public Policy' in *Nations and Nationalism*, 3, 1, 1997, pp 113-37, and more fully B. Houlihan, *Sport, Policy and Politics. A Comparative Analysis* (London 1997) which uses Ireland as one of its case studies.

11 Bale, 'Sport and National Identity', p. 18.

12 Horkheimer quoted in W.J. Morgan, 'Toward a Critical Theory of Sport' in *Journal of Sport and Social Issues*, 1983, 7, 1, p. 32.

13 P.C. McIntosh, 'Sport, Politics and Internatonalism' in M. Hart (ed.), *Sport in the Sociocultural Process* (Dubuque 1972), p. 304.

14 'Can I go Home Now? Does the World Cup really need the third place play-off?' in *Total Sport. World Cup '98 Supplement*, August 1998, p. 45.

15 RSVP to an invitation to attend an athletic meeting at the Wangamui Domain from George Bernard Shaw, *Auckland Star*, 1934 in *Dictionary of Quotations* (London 1996), p. 342.

16 For an exploration of such links, and an under-
    standing of the issue of patriotism see S. Pope,
    *Patriotic Games. Sporting Traditions in the American
    Imagination, 1876-1926* (Oxford 1997).

17 For an exploration of the links between sport and
    politics and a host of examples see, R. J. Paddick,
    'Sport and Politics: The (Gross) Anatomy of their
    Relationships' in *Sporting Traditions*, 1, 2, 1985, p.
    56.

18 See J.M. Leiper, 'Politics and Nationalism in the
    Olympic Games' in J.O. Segrave and D. Chu, *The
    Olympic Games in Transition* (Champaign 1988), p.
    331.

19 Ibid., p. 329.

20 McIntosh, 'Sport, Politics and Internationalism',
    p. 296.

21 For an example of the extremes in politics and
    their relationship with sport see, P. Arnaud and J.
    Riordan (eds), *Sport and International Politics. The
    Impact of Fascism and Communism on Sport*
    (London 1998).

22 H. Edwards, 'Sportpolitics: Los Angeles 1984 –
    the Olympic Tradition Continues' in *Sociology of
    Sport Journal*, 1, 1984, p. 172.

23 W. Paish and T. Duffy, *Athletics in Focus* (London
    1976), p. 130.

24 E. Hobsbawm, *Nations and Nationalism since 1780.
    Programme, Myth, Reality* (Cambridge 1990), p.
    143.

25 B. Stoddart, 'Caribbean Cricket: The Role of
    Sport in Emerging Small Nation Politics' in
    International Journal, 43, 1988, pp 618-19.

26 Questions asked by Chas Critcher and discussed
    in D.L. Andrews and J.W. Loy, 'British Cultural
    Studies and Sport: Past Encounters and Future
    Possibilities' in *Quest*, 45, 1993, p. 264.

27 Many colonial sports are seen as having been
    transplanted and therefore some may disagree with
    my point. What I am suggesting is that the reloca-
    tion of sport, even if conducted by an outside force
    (invader, media, etc.), can only succeed if it
    becomes representative of the nation into which it
    is moved. Caribbean cricket succeeds (as with all
    colonial cricket) as it becomes representative of
    Caribbean nationalism and jettisons its links with
    Britishness. American Football has failed in the
    UK because it could not be unamericanised and
    has thus failed to develop linkages with British
    nationalism. This problematic in the diffusion of
    games is one that I feel A. Guttmann's *Games and
    Empire. Modern Sports and Cultural Imperialism*
    (New York 1994) deals with weakly.

28 N. Baker, 'Sport and National Prestige: The Case
    of Britain 1945-48' in *Sporting Traditions*, 12, 2,
    1996, p. 83.

29 Ibid., p. 89.

30 G.T. Stewart, 'The British Reaction to the
    Conquest of Everest' in *Journal of Sport History*, 7,
    1, 1980, p. 37.

31 See Stoddart, 'Caribbean Cricket', p. 632.

32 L. Burgener, 'Sport and Politics' in *Olympic
    Review*, 141/2, 1979, p. 433.

33 McIntosh, 'Sport, Politics and Internationalism',
    p. 297.

34 The importance of Canadian ice hockey is of
    great value in this respect, especially when a home

    team wins the Stanley Cup. Also highly illustra-
    tive is the Ben Johnson case. Celebrated for win-
    ning gold in Seoul in 1988 (especially as he had
    beaten Carl Lewis from the US), Johnson brought
    disgrace on the Canadian nation as a result of his
    failed drug test. For details see S.J. Jackson, D.L.
    Andrews and C. Cole, 'Race, Nation, Authenticity
    of Identity. Interrogating the Everywhere Man
    (Michael Jordan) and the Nowehere Man (Ben
    Johnson)' in Cronin, and Mayall, *Sporting
    Nationalisms*, pp 82-103.

35 Ehn, B., 'National Feeling in Sport. The Case of
    Sweden' in *Ethnologia-Europea*, 19, 1, 1989, pp 57-
    8.

36 J. Maguire, 'Sport, Identity, Politics and
    Globalization: Diminishing Contrasts and
    Increasing Varieties' in *Sociology of Sport Journal*,
    11, 4, 1994, p. 409.

37 J. Coote, *Olympic Report 1968. Mexico and Grenoble*
    (London 1968), p. 28.

38 J.D. Reed, 'Gallantly Screaming' in *Sports
    Illustrated*, 3 January 1977, p. 54.

39 McIntosh, 'Sport, Politics and Internationalism',
    p. 295.

40 R. Swierczewski, 'The Athlete – the Country's
    Representative as a Hero', p. 90.

41 Ibid., p. 93.

42 D. Hannigan, *The Garrison Game* (Edinburgh
    1998), p. 106.

43 Tatz, 'The Corruption of Sport', p. 5.

44 Reed, 'Gallantly Screaming', p. 60.

45 McIntosh, 'Sport, Politics and Internationalism',
    p. 297.

46 For a discussion of the Rugby World Cup and
    South African sport see D. Booth, *The Race Game.
    Sport and Politics in South Africa* (London 1998)
    and J. Nauright, *Sport, Cultures and Identities in
    South Africa* (London 1997).

47 A. Guttmann, *The Games Must Go On. Avery
    Brundage and the Olympic Movement* (New York
    1984), p. 138.

48 See Leiper, 'Politics and Nationalism in the
    Olympic Games', p. 334.

49 For a useful coverage of some of these issues see
    G. Jarvie, 'A World in Union?' in *Sport and
    Leisure*, January/February 1992, pp 12-13, and for
    a critique of the ordinariness of the national
    anthem see T. Frayne, 'Why Play National
    Anthems Anyway?' in *Macleans (Toronto)*, 109, 15,
    8 April 1996, p. 60.

50 For details of O'Callaghan's career see L.
    Naughton and J. Watterson, *Irish Olympians*
    (Dublin 1992).

51 H.E. Wilson, Jr., 'The Golden Opportunity:
    Romania's Political Manipulation of the 1984 Los
    Angeles Olympic Games' in *Olympika* 3, 1994, p.
    92.

52 Ibid.

53 Dyreson, *Making the American Team*, p. 7.

54 Tatz, 'The Corruption of Sport', p. 6.

55 For a critique of the way in which links between
    nationalism and Olympism have often been mis-
    appropriated or misunderstood see J. Hargreaves,
    'Olympism and Nationalism: Some Preliminary
    Consideration' in *International Review for the
    Sociology of Sport* 27, 1, 1992, pp 119-35, and for

an historically based response see W.J. Morgan, 'Cosmopolitanism, Olympism and Nationalism: A Critical Interpretation of Coubertin's Ideal of International Sporting Life' in *Olympika*, 4, 1995, pp 79-92.

56 A. Guttmann, *The Olympics. A History of the Modern Games* (Urbana 1992), p. 171.

57 For a general discussion of new nations and their use of sport see B. Houlihan, *Sport and International Politics* (London 1994).

58 D.B. Kanin, 'The Olympic Boycott in Diplomatic Context' in *Journal of Sport and Social Issues*, 4, 1, 1980, p. 4. Dr Kanin served as a resource person for the Central Intelligence Agency (CIA) during the 1980 Olympic Games. Such employment may explain the overtly political and seemingly anti-Soviet slant of his article.

59 J. Coote, *Olympic Report '76* (London 1976), p. 144.

60 For a full discussion of this situation see J. Hargreaves and M. Garcia Ferrando, 'Public Opinion, National Integration and National Identity in Spain: The Case of the Barcelona Olympic Games' in *Nations and Nationalism*, 3, 1, 1997, pp 65-87.

61 Maguire, 'Sport, Identity, Politics and Globalisation', pp 398-427.

62 Ibid., p. 400.

63 See also J. Maguire, 'Globalisation, Sport and National Identities: The Empire Strikes Back?' in *Society and Leisure*, 16, 2, 1993, pp 293-322.

64 Maguire., 'Sport, Identity, Politics and Globalisation', p. 415.

65 See D. Sabo, S.C. Jansen, D. Tate, M.C. Duncan and S. Leggett, 'Televising International Sport: Race, Ethnicity and Nationalistic Bias' in *Journal of Sport and Social Issues*, 21, February 1996, pp 7-21.

66 See Maguire and Tuck, 'Global Sports and Patriot Games'.

67 See Cronin, 'Which Nation, Which Flag? Boxing and National Identities in Ireland'.

68 For details see H. O'Donnell, 'Mapping the mythical: a geopolitics of national sporting stereotypes' in *Discourse and Society*, 5, 3, 1994, pp 374-5.

69 R. Fotheringham, 'Sport and Nationalism on Australian Stage and Screen; From Australia Felix to Gallipoli' in *Australian Drama Studies*, 1, 1, 1982, pp 79-81.

70 A. Briggs, 'The Media and Sport in the Global Village' in R.C. Wilcox (ed.), *Sport in the Global Village* (Morgantown 1994), p. 20.

71 J. Hunter, 'Nationalism and Sport: A Case for Separateness, to Mutual Advantage' in B. Svoboda and A. Rychteck, *Physical Activity for Life: East and West, South and North. Proceedings of 9th Biennial Conference of ISCPES* (Prague 1995), p. 128.

72 Hargreaves and Ferrando, 'Public Opinion, National Integration and National Identity in Spain', p. 73.

4 / GAELIC GAMES

1 M. de Búrca, *The GAA. A History of the Gaelic Athletic Association* (Dublin 1980), p. 266.

2 T. Humphries, *Green Fields. Gaelic Sport in Ireland* (London 1996), p. 9.

3 Ibid., p. 144. This was a chant that echoed round Croke Park, especially from the massed ranks on Hill 16, when the new phenomenon, Jason Sherlock, galvanised Dublin Gaelic football in 1995.

4 See N. Garnham, 'hurling' in S.J. Connolly, *The Oxford Companion to Irish History* (Oxford 1998), p. 252.

5 Humphries, *Green Fields*, p. 158.

6 B. Ó hEithir, *Over the Bar* (Dublin 1984), p. 215.

7 I. Prior, *The History of Gaelic Games* (Belfast 1997), p. 14.

8 Ó hEithir, *Over the Bar*.

9 de Búrca, *The GAA*, pp 1-2.

10 M. Dames, *Mythic Ireland* (London 1996), p. 106.

11 W. Sayers, 'Games, Sport and Para-Military Exercise in Early Ireland' in *Aethlon*, 10, 1, 1992, p. 106.

12 Ibid., p. 119.

13 For an attempt at explaining the Aonach Tailteann and its importance within ancient sporting history see S. Egan, 'The Aonach Tailteann and the Tailteann Games Origin, Functions and Ancient Associations' in *CAPHER Journal*, May-June 1980, pp 3-5 and p. 38.

14 A. Ó Maolfabhail, *Camán: 2,000 Years of Hurling in Ireland* (Dublin 1973).

15 de Búrca, *The GAA*, pp 1-7.

16 Ibid., p. 4.

17 Ibid., p. 5.

18 H. Dan MacLennan, *Not an Orchid ...* (Inverness 1995) p. 45.

19 N. Struna, 'Remodelling Historical Change; the Practice of Moving Away From'. Unpublished paper presented to the British Society of Sports History Annual Conference, Edinburgh 1998.

20 M. Tierney, 'The Public and Private Image of the GAA – A Centenary Appeal' in *The Crane Bag: Media and Popular Culture*, 8, 2, 1984, p. 161.

21 John Sugden and Alan Bairner, *Sport, Sectarianism and Society in a Divided Ireland* (Leicester 1993).

22 For a useful general coverage of this period, and the ensuing battle for the control of Irish athletics see P. Griffin, *The Politics of Irish Athletics, 1850-1990* (Ballinamore 1990). For a brief overview see H. Smulders, 'Sport and Politics. The Irish Scene 1884-1921', in *Review of Sport and Leisure*, 2, June 1977, pp 116-29.

23 See 'A Word on Irish Athletics' in *United Ireland* and the *Irishman*, both 11 October 1884.

24 M. de Búrca, *Michael Cusack and the GAA* (Dublin 1989) p. 96.

25 For details of Davin's life and sporting career see S. Ó Riain, *Maurice Davin (1842-1927) First President of the GAA* (Dublin 1996).

26 *United Ireland*, 18 October 1884.

27 For details of the controversy that surrounds those who attended the meeting and their political affiliations see de Búrca, *Michael Cusack*, pp 102-6, and W.F. Mandle, *The Gaelic Athletic Association and Irish Nationalist Politics, 1884-1924* (London 1987), pp 6-8.

28 Mandle, *The GAA and Irish Nationalist Politics*.

29 *Freeman's Journal*, 24 December 1884, *United Ireland*, 27 December 1884 and *Irishman*, 27 December 1884.
30 Ibid.
31 Foster, *Modern Ireland*, p. 454.
32 F.S.L. Lyons, *Ireland Since the Famine* (London 1971), p. 226.
33 T. Brown, *Ireland. A Social and Cultural History, 1922-85* (London 1981).
34 *United Ireland*, 11 October 1884.
35 Sugden and Bairner, *Sport, Sectarianism and Society*, p. 30.
36 See R.F. Foster, *Paddy and Mr Punch Connections in Irish and English History* (London 1994), p. xv.
37 P. Rouse, 'The Politics of Culture and Sport in Ireland: A history of the GAA Ban on Foreign Games, 1884-1971. Part One: 1884-1921' *International Journal for the History Of Sport*, 10, 3, 1993, p. 349.
38 Mandle, *The GAA and Irish Nationalist Politics*.
39 de Búrca, *The GAA*.
40 Rouse, ' The Politics of Culture and Sport in Ireland: A history of the GAA Ban on Foreign Games, 1884-1971. Part One: 1884-1921'.
41 Ibid., pp 338-9.
42 Mandle, *The GAA and Irish nationalist politics*, pp 106-7.
43 Ibid., p. 118.
44 Ibid., p. 178.
45 de Búrca, *The GAA*, pp 149-50.
46 Mandle, *The GAA and Irish Nationalist Politics*, p. 194.
47 Sugden and Bairner, *Sport, Sectarianism and Society*, p. 33.
48 See de Búrca, *The GAA*, pp 154-8 and Mandle, *The GAA and Irish Nationalist Politics*, pp 206-8.
49 P.D. Mehigan, *Hurling. Ireland's National Game* (Dublin 1946), p. 112.
50 P.J. Devlin, *Our Native Games* (Dublin 1934), p. 76.
51 See B. Hüppauf, 'The Birth of Fascist Man from the Spirit of the Front: From Langemarck to Verdun' in J. Milful (ed.), *The Attractions of Fascism* (New York 1990).
52 *Gaelic Weekly* awards banquet, 16 March 1966.
53 Quoted by Mac Lua, *Steadfast Rule*, p. 119.
54 Ó Ceallaigh, *The Story of the GAA*, p. 12.
55 Mandle, *The GAA and Irish Nationalist Politics*, p. 221.
56 See B.Stoddart, 'Caribbean Cricket: The Role of Sport in Emerging Small Nation Politics' in H.McD Beckles, and B. Stoddart, *Liberation Cricket. West Indies Cricket Culture* (Manchester 1995), p. 239.
57 The lack of work that tackles the GAA at a variety of levels should be contrasted with the excellent work of Joseph Arbena who has examined Central America, its sport and politics with a very wide and thus highly engaging agenda. See for example, J. Arbena, 'The Diffusion of Modern European Sport in Latin America: A Case Study of Cultural Imperialism? in *South Eastern Latin Americanist*, 4, 1990, pp 1-8, and J. Arbena, 'Sport and Nationalism in Latin America, 1880-1970: The Paradox of Promoting and Performing

European Sports' in *History of European Ideas*, 16, 4-6, 1993, pp 837-44.
58 For example see G.B. Brock, *The Gaelic Athletic Association in County Fermanagh* (Eniskillen 1984) or V. Carmody, K. O'Shea and J. Molyneaux, *Listowel and the Gaelic Athletic Association* (Listowel 1985).
59 For a critique of the GAA and its use of historical myth see M. Cronin, 'Defenders of the Nation? The Gaelic Athletic Association and Irish Nationalist Identity' in *Irish Political Studies* 11, 1986.
60 T.F. O'Sullivan, *Story of the GAA* (Dublin 1916).
61 Devlin, *Our Native Games*.
62 Ibid., p. 68.
63 P.D.Mehigan, *Gaelic Football* (Dublin 1941).
64 Mehigan, *Hurling* .
65 Mehigan, *Gaelic Football*, p. 18.
66 Ibid., p. 22.
67 See Lee, *Ireland 1912-85*, p. 241.
68 E.N.M. O'Sullivan, *The Art and Science of Gaelic Football* (Tralee 1958).
69 O'Sullivan, *Art and Science*, p. viii.
70 B.MacLua, *The Steadfast Rule: A History of the GAA Ban* (Dublin 1967).
71 Ó Maolfabhail, *Camán: 2,000 Years of Hurling in Ireland*.
72 Ibid., p. 53.
73 Ibid.
75 de Búrca, *The GAA*.
76 Humphries, *Green Fields*.
77 Ibid., pp 116-17.
78 Ibid., p. 3.
79 Holt, *Sport and the British*, p. 240.
80 For example see Garvin, *Evolution of Irish Nationalist Politics*.
81 See T.A. O'Donoghue, 'Sport, Recreation and Physical Education: The Evolution of a National Policy of Regeneration in Eire, 1926-48' in *British Journal of Sports History*, 3, 2, 1986, pp 216-33, and H. Smulders, 'Irish Representation in International Sport Events, 1922-32. The Dialectics of Autonomy and Internationalism in Sport' in *Proceedings of the VIth International Congress of the International Association for the History of Physical Education and Sport* (Dartford 1977).
82 Mandle, *The GAA and Irish Nationalist Politics*.
83 Ibid., jacket notes.
84 Ibid., pp 13-15.
85 W.F. Mandle, 'The GAA and Popular Culture, 1884-1924' in O.MacDonagh, W.F. Mandle and P. Travers, *Irish Culture and Irish Nationalism* (London, 1983).
86 Ibid., p. 105.
87 P. Rouse, 'The Politics of Culture and Sport in Ireland: A History of the GAA Ban on Foreign Games 1884-71. Part One: 1884-1921' in *International Journal of the History of Sport* 10, 3 (1993).
88 Ibid., p. 333.
89 Sugden and Bairner, *Sport, Sectarianism and Society in a Divided Ireland*.
90 Ibid., p. 30.
91 M. Mullan, 'The Devolution of the Irish Economy in the Nineteenth Century and the

Bifurcation of Irish Sport' in *International Journal of the History of Sport*, 13, 2 (1996), M. Mullan, 'Sport as Institutionalised Charisma', in *Journal of Sport and Social Issues*, 19, 3, 1995, pp 285-306, and M. Mullan, 'Opposition, Social Closure and Sport: The Gaelic Athletic Association in the 19th Century' in *Sociology of Sport Journal*, 12, 3, 1995, pp 268-89.

92 Ibid., pp 42-3.
93 Sugden and Bairner, *Sport, Sectarianism and Society*, p. 30.
94 N. Wigglesworth, *The Evolution of English Sport* (London, 1996), p. 7.
95 For details see work such as Holt, *Sport and the British*.
96 C. Ó Gráda, *Ireland. A New Economic History* (London, 1994), p. 213.
97 Some attempts were made by the Church of England to promote rational recreation but this is relatively short lived. For details see K.S. Inglis, *The Churches and Working Class in Victorian England* (London, 1963).
98 K. Whelan, 'The Geography of Hurling' in *History Ireland* 1, 1 (1993), p. 28.
99 *United Ireland*, 18 October 1884.
100 O'Sullivan, *Art and Science*, p. 17.
101 *United Ireland*, 8 November 1884.
102 Mehigan, *Gaelic Football*, pp 18-19.
103 Mandle, 'The GAA and Popular Culture', p. 113.
104 T. Collins, 'Class, Community and Commercialisation in the Formation of the Northern Rugby Football Union', Unpublished PhD (Sheffield Hallam University, 1997), p. 18.
105 For example see J.A.Mangan, 'Games Field and Battlefield: A Romantic Alliance in Verse and the Creation of a Militaristic Masculinity' in J.Nauright and T.J.L. Chandler, *Making Men. Rugby and Masculine Identity* (London, 1996).
106 S.P. O'Ceallaigh, *Story of the GAA* (Limerick 1977) p. 17.
107 *United Ireland*, 27 June 1885.
108 *United Ireland*, 11 October 1884.
109 J.A. Mangan, *Athleticism in the Victorian and Edwardian Public School* (Cambridge, 1981).
110 For examples see L.P. Curtis Jr, *Apes and Angels: The Irishman in Victorian Caricature* (Newton Abbot, 1971) and J. Darby, *Dressed to Kill. Cartoonists and the Northern Ireland Conflict* (Belfast, 1983).
111 *Irish Daily Independent*, 1 May 1895.
112 *United Ireland*, 21 March 1885.
113 M. Tierney, *Croke of Cashel. The Life of Archbishop William Croke, 1823-1902* (Dublin, 1978), p. 190.
114 For a discussion of many of themes relating to the international isolation of Gaelic games see M. Cronin 'When the World Soccer Cup is played on Roller Skates: The Attempt to Make Gaelic Games International: The Meath-Australia Matches of 1967-8' in Cronin and Mayall, *Sporting Nationalisms*, pp 170-88.
115 A. Guttmann, 'Games and Empires. Ludic Diffusion as Cultural Imperialism?' in G. Pfister, T. Niewerth and G. Steins (eds), *Games of the World Between Tradition and Modernity. Proceedings of the 2nd ISHPES Congress* (Berlin 1995), p. 296.
116 Dyreson, *Making the American Team*, p. 2.

117 J. Galtung, ''The Sport System as a Metaphor for the World System' in F. Landry, M. Landry and M.Yerlès (eds), *Sport. The Third Millennium* (Sainte-Foy 1991), p. 150.
118 B. Stoddart, 'Sport, Cultural Imperialism and Colonial Response in the British Empire' in *Comparative Studies in Society and History*, 30, 4, 1988, p. 651.
119 Guttmann, *Games and Empire*.
120 J.A. Mangan (ed.) *The Cultural Bond: Sport, Empire and Society* (London 1992) and *The Games Ethic and Imperialism* (New York 1986).
121 B. Stoddart and K.A.P. Sandiford (eds), *The Imperial Game. Cricket, Culture and Society* (Manchester 1998).
122 For a useful overview of the Guttmann line and its consequences for understanding the GAA, see Mullan, 'Sport as Institutionalised Charisma'.
123 Guttmann, *Games and Empires*, p. 168.
124 Ibid., p. 158.
125 See M. Cronin, 'Enshrined in Blood. The Naming of Gaelic Athletic Association Grounds and Clubs' in *The Sports Historian*, 18, 1, 1998, pp 91-104.
126 The 1926 All-Ireland final between Kerry and Kildare is often reputed to be the first 'national' sporting events ever broadcast live in Europe.
127 R. Boyle, 'From our Gaelic Fields: Radio, Sport and Nation in Post-Partition Ireland' in *Media, Culture and Society*, 14, 1992, pp 623-36.
128 J. Riordan, 'State and Sport in Developing Societies' in *International Review for the Sociology of Sport*, 21, 4, 1986, p. 297.

5 / SOCCER

1 *Irish News*, 10 June 1988.
2 Banner of Irish supporters at the 1990 World Cup Finals, in M. Hunt, *There We Were – Italia '90* (Nass 1991), p. 274.
3 Report on the ceremonies at the Ireland v. Scotland international at Dalymont Park, 15 March 1913, in P. Byrne, *Football Association of Ireland. 75 Years* (Dublin 1996), p. 19.
4 See for example the work of Richard Giulianotti, 'Back to the Future: An Ethnography of Ireland's Football Fans at the 1994 World Cup Finals in the USA' in *International Review for the Sociology of Sport*, 31, 3, 1996, pp 323-47, and M. Free, 'Angels With Drunken Faces? Travelling Republic of Ireland Supporters and the Construction of Irish Migrant Identity in England' in A. Brown (ed.), *Fanatics! Power, Identity and Fandom in Football* (London 1998), pp 219-32.
5 Sugden and Bairner, *Sport, Sectarianism and Society*, p. 71.
6 E. Corry, *Going to America. World Cup USA 1994* (Dublin 1994), p. 84.
7 Sugden and Bairner, *Sport, Sectarianism and Society*, p. 71.
8 For a similar discussion of a different nation, see M. Goksøyr, 'Norwegian Football's Function as a Carrier of Nationalism' in G. Pfister, T. Niewerth and G. Steins (eds), *Games of the World Between Tradition and Modernity. Proceedings of the 2nd ISHPES Congress* (Berlin 1995), pp 367-73.

9   See Byrne, *Football Association of Ireland*, p. 15. Neal Garnham identifies the same key date as the official origins of soccer, but acknowledges that games had been played on an informal basis in Ulster since the 1860s. For details see 'Soccer' in S.J. Connolly (ed.) *The Oxford Companion to Irish History*, p. 516.

10 Appendix to formation minutes of the IFA in M. Brodie, *100 Years of Irish Football* (Belfast 1980), p. 1.

11 N. Garnham, 'Politics and Association Football in Ireland, 1880-1932', unpublished paper presented to the British Society of Sports History Annual Conference, Edinburgh 1998.

12 Byrne, *Football Association of Ireland*, p. 20.

13 Ibid..

14 For full details of all Ireland's international matches see, D. Cullen, *Ireland on the Ball. International Matches of the Republic of Ireland Soccer Team. A Complete Record, March 1926 to June 1993* (Dublin 1993).

15 For details of the chaotic process of division see Brodie, *100 Years of Irish Football*.

16 H.F. Moorehouse, 'One State, Several Countries: Soccer and Nationality in a United Kingdom' in J.A. Mangan, *Tribal Identities. Nationalism, Europe, Sport* (London 1996), p. 58.

17 For full discussion of these issues, see Ibid., pp 58-64.

18 Corry, *Going to America*, p. 153.

19 For a discussion of the Diaspora and their sporting connections see M.F. Black, 'Cultural Identity: Sport, Gender, Nationalism and the Irish Diaspora', unpublished PhD thesis, University of Michigan, 1997, and A. Hughes, 'The Irish Community', in P.A. Mosely, R. Cashman, J. O'Hara and H. Weatherburn (eds), *Sporting Immigrants. Sport and Ethnicity in Australia* (Crows Nest, NSW 1997), pp 73-87.

20 A. Grundligh, 'Playing for Power? Rugby, Afrikaner Nationalism and Masculinity in South Africa, *c.*1900-*c.*1970' in Nauright and Chandler, *Making Men*, p. 186.

21 Billig, *Banal Nationalism*, p. 125.

22 Hobsbawm, *Nations and Nationalism since 1780*, p. 143.

23 G. Jarvie, 'Sport, Nationalism and Cultural Identity' in L. Allison (ed.), *The Changing Politics of Sport* (Manchester, 1993), pp 74-5.

24 Goksøyr, 'Norwegian Football's Function', p. 370.

25 By way of example is the Republic of Ireland team for a 1966 European Championship qualifier versus Spain. The team contained only four players from the English first division (all defenders), six from the lower reaches of the English league and one Shamrock Rovers player. The Irish lost the game 2-0.

26 M. Goksøyr, 'Phases and Functions of Nationalism: Norway's Utilization of International Sport in the Late Nineteenth and Early Twentieth Centuries' in Mangan, *Tribal Identities*, p. 142.

27 For a good general coverage of Charlton and his career see S. McGarrigle, *The Complete Who's Who of Irish International Football, 1945-96* (Edinburgh 1996), pp 202-5.

28 Byrne, *Football Association of Ireland*, p. 131.

29 J. Charlton, *The Autobiography* (London 1996), p. 242.

30 Corry, *Going to America*, p. 239.

31 N. Blain, R. Boyle, and H. O'Donnell, *Sport and National Identity in the European Media* (Leicester 1993), p. 45.

32 Charlton, *Autobiography*, pp 279-81.

33 D. Bolger, *In High Germany: A Dublin Quartet* (London 1992), p. 107.

34 Roddy Doyle, *The Van* (London 1991).

35 Ibid., pp 178-83.

36 P. Rowan, *The Team That Jack Built* (Edinburgh 1994), p. 135.

37 Eamon Dunphy, 'Patron Saint of Ireland' in *The Independent on Sunday*, 12 June 1994, p. 20.

38 M. Hunt, *Here We Go – US '94. Republic of Ireland's Route to the World Cup* (Naas 1993), p 197.

39 There are a wealth of newspaper reports that explore the legendary victory over Italy, but for a taste see Rogan Taylor in the *Independent*, 20 June 1994, p. 38, who was in Italy, or Helen Birch in the *Independent*, 20 June 1994, p. 2, who was in Kilburn.

40 Joseph O'Connor, *The Secret World of the Irish Male* (London 1994), p. 203.

41 Roddy Doyle, 'Republic is a beautiful word – Republic of Ireland 1990' in Nick Hornby (ed.), *My favourite year – a collection of new football writing* (London 1993 pp 7-21), pp 20-1.

42 D. Watson, *Dancing in the Streets. Tales from World Cup City* (London 1994), p. 82.

43 Corry, *Going to America*, p. 327.

44 S. Ryan, *The Boys in Green. The FAI International Story* (Edinburgh 1997), p. 205.

45 *Independent on Sunday*, 20 June 1994, p. 3.

46 *Independent on Sunday*, 20 June 1994, p. 17.

47 M. Engel, 'Outrage puts damper on Ireland's euphoria' in the *Guardian*, 20 June 1994, p. 15

48 O'Connor, *The Secret World of the Irish Male*, pp 244-5.

49 J. Joyce, 'How Irish Euphoria Turned to Horror', the *Guardian*, 20 June 1994, p. 1.

50 R. Giulianotti, 'All the Olympians: A Thing Never Known Again?' Reflections on Irish Football Culture and the 1994 World Cup Finals' in *Irish Journal of Sociology*, 6, 1996, pp 101-26.

51 M. Holmes, 'Symbols of National Identity and Sport: The Case of the Irish Football Team' in *Irish Political Studies*, 9, 1993, pp 81-98.

52 Summation by Alan Bairner, 'Sportive Nationalism and Nationalist Politics: A Comparative Analysis of Scotland, the Republic of Ireland and Sweden' in *Journal of Sport and Social Issues*, 20, 3, 1996, p. 325. In believing that Charlton was responsible for creating a more mature attitude towards the British, one should observe the results of Marcus Free's work. 'En route to Liverpool in December 1995 for Ireland's play off against Holland for the Euro '96 finals, his Birmingham Irish flag was flying from the car window: "this'll show these English fuckers". When I pointed out that we were getting nothing but honks of support from passing traffic, he muttered "patronising bastards!" Quoted by Free, 'Angels With Drunken Faces', pp 231-2.

53 Bairner, 'Sportive Nationalism', p. 327.

6 / NORTHERN IRELAND AND THE TROUBLES

1 *Irish Times*, 11 July 1996. The widespread rioting that followed an RUC decision not to allow Portadown Orange Order members to march down the Garvaghy Road caused the difficulties.
2 *Irish Times*, 17 October 1997. Comments by Donaldson were in response to the decision by Mo Mowlam that the GAA and its activities would not come under the jurisdiction of the Northern Ireland Parades Commission.
3 *The Guardian*, 17 May 1997. Words written by Seamus Heaney in honour of his friend and GAA devotee, Sean Brown of Bellaghy, Co. London-derry, who was murdered by loyalist gunmen.
4 There have been attempts over the years to use sport as a means of reconciliation. For details of the Belfast United Scheme see rather idealistically R. Demack, 'Bridge Over Troubled Water' in *Sports Illustrated*, 75, 23, 1991, pp 16-23, and more realistically, J. Sugden, 'Belfast United: Encouraging Cross-Community Relations through Sport in Northern Ireland' in *Journal of Sport and Social Issues*, 15, 1, 1991, pp 59-80. There have also been claims made at various times that individual athletes transcend the division and bring about unity. One example that is often cited is Barry McGuigan, the former Boxing World Champion. By way of illustration see, C. Gammon, 'They're All For One' in *Sports Illustrated*, 62, 7, 1985, pp 26-34.
5 Finn, 'Sporting Symbols, Sporting Identities, p. 33.
6 For a general coverage of leisure based initiatives that were planned to bring communities together see J. Sugden, 'Patterns of Division. Sport and Leisure in Northern Ireland' in *Journal of Physical Education, Recreation and Dance*, April 1989, J. Sugden and A. Bairner, 'Northern Ireland: The Politics of Leisure in a Divided Society' in *Leisure Studies*, 5, 1986, pp 341-52, J. Sugden and A. Bairner, 'Ma, There's a Helicopter on the Pitch! Sport, Leisure and the State in Northern Ireland' in *Sociology of Sport Journal*, 9, 1992, pp 154-66, and M.H. Duncan, 'The Effects of Social Conflict on Recreation Patterns in Belfast, Northern Ireland', unpublished PhD thesis, San Diego, 1975. All conclude that despite the money that has been poured into leisure provision in Northern Ireland, the effect has been 'to reinforce rather than to break down sectarian identities', in Sugden and Bairner, 'Northern Ireland, The Politics of Leisure in a Divided Society', p. 351.
7 V. Duke and L. Crolley, *Football, Nationality and the State* (London 1996).
8 Ibid., p. 4.
9 For example see S. Kuper, *Football against the Enemy* (London 1994) or J. Williams, E. Dunning, and P. Murphy, *Hooligans Abroad* (London 1984).
10 J.G. Kellas, *The Politics of Nationalism and Ethnicity* (London, 1991), pp 23-4.
11 B. Jenkins, and S.A Sofos (eds), *Nation and Identity in Contemporary Europe* (London 1996), p. 11.
12 M. Guibernau, *Nationalisms. The Nation-State and Nationalism in the Twentieth Century* (Cambridge 1996), p. 102.
13 Ibid., p. 103.
14 J. Breuilly, 'The Sources of Nationalist Ideology' in J. Hutchinson, and A.D. Smith, *Nationalism* (Oxford 1994), p. 111.
15 Boyce, *Nationalism in Ireland*.
16 For example, J. Ruane, and J. Todd, *The Dynamics of Conflict in Northern Ireland* (Cambridge 1996).
17 Hutchinson, *Dynamics of Cultural Nationalism*.
18 This has been attempted in part by Sugden and Bairner, *Sport, Sectarianism and Society*.
19 Hutchinson, *Dynamics of Cultural Nationalism*, p. 9.
20 Ibid.
21 There have been attacks on GAA members and premises since 1991 and the UDA decision that the GAA was an acceptable target. There has also been harassment from security forces. The actual playing of the games however does not bring the GAA into conflict as no rival teams or supporters are from the opposing identity.
22 Kellas, *Politics of Nationalism and Ethnicity* p. 21.
23 Ibid., pp 21-2.
24 Guibernau, *Nationalisms*, p. 81.
25 Smith, *Nations and Nationalism in a Global Era*, p. 13.
26 J. Sugden, 'Sport, Community Relations and Community Conflict in Northern Ireland' in S. Dunn (ed.), *Facets of the Conflict in Northern Ireland* (London 1995), p. 211.
27 *New Framework For Agreement*, February 1995, article 4.
28 *Gaelic Review*, September 1987.
29 Adam's address to Sinn Fein Ard-Fheis, March 1995.
30 *New Framework For Agreement*, article 50, February 1995.
31 *Financial Times*, 9 October 1993.
32 Sugden and Bairner, *Sport, Sectarianism and Society*, p. 34.
33 J. McGarry and B. O'Leary, *Explaining Northern Ireland* (Oxford 1995), p. 224.
34 Sugden and Bairner, *Sport, Sectarianism and Society*, p. 35.
35 *The Independent*, 9 October 1991.
36 *The Guardian*, 16 November 1991.
37 See Sugden and Bairner, *Sport, Sectarianism and Society*, pp 35-6.
38 *Irish Times*, May 1973.
39 *The Observer*, 4 September 1994.
40 *Irish Times*, 11 April 1995.
41 Ibid.
42 J. Bradley, *Sport, Culture, Politics and Scottish Society. Irish Immigrants and the Gaelic Athletic Association* (Edinburgh 1998), p. 112.
43 *Irish Times*, 11 April 1995.
44 *Dublin Evening Herald*, 4 April 1995.
45 *Irish Times*, 4 January 1996.
46 Ibid.
47 Ibid.
48 *Irish Times*, 8 April 1996.
49 *Irish Times*, 14 April 1997.
50 *Irish Times*, 22 October 1997.
51 *Irish Times*, 25 October 1997.

52 *Irish Times*, 4 November 1997.
53 *Irish Times*, 13 April 1998.
54 Ibid.
55 *Irish Times*, 15 April 1998.
56 For outline of procedures and debates see *Irish Independent*, 20 April 1998 and *Irish Times*, 20 April.
57 *Irish Independent*, 20 April 1998.
58 *Irish Times*, 25 April 1998.
59 *Irish Times*, 2 May 1998.
60 *Irish Times*, 28 May 1998.
61 *Irish Times*, 20 May 1998.
62 *Irish Independent*, 22 May 1998.
63 *Irish Independent*, 25 May 1998.
64 Ibid.
65 *Irish Times*, 26 May 1998.
66 *GAA Discussion Board*, 26 May 1998, http://www.gaa.ie/discussions.
67 *An Phoblacht*, 28 May 1998.
68 *Andersontown News*, 30 May 1998.
69 See for example the *Irish Times* which stated that 'perceptions of the GAA will be damaged by upholding this provision in the face of the current climate' and the *Irish Independent* that suggested 'failure to remove this rule would take the GAA out of the mainstream of national sentiment and line it up with the motley crew in the North who voted no in the referendum', both 30 May 1998.
70 *Irish Times*, 1 June 1998.
71 *Belfast Telegraph* and *Irish Independent*, both 1 June 1998.
72 *Irish News*, 2 June 1998.
73 *Irish Echo*, 3 June 1998.
74 *Andersontown News* and the *Irish Post*, both 6 June 1998.
75 See for discussion of Clifford's statement, *Irish Independent, Ireland Today, Irish News* and *Irish Times*, 8 June 1998, and *Irish News* 9 June 1998.
76 *Irish Times*, 8 June 1998.
77 See *Irish Times*, 18 June 1998 and 1 July 1998.
78 *Irish Times*, 3 April 1995.
79 D. Murray, 'Culture, Religion and Violence in Northern Ireland' in S. Dunn (ed.), *Facets of the Conflict in Northern Ireland* (London 1995), p. 228.
80 J. Sugden and S. Harvie, Sport and Community Relations in Northern Ireland (Coleraine 1995), p. 95
81 For useful coverage of some of the themes dealt with here see J. Sugden and A. Bairner, 'Sectarianism and Soccer Hooliganism in Northern Ireland' in T. Reilly, A. Lees, K. Davids and W.J. Murphy (eds), *Science and Football* (London 1988), pp 572-8, and J. Sugden and A. Bairner, 'Observe the Sons of Ulster: Football and Politics in Northern Ireland' in A. Tomlinson and G. Whannel, *Off the Ball. The Football World Cup* (London 1986), pp 146-57.
82 See Sugden and Bairner, *Sport, Sectarianism and Society*, p. 82.
83 For full details of the match see J. Kennedy, *Belfast Celtic* (Belfast 1989), pp 91-102.
84 Interview with Frank Curran, 28 November 1995, Derry.
85 For a straightforward account of Derry City's

performance in the League and Cup see W.H.W. Platt, *A History of Derry City Football and Athletic Club, 1929-72* (Coleraine 1986).
86 *Londonderry Sentinel*, 25 August 1971.
87 *Londonderry Sentinel*, 1 September 1971.
88 *Londonderry Sentinel*, 15 September 1971.
89 Ibid.
90 Ibid.
91 *Londonderry Sentinel*, 22 September 1971.
92 *Londonderry Sentinel*, 18 October 1972.
93 *Irish News*, 14 October 1972.
94 *Irish News*, 14 October 1972.
95 *The Sentinel*, 14 March 1984.
96 Ibid.
97 *The Sentinel*, 28 March 1984.
98 FAI Records, Executive Committee Minutes, 11 May 1984.
99 FAI Records, Council Minutes, 30 June 1984.
100 *The Sentinel*, 18 July 1984.
101 *The Sentinel*, 17 October 1984.
102 FAI Records, Council Minutes, 30 November 1984 and Executive Committee Minutes, 9 November 1984.
103 *Irish Times*, 24 November 1984.
104 *Irish Times*, 2 February 1985.
105 *The Sentinel*, 24 July 1985.
106 *The Sentinel* 11 November 1985.
107 See Sugden and Bairner, *Sport, Sectarianism and Society*, pp 87-9.
108 Ibid., p. 89.
109 Ibid.
110 *Building Trust in Ireland. Studies Commissioned by the Forum for Peace and Reconciliation* (Dublin 1996), p. 41.
111 A. Bairner, 'The arts and sport' in Aughey, A. and Morrow, D. (eds), *Northern Ireland Politics* (London 1996) p. 172.
112 *The Sentinel*, 24 July 1985.
113 Interview with Frank Curran.
114 Sugden and Bairner, *Sport, Sectarianism and Society*, p. 87.
115 *Irish Times*, 26 October 1996.

CONCLUSIONS: SPORT AND THE EVER-CHANGING SENSE OF IRISHNESS

1 *Irish Times*, 29 May 1998.
2 For details of the Donegal Celtic versus RUC match and the struggle that surrounded it see, *An Phoblacht*, 12 and 19 November 1998, *Irish News*, 16 November 1998 and *Guardian*, 14 November 1998.
3 *Irish Times*, 27 July 1998.
4 For the highly positive reporting on the Cliftonville versus Linfield game see *Guardian*, 21 November 1998, *Irish News*, 23 November 1998, *Belfast News*, 21 November 1998 and *Belfast Telegraph*, 21 November 1998.
5 *Guardian*, 26 September 1998.
6 For a useful discussion of the ninety minute patriot ideal and coverage of Jim Sillars's, of the Scottish National Party, speech where the phrase was first used, see G. Jarive and J. Maguire, *Sport and Leisure in Social Thought* (London 994), pp 95-7.

Bibliography

For ease of reference the bibliography has been divided into sections which relate to specific areas covered in the book.

ARCHIVES

Football Association of Ireland, Merrion Square, Dublin.
National Archive of Ireland, Bishop Street, Dublin

NEWSPAPERS AND MAGAZINES

An Phoblacht	*The Guardian*	*The Irishman*
Andersontwon News	*The Independent*	*Londonderry Sentinel.*
Belfast Telegraph	*Irish Daily Independent*	*The Observer*
Dublin Evening Herald	*Irish Echo*	*Sports Illustrated*
Financial Times	*Irish Independent*	*The Sentinel*
Freeman's Journal	*Irish News*	*Total Sport*
Gaelic Review	*Irish Post*	*United Ireland*
Gaelic Weekly	*Irish Times*	

IRISH HISTORY, NATIONALISM AND NATIONAL IDENTITY

Aretxaga, Begoña, *Shattering Silence. Women, Nationalism and Political Subjectivity in Northern Ireland* (Princeton 1997)

Aughey, Arthur, 'Obstacles to Reconciliation in the South' in Forum for Peace and Reconciliation, *Building Trust in Ireland* (Belfast 1996), pp 1-52

Bolger, Dermot, *In High Germany: A Dublin Quartet* (London 1992)

Bourke, Joanna, *Husbandry to Housewifery* (Oxford 1993)

Boyce, D.G. and O'Day, A. (eds), *The Making of Modern Irish History. Revisionism and the Revisionist Controversy* (London 1996)

—, *Nationalism in Ireland* (London 1995, 3rd edition)

Brown, Terence, *Ireland. A Social and Cultural History, 1922-85* (London 1985)

Connolly, S.J. (ed.), *The Oxford Companion to Irish History* (Oxford 1998)

Coogan, Tim Pat, *De Valera. Long Fellow, Long Shadow* (London 1993)

Cronin, Sean, *Irish Nationalism. A History of its Roots and Ideology* (Dublin 1980)

Dames, Michael, *Mythic Ireland* (London 1996)

Doyle, Roddy, *The Van* (London 1991)

Dudley Edwards, Ruth, *Patrick Pearse: The Triumph of Failure* (London 1977)

Dunne, T., *Theobold Wolfe Tone: Colonial Outsider* (Cork 1982)

Elliott, Marianne, 'Religion and Identity in Northern Ireland' in Van Horne, Winston A., *Global Convulsions. Race, Ethnicity and Nationalism at the End of the Twentieth Century* (New York 1997), pp 149-68

Fitzpatrick, David, *Oceans of Consolation: Personal Accounts of Irish Migration to Australia* (Oxford 1995)

—, 'The Geography of Irish Nationalism 1910-21' in *Past and Present*, 78, 1978

Foster, Roy, *Modern Ireland 1600-1972* (London 1989)

—, *Paddy and Mr Punch. Connections in Irish and English and Irish History* (London 1993)

—, 'Storylines: Narratives and Nationality in Nineteenth Century Ireland' in Cubitt, Geoffrey (ed.), *Imagining Nations* (Manchester 1998), pp 38-56

Garvin, Tom, 'Hibernian Endgame? Nationalism in a Divided Ireland' in Caplan, Richard and Feffer, John (eds), *Europe's New Nationalism. States and Minorities in Conflict* (Oxford 1996), pp 184-94
—, *1922. The Birth of Irish Democracy* (Dublin 1996)
—, *Nationalist Revolutionaries in Ireland, 1858-1928* (Oxford 1987)
—, *The Evolution of Irish Nationalist Politics* (Dublin 1981)
Hennessey, Thomas, 'Ulster Unionist Territorial and National Identities 1886-1893: Province, Island, Kingdom and Empire' in *Irish Political Studies*, 8, 1993, pp 21-36
Hussey, Gemma, *Ireland Today. An Anatomy of a Changing State* (London 1993)
Hutchinson, John, *The Dynamics of Cultural Nationalism. The Gaelic Revival and the Creation of the Irish Nation State* (London 1987)
Kearney, Richard, *Postnationalist Ireland. Politics, Culture, Philosophy* (London 1997)
Keogh, Dermot, *Twentieth Century Ireland: Nation and State* (Dublin 1994)
Kiberd, Declan, *Inventing Ireland* (London 1995)
Kirkland, Richard, *Literature and Culture in Northern Ireland Since 1965: Moments of Danger* (London 1996)
Lee, J.J., *Ireland 1912-85: Politics and Society* (Cambridge 1989)
Lyons, F.S.L., *Ireland Since the Famine* (London 1971)
MacLaughlin, J. (ed.), *Location and Dislocation in Contemporary Irish Society: Emigration and Irish Identities* (Cork 1997)
Moran, Sean F., *Patrick Pearse and the Politics of Redemption: The Mind of the Easter Rising 1916* (Washington 1994)
Murray, Dominic, 'Culture, Religion and Violence in Northern Ireland' in Dunn, S. (ed.), *Facets of the Conflict in Northern Ireland* (London 1995)
Ó Gráda, Cormac, *Ireland. A New Economic History* (London 1994)
O'Brien, Conor Cruise, *Ancestral Voices. Religion and Nationalism in Ireland* (Dublin 1994)
O'Connor, Joseph, *Sweet Liberty: Travels in Irish America* (London 1996)
—, *The Irish Male at Home and Abroad* (Dublin 1996)
—, *The Secret World of the Irish Male* (London 1994)
Orr, Martin, 'The National Question and the Struggle Against British Imperialism in Northern Ireland' in Berberoglu, Berch (ed.), *The National Question. Nationalism, Ethnic Conflict and Self-Determination in the 20th Century* (Philadelphia 1995), pp 158-79
Ruane, J. and Todd, J., *The Dynamics of Conflict in Northern Ireland* (Cambridge 1996)
Ryle Dwyer, Terence, *De Valera. The Man and the Myths* (Swords 1991)
Thuente, Mary Helen, *The Harp Re-Strung. The United Irishmen and the Rise of Irish Literary Nationalism* (Syracuse 1994)
Tierney, Mark, *Croke of Cashel. The Life of Archbishop William Croke, 1823-1902* (Dublin 1978)
Walker, Graham, 'Empire, Religion and Nationality in Scotland and Ulster before the First World War' in Wood Ian S. (ed.), *Scotland and Ulster* (Edinburgh 1994), pp 97-115
Waters, John, *An Intelligent Person's Guide to Modern Ireland* (London 1997)
—, *Jiving at the Crossroads* (Belfast 1991)

IRISH SPORT

Bairner, Alan, 'Sportive Nationalism and Nationalist Politics: A Comparative Analysis of Scotland, the Republic of Ireland and Sweden' in *Journal of Sport and Social Issues*, 20, 3, 1996, pp 314-34
—, 'The Arts and Sport' in Aughey, A. and Morrow, D. (eds), *Northern Ireland Politics* (London 1996)
—, 'Up to their Knees? Football, Sectarianism, Masculinity and Protestant Working-Class Identity' in P. Shirlow and M. McGovern (eds), *Who Are The People? Unionism, Protestantism and Loyalism in Northern Ireland* (London 1997), pp 95-113
Black, Michael Francis, 'Cultural Identity: Sport, Gender, Nationalism and the Irish Diaspora', PhD thesis, University of Michigan, Michigan, 1997.
Boyle, Raymond, 'From our Gaelic Fields: Radio, Sport and Nation in Post-Partition Ireland' in *Media, Culture and Society*, 14, 1992, pp 623-36
Bradley, Joseph, M., *Sport, Culture, Politics and Scottish Society. Irish Immigrants and the Gaelic Athletic Association,* (Edinburgh 1998)
Brock, Gabriel, B., *The Gaelic Athletic Association in County Fermanagh* (Eniskillen 1984)
Brodie, Malcolm, *100 Years of Irish Football* (Belfast 1990)
Byrne, Peter, *Football Association of Ireland. 75 Years* (Dublin 1996)

Carmody, Vincent, O'Shea, Kieran and Molyneaux, John, *Listowel and the Gaelic Athletic Association* (Listowel 1985)
Charlton, Jack and Byrne, Peter, *Jack Charlton's American World Cup Diary* (London 1994)
—, *Jack Charlton. The Autobiography* (London 1996)
Corry, Eoghan, *Going to America. World Cup USA 1994* (Dublin 1994)
Cronin, Mike, 'When the World Soccer Cup is Played on Roller Skates: The Attempt to Make Gaelic Games International: The Meath-Australia Matches of 1967-8' in Cronin, M. and Mayall, D. (eds), *Sporting Nationalism. Identity, Ethnicity, Immigration, Assimilation* (London 1998)
—, 'Blueshirts, Sports and Socials' in *History Ireland*, 2, 3, 1994, pp 43-7
—, 'Defenders of the Nation? The Gaelic Athletic Association and Irish Nationalist Identity' in *Irish Political Studies*, 11, 1996, pp 1-19
—, 'Enshrined in Blood: The Naming of Gaelic Athletic Association Grounds and Clubs' in *The Sports Historian*, 18, 1, 1998, pp 90-104
—, 'Soccer, Sectarianism and the Troubles: The Fall and Rise of Derry City Football Club' in *Sporting Heritage*, 2, pp 7-24
—, 'Sport and a sense of Irishness' in *Irish Studies Review*, 9, 1994, pp 13-18
—, 'Which Nation, Which Flag? Boxing and National Identities in Ireland' in *International Review for the Sociology of Sport*, 32, 2, 1997, pp 131-46
Cullen, Donal, *Ireland On the Ball. International Soccer Matches of the Republic of Ireland Soccer Team. A Complete Record March 1926 to June 1993* (Dublin 1993)
Cumann Lúthcleas Gael, *A Century of Service, 1884-1984* (Dublin 1984)
Curran, Frank, *The Derry City Story, 1928-86* (Donegal 1986)
de Búrca, Marcus, *Michael Cussack and the GAA* (Dublin 1989)
—, *The GAA. A History of the Gaelic Athletic Association* (Dublin 1980)
Demack, Richard, 'Bridge Over Troubled Water. In Northern Ireland People Are Working to Make Sport a Common Denominator for Protestants and Catholics' in *Sports Illustrated*, 75, 22, 1991, pp 16-23
Devlin, P.J., *Our Native Games* (Dublin 1935)
Doyle, Roddy, 'Republic is a Beautiful Word' in Hornby, Nick (ed.), *My Favourite Year. A Collection of New Football Writing* (London 1993), pp 7-21
Duncan, Mary Hackett, 'The Effects of Social Conflict on Recreation Patterns in Belfast, Northern Ireland'. PhD thesis, United States International University, San Diego, 1975
Egan, Sean, 'The Aonach Tailteann and the Tailteann Games Origin, Function and Ancient Associations' in *CAPHER Journal*, May-June 1980, pp 3-5, 38
Finn, Gerry P.T., 'Sporting Symbols, Sporting Identities: Soccer and Intergroup Conflict in Scotland and Northern Ireland' in Wood, Ian S. (ed.), *Scotland and Ulster* (Edinburgh 1994), pp 33-55
Free, Marcus, 'Angels' With Drunken Faces? Travelling Republic of Ireland Supporters and the Construction of Irish Migrant Identity in England' in Brown, Adam (ed.), *Fanatics! Power, Identity and Fandom in Football* (London 1998), pp 219-232
Fulham, Brendan, *Giants of the Ash* (Dublin 1992)
Garnham, Neil, 'Politics and Association Football in Ireland 1880-1922', unpublished paper delivered at the British Society of Sports History Annual Conference, Edinburgh, 1998
Giulianotti, Richard, 'All the Olympians: A Thing Never Known Again? Reflections on Irish Football Culture and the 1994 World Cup Finals' in *Irish Journal of Sociology*, 6, 1996, pp 101-26.
—, 'Back to the Future: An Ethnography of Ireland' Football Fans at the 1994 World Cup Finals in the USA' in *International Review for the Sociology of Sport*, 31, 3, 1996, pp 323-47
Griffin, Padraig, *The Politics of Irish Athletics* (Ballinamore 1990)
Hannigan, Dave, *The Garrison Game. The State of Irish Football* (Edinburgh 1998)
Healy, Paul, *Gaelic Games and the Gaelic Athletic Association* (Boulder 1998)
Holmes, Michael, 'Symbols of National Identity and Sport: The Case of the Irish Football Team' in *Irish Political Studies*, 9, pp 91-8
Hughes, Anthony, 'The Irish Community' in Mosely, P.A., Cashman, R., O'Hara, J. and Weatherburn, H. (eds), *Sporting Immigrants. Sport and Ethnicity in Australia* (Crows Nest, NSW 1997)
Humphries, Tom, *Green Fields. Gaelic Sport in Ireland* (London 1996)
—, *The Legend of Jack Charlton* (London 1994)
Hunt, Mary, *Here We Go – US '94. Republic of Ireland's Route to the World Cup* (Dublin 1993)
—, *There We Were – Germany '88* (Kilkenny 1989)
—, *There We Were – Italia '90* (Dublin 1991)
Kennedy, J., *The Belfast Celtic Story* (Belfast 1989)

King, Seamus J., *A History of Hurling* (Dublin 1992)

—, *The Clash of the Ash in Foreign Fields: Hurling Abroad* (Cashel 1998)

Lennon, Joe, *The Playing Rules of Football and Hurling, 1884-1995* (Dublin 1997)

MacLua, Brendan, *The Steadfast Rule. A History of the GAA Ban* (Dublin 1967)

Malcolm, Elizabeth, 'Popular Recreation in Nineteenth Century Ireland' in MacDonagh, O., Mandle, W.F., and Travers, P. (eds) *Irish Culture and Nationalism 1750-1950* (Canberra 1983)

Mandle, W.F., 'Sport as Politics. The Gaelic Athletic Association 1814-196' in Cashman, Richard and McKernan, M. (eds), *Sport in History* (Brisbane 1980)

—, *The Gaelic Athletic Association and Irish Nationalist Politics, 1884-1924* (London 1987)

—, 'The Gaelic Athletic Association and Popular Culture 1884-1924' in MacDonagh, O., Mandle, W.F. and Travers, P. (eds), *Culture and Nationalism in Ireland 1750-1950* (Canberra 1983)

—, 'The Irish Republican Brotherhood and the Beginnings of the Gaelic Athletic Association' in *Irish Historical Studies*, 20, 80, 1977, pp 418-38

McDermott, Peter, *Gaels in the Sun. Detailed Account of Meath's Historic Trip to Australia* (Drogheda 1970)

McGarrigle, Stephen, *The Complete Who's Who of Irish International Football, 1945-96* (Edinburgh 1996)

Meenan, Patrick N., *St. Patrick's Blue and Saffron. A Miscellany of UCD Sport* (Dublin 1997)

Mehigan, P.D., *Gaelic Football* (Dublin 1941)

—, *History of Hurling* (Dublin 1946)

Mullan, Michael L., 'Opposition, Social Closure and Sport: The Gaelic Athletic Association in the 19th Century' in *Sociology of Sport Journal*, 12, 3, 1995, pp 268-89

—, 'Sport as Institutionalized Charisma' in *Journal of Sport and Social Issues*, 19, 3, 1995, pp 285-306

—, 'The Devolution of the Irish Economy in the Nineteenth Century and the Bifurcation of Irish Sport' in *International Journal for the History of Sport*, 13, 2, 1996

Naughton, Lindie and Watterson, Johnny, *Irish Olympians* (Dublin 1992)

O'Brien, Michael, *The Struggle for Páirc Tailteann* (Navan 1994)

O'Hehir, Michael, *My Life and Times* (Dublin 1996)

Ó hEithir, Breandán, *Over the Bar* (Dublin 1984)

Ó Kelly, Derek and Blair, Shay (eds), *What's the Story? True Confessions of the Republic of Ireland Soccer Supporters* (Dublin 1992)

Ó Maolfabhail, A., *Camán: 2,000 Years of Hurling in Ireland* (Dublin 1973)

Ó Riain, Séamus, *Maurice Davin (1842-1927). First President of the GAA* (Dublin 1997)

O' Ceallaigh, S.P., *Story of the GAA* (Limerick 1977)

O' Sullivan, T.F., *Story of the GAA* (Dublin 1916)

O'Sullivan, E.N.M., *The Art and Science of Gaelic Football* (Tralee 1958)

O'Donoghue, Thomas A., 'Sport, Recreation and Physical Education: The Evolution of a National Policy of Regeneration in Eire, 1926-48' in *The British Journal of Sports History*, 3, 2, 1986, pp 216-33

Platt, W.H.W., *A History of Derry City Football and Athletic Club, 1929-72* (Coleraine 1986)

Prior, Ian, *The History of Gaelic Games* (Belfast 1997)

Puirseal, Padraig, *Scéal na Camógaíochta* (Kilkenny 1984)

Rafferty, Eamonn, *Talking Gaelic. Leading Personalities on the GAA* (Dublin 1997)

Rouse, Paul, 'The Politics of Culture and Sport in Ireland: A History of the GAA Ban on Foreign Games 1884-71. Part One: 1884-1921' in *International Journal for the History of Sport*, 10, 3, 1993

Rowan, Paul, *The Team That Jack Built* (Edinburgh 1994)

Ryan, Sean, *The Boys in Green. The FAI International Story* (Edinburgh 1997)

Sayers, William, 'Games, Sport and Para-Military Exercise in Early Ireland' in *Aethlon*, 10, 1, 1992, pp 105-23

Smulders, Herman, 'Sport and Politics. The Irish Scene 1884-1921' in *Review of Sport and Leisure*, 2, 1977, pp 116-29

—, 'Irish Representation in International Sport Events, 1922-1932. The Dialectics of Autonomy and Internationalism in Sport' in *HISPA VIth Intenrational Congress Proceedings* (Dartford 1977)

Stapleton, Frank, *Frankly Speaking* (Dublin 1991)

Sugden, John and Bairner, Alan, 'Ireland and the World Cup: Two Teams in Ireland, There's Only Two Teams in Ireland …' in Sugden, John and Tomlinson, Alan (eds), *Hosts and Champions. Soccer Cultures, National Identities and the USA World Cup* (Aldershot 1994), pp 119-39.

— and Bairner, Alan, 'Ma, There's a Helicopter on the Pitch! Sport, Leisure and the State in Northern Ireland' in *Sociology of Sport Journal*, 9, 1992, pp 154-66

— and Bairner, Alan, 'Northern Ireland: The Politics of Leisure in a Divided Society' in *Leisure Studies*, 5, 1986, pp 341-52

— and Bairner, Alan, 'Sectarianism and Soccer Hooliganism in Northern Ireland' in Reilly, T., Lees, A., Davids, K., and Murphy, W.J. (eds), *Science and Football* (London 1988), pp 572-8.
— and Bairner, Alan, *Sport, Sectarianism and Society in a Divided Ireland* (Leicetser 1993)
— and Harvie, Scott, *Sport and Community Relations in Northern Ireland* (Coleraine 1995)
—, 'Belfast United: Encouraging Cross-Community Relations through sport in Northern Ireland' in *Journal of Sport and Social Issues*, 15, 1, 1991, pp 59-80
—, 'Patterns of Division. Sport and Leisure in Northern Ireland' in *Journal of Physical Education, Recreation and Dance*, April 1989, pp 51-54
—, 'Sport, Community Relations and Community Conflict in Northern Ireland' in Dunn, Seamus (ed.), *Facets of the Conflict in Northern Ireland* (New York 1995)
Tierney, Mark, 'The Public and Private Image of the GAA – A Centenary Appraisal' in *The Crane Bag: Media and Popular Culture*, 8, 2, 1984, pp 161-5
Tobin, Colm, 'Ireland's War on Eamon Dunphy' in Williams, G. (ed.), *The Esquire Book of Sports Writing* (London 1995)
Van Esbeck, E., *The Story of Irish Rugby* (London 1986)
Watson, Don, *Dancing in the Streets. Tales from World Cup City* (London 1994)
Whelan, Kevin, 'The Geography of Hurling' in *History Ireland*, 1, 1, 1993
Wolff, Alexander, 'A Day to be Irish. In a Game Between the Ancestral Lands of Millions of Americans, Ireland Beat Italy 1-0' in *Sports Illustrated*, 80, 25, June 1994, pp 56-62
—, 'Here Come the Lads' in *Sports Illustrated*, 80, 23, June 1994, pp 60-70
—, 'Peacefully Done' in *Sports Illustrated*, , 79, 29, November 1994, pp 80-85

SPORT

Andrews, David L. and Loy, John W., 'British Cultural Studies and Sport: Past Encounters and Future Possibilities' in *Quest*, 45, 1993, pp 255-76
—, 'The (Trans)National Basketball Association: American Commodity Sign Culture and Global-Local Conjuncturalism' in Cvetkovich, Ann and Kellner, Douglas (eds) *Articulating the Global and the Local. Globalization and Cultural Studies* (Boulder 1997), pp 72-101
Arbena, Joseph L., 'Sport and Nationalism in Latin America, 1880-1970: The Paradox of Promoting and Performing European Sports' in *History of European Ideas*, 16, 4-6, 1993, pp 837-44
—, 'The Diffusion of Modern European Sport in Latin America: A Case Study of Cultural Imperialism' in *South Eastern Latin Americanist*, L, 4, 1990, pp 1-8
Arnaud, Pierre and Riordan, James (eds), *Sport and International Politics. The Impact of Fascism and Communism on Sport* (London 1998)
Baker, Norman, 'Sports and National Prestige: The Case of Britain 1945-48' in *Sporting Traditions*, 12, 2, 1996, pp 81-97
Bale, John, 'Sport and National Identity: A Geographical View' in *The British Journal of Sports History*, 3, 1, 1986, pp 18-41
Beckles, H. McD., and Stoddart, Brian (eds), *Liberation Cricket. West Indies Cricket Culture* (Manchester 1995)
Blain, Neil, Boyle, Raymond and O'Donnell, Hugh, *Sport and National Identity in the European Media* (Leicester 1993)
Booth, Doug, *The Race Game. Sport and Politics in South Africa* (London 1998)
Bradley, Joseph M., 'We Shall Not Be Moved! Mere Sport, Mere Songs? A Tale of Scottish Football' in Brown, Adam (ed.), *Fanatics! Power, Identity and Fandom in Football* (London 1998), pp 203-218
Briggs, Asa, 'The Media and Sport in the Global Village' in Wilcox, Ralph C. (ed.), *Sport in the Global Village* (Morgantown 1994)
Brown, Adam (ed.), *Fanatics! Power, Identity and Fandom in Football* (London 1998)
Burgener, Louis, 'Sport and Politics' in *Olympic Review*, 141, 1979, pp 431-4
Butlin, R., 'Every Four Years We Become a Nation' in Royle, N (ed.), *The Agony and the Ecstacy. New Writing for the World Cup* (London 1998)
Caldwell, Geoffrey, 'Sport and Politics. International Sport and National Identity' in *International Social Science Journal*, 34, 2, 1982, pp 173-83
Carrington, Ben, 'Football's Coming Home. But Whose Home? And do We Want it? Nation, Football and the Politics of Exclusion' in Brown, Adam (ed.), *Fanatics! Power, Identity and Fandom in Football* (London 1998), pp 101-23
Coote, James (ed.), *Olympic Report '76* (London 1976)

—, *Olympic Report 1968. Mexico and Grenoble* (London 1968)

Cronin, Mike and Mayall, David. (eds), *Sporting Nationalisms. Identity, Ethnicity, Immigration, Assimilation* (London 1998)

Davies, Pete, *All Played Out. The Full Story of Italia '90* (London 1990)

Duke, Vic and Crolley, Liz, *Football, Nationality and the State* (London 1996)

Dyreson, Mark, *Making the American Team. Sport, Culture and the Olympic Experience* (Urbana 1988)

Edwards, Harry, 'Sportpolitics: Los Angeles 1984 – The Olympic Tradition Continues' in *Sociology of Sport Journal*, 1, 1984, pp 172-83

Ehn, Billy, 'National Feeling in Sport. The Case of Sweden' in *Ethnologia-Europea*, 19, 1, 1989, pp 56-66

Fotheringham, Richard, 'Sport and Nationalism on Australian Stage and Screen; from Australia Felix to Gallipoli' in *Australian Drama Studies*, 1, 1, 1982, pp 65-88

Frayne, Trent, 'Why Play National Anthems Anyway' in *Macleans (Toronto)*, 109, 15, 1996, p. 60

Goksøyr, Matti, 'Norwegian Football's Function as a Carrier of Nationalism' in Pfister, Gertrud, Niewerth, Toni and Steins, Gerd (eds), *Games of the World Between Tradition and Modernity. Proceedings of the 2nd ISHPES Congress, Berlin 1993* (Berlin 1995) pp 368-73

—, 'Phases and Functions of Nationalism: Norway's Utilization of International Sport in the Late Nineteenth and Early Twentieth Century' in Mangan, J.A. (ed.), *Tribal Identities. Nationalism, Europe, Sport* (London 1996)

Guttmann, Allen, 'Games and Empires. Ludic Diffusion as Cultural Imperialism?' in Pfister, G., Niewerth, T., and Steins, G. (eds), *Games of the World Between Tradition and Modernity. Proceedings of the 2nd ISHPES Congress* (Berlin 1995)

—, *Games and Empires. Modern Sports and Cultural Imperialism* (New York 1994)

—, *The Games Must Go On. Avery Brundage and the Olympic Movement* (New York 1984)

—, *The Olympics. A History of the Modern Games* (Urbana 1992)

Hargreaves, John and Ferrando, Manuel Garcia, 'Public Opinion, National Integration and National Identity in Spain: The Case of the Barcelona Olympic Games' in *Nations and Nationalism*, 3, 1, 1997, pp 65-87

—, 'Olympism and Nationalism: Some Preliminary Consideration' in *International Review for the Sociology of Sport*, 27, 2, 1992, pp 119-37

Hart, Marie, *Sport in the Sociocultural Process* (Dubuque 1972)

Heinila, Kalevi, 'Sport and International Understanding – Acontradiction in Terms?' in *Sociology of Sport Journal*, 2, 3, 1985, pp 240-48

Holt, Richard, 'Amateurism and its Interpretation: The Social Origins of British Sport' in *Innovation*, 5, 4, 1992, pp 19-31

—, *Sport and the British* (Oxford 1989)

Hornby, N. (ed.), *My Favourite Year. A Collection of New Football Writing* (London 1993)

Houlihan, Barry, 'Sport, National Identity and Public Policy' in *Nations and Nationalism*, 3, 1, 1997, pp 113-37

Houlihan, Barry, *Sport and International Politics* (London 1994)

—, *Sport, Policy and Politics. A Comparative Analysis* (London 1997)

Hunter, John, 'Nationalism and Sport: A Case for Separateness, to Mutual Advantage' in Svoboda, Bohumil and Rychteck˝, Antonín, *Physical Activity for Life: East and West, South and North. The Proceedings of the 9th Biennial Conference of International Society for Comparative Physical Education* (Prague 1995)

Jackson, Steven, J., Andrews, David, L. and Cole, Cheryl, 'Race, Nation and Authenticity of Identity: Interrogating the 'Everywhere' Man (Michael Jordan) and the 'Nowhere' Man (Ben Johnson)', in Cronin, M. and Mayall, D. (eds), *Sporting Nationalisms. Identity, Ethnicity, Immigration and Assimilation* (London 1998), pp 82-102

Jarvie, Grant and Maguire, Joseph, *Sport and Leisure in Social Thought* (London 1994)

— and Walker, Graham (eds), *Scottish Sport in the Making of the Nation. Ninety Minute Patriots?* (London 1994)

—, 'A World in Union?' in *Sport and Leisure*, Jan/Feb 1992, pp 12-13

—, 'Leisure and Cultural Identity: Modern Scotland 1920-1939' in *Scottish Journal of Physical Education*, 15, 3, 1987, pp 48-52

—, 'Sport, Nationalism and Cultural Identity' in Allison, Lincoln (ed.), *The Changing Politics of Sport* (Manchester 1993)

Kanin, David B., 'The Olympic Boycott in Diplomatic Context' in *Journal of Sport and Social Issues*, 4, 1, 1980, pp 21-4

Kuper, Simon, *Football Against the Enemy* (London 1994)

Landry, Fernand, Landry, Marc and Yerlès, Magdeleine, *Sport... The Third Millennium* (Sainte-Foy 1991)

Leiper, Jean M., 'Politics and Nationalism in the Olympic Games' in Segrave, Jeffrey O. and Chu, Donald (eds), *The Olympic Games in Transition* (Champaign 1988), pp 329-44

MacLennan, Hugh Dan, *Not an Orchid ...* (Inverness 1995)

Maguire, Joseph and Tuck, Jason, 'Global Sports and Patriot Games: Rugby Union and National Identity in a United Sporting Kingdom Since 1945' in Cronin, M. and Mayall, D. (eds), *Sporting Nationalisms. Identity, Ethnicity, Immigration, Assimilation* (London 1998), pp 103-26

—, 'Globalisation, Sport and National Identities: The Empires Strike Back?' in *Society and Leisure*, 16, 2, 1993, pp 293-322

—, 'Sport, Identity, Politics and Globalization: Diminishing Contrasts and Increasing Varieties' in *Sociology of Sport Journal*, 11, 4, 1994, pp 398-427

Mangan, J.A. (ed.), *The Cultural Bond: Sport, Empire and Society* (London 1992)

—, *Athleticism in the Victorian and Edwardian Public School* (Cambridge 1981)

—, *The Games Ethic and Imperialism* (New York 1986)

Moorehouse, H.F., 'One State, Several Countries: Soccer and Nationality in a United Kingdom' in J.A. Mangan (ed.), *Tribal Identities. Nationalism, Europe, Sport* (London 1996)

Morgan, William J., 'Cosmopolitanism, Olympism and Nationalism: A Critical Interpretation of Coubertin's Ideal of International Sporting Life' in *Olympika*, 4, 1995, pp 79-91

—, 'Toward a Critical Theory of Sport' in *Journal of Sport and Social Issues*, 7, 1, 1983, pp 24-34

Naul, Roland (ed.), *Contemporary Studies in the National Olympic Games Movement* (Frankfurt 1997)

Nauright, John and Chandler, Timothy J.L. (eds), *Making Men. Rugby and Masculine Identity* (London 1996)

—, *Sport, Cultures and Identities in South Africa* (London 1997)

O'Donnell, Hugh, 'Mapping the Mythical: A Geopolitics of National Sporting Stereotypes' in *Discourse and Society*, 5, 3, 1994, pp 345-80

Paddick, Robert J., 'Sport and Politics: The (Gross) Anatomy of their Relationships' in *Sporting Traditions*, 1, 2, 1985, pp 51-66

Paish, Wilf and Duffy, Tony, *Athletics in Focus* (London 1976)

Pope, S.W., *Patriotic Games. Sporting Traditions in the American Imagination, 1876-1926* (Oxford 1997)

Reed, J.D., 'Gallantly Screaming' in *Sports Illustrated*, 3 January 1977, pp 52-60

Riordan, Jim, 'State and Sport in Developing Societies' in *International Review for the Sociology of Sport*, 21, 4, 1986, pp 287-303

Rowe, David, *Popular Cultures. Rock Music, Sport and the Politics of Pleasure* (London 1995)

Sabo, D., Jansen, S.C., Tate, D., Duncan, M.C, and Leggett, S., 'Televising International Sport: Race, Ethnicity and Nationalistic Bias' in *Journal of Sport and Social Issues*, 21, February 1996, pp 7-21

Segrave, Jeffrey O. and Chu, Donald (eds), *The Olympic Games in Transition* (Champaign 1988)

Stewart, Gordon T., 'The British Reaction to the Conquest of Everest' in *Journal of Sport History*, 7, 1, 1980, pp 21-39

Stoddart, Brian and Sandiford, K.A.P. (eds), *The Imperial Game. Cricket, Culture and Society* (Manchester 1988)

—, 'Caribbean Cricket: The Role of Sport in Emerging Small Nation Politics' in *International Journal*, XLIII, 4, 1988, pp 618-42

—, 'Sport, Cultural Imperialism and Colonial Response in the British Empire' in *Comparative Studies in Society and History*, 30, 4, 1988, pp 649-73

Struna, Nancy, 'Remodelling Historical Change; the Practice of Moving Away From', unpublished paper presented to the British Society of Sports Historians Annual Conference, Edinburgh 1998

Sugden, John and Tomlinson, Alan (eds), *Hosts and Champions. Soccer Cultures, National Identities and the USA World Cup* (Aldershot 1994)

Swierczewski, Ryszard, 'The Athlete – The Country's Representative as a Hero' in *International Review of Sport Sociology*, 3, 13, 1978, pp 89-100

Tatz, Colin, 'The Corruption of Sport' in *Current Affairs Bulletin*, 59, 4, 1982, pp 4-16

Tomlinson, Alan, and Whannel, Garry, *Off the Ball. The Football World Cup* (London 1986)

Wigglesworth, N., *The Evolution of English Sport* (London 1996)

Williams, John, Dunning, Eric and Murphy, Paul, *Hooligans Abroad* (London 1984)

Wilson, Harold E., 'The Golden Opportunity: Romania's Manipulation of the 1984 Los Angeles Games' in *Olympika*, 3, 1994, pp 83-97

NATIONALISM AND NATIONAL IDENTITY

Alter, Peter, *Nationalism* (London 1994, revised edition)
Anderson, Benedict, *Immagined Communities. Reflections on the Origin and Spread of Nationalism* (London 1991, revised edition)
Angus, Ian, *National Identity, Cultural Plurality and Wilderness* (Montreal 1997)
Axtmann, Roland, 'Collective Identity and the Democratic Nation-State in the Age of Globalization' in Cvekovich, Ann and Kellner, Douglas (eds) *Articulating the Global and the Local. Globalization and Cultural Studies*, pp 33-54.
Balcells, Albert, *Catalan Nationalism. Past and Present* (London 1996)
Berlin, Isaiah, *Against the Current. Essays in the History of Ideas* (London 1979)
Billig, Michael, *Banal Nationalism* (London 1995)
Bodnar, John, *Remaking America. Public Memory, Commemoration and Patriotism in Twentieth Century* (Princeton 1992)
Breuilly, John, *Nationalism and the State* (Manchester 1982)
Calhoun, Craig, *Nationalism* (Buckingham 1997)
Chai, Sun-Ki, 'A Theory of Ethnic Group Boundaries' in *Nations and Nationalism*, 2, 2, 1996, pp 281-307
Colley, Linda, *Britons* (London 1996)
Connerton, Paul, *How Societies Remember* (Cambridge 1989)
Connor, Walker, *Ethnonationalism. The Quest for Understanding* (Princeton 1994)
Cubitt, Geoffrey (ed.), *Imagining Nations* (Manchester 1998)
Cvekovich, Ann and Kellner, Douglas (eds) *Articulating the Global and the Local. Globalization and Cultural Studies* (Boulder 1997)
— and Kellner, Douglas (eds) *Articulating the Global and the Local. Globalization and Cultural Studies* (Boulder 1997)
DaSilva, Fabio B. and Faught, Jim, 'Nostalgia: A Sphere and Process of Contemporary Ideology' in *Qualitative Sociology*, 5, 1, 1982, pp 47-61
Delanty, Gerard, *Inventing Europe. Idea, Identity, Reality* (London 1995)
Drummond, Phillip, Paterson, Richard and Willis, Janet (eds), *National Identity and Europe. The Television Revolution* (London 1993)
Eatwell, Roger (ed.), *European Political Cultures. Conflict or Convergence?* (London 1997)
Eley, Geoff and Suny, Ronald Grigor, *Becoming National. A Reader* (New York 1996)
Fredrickson, G.M., *The Comparative Imagination. On the History of Racism, Nationalism and Social Movements* (London 1997)
Gellner, Ernest, *Culture, Identity and Politics* (Cambridge 1987)
—, *Encounters With Nationalism* (Oxford 1994)
—, *Nations and Nationalism* (Oxford 1983)
Gills, John R., 'Memory and Identity: The History of a Relationship' in in Gills, John R. (ed.), *Commemorations. The Politics of National Identity* (Princeton 1994), pp 3-24
Grant, Susan-Mary, 'When is a Nation Not a Nation? The Crisis of American Nationality in the mid-nineteenth century' in *Nations and Nationalism*, 2, 1, 1996, pp 105-29
Greenfield, Liah, *Nationalism. Five Roads to Modernity* (Harvard 1992)
Griffin, Roger, 'Nationalism' in Eatwell, R. and Wright, A. (eds), *Contemporary Political Ideologies* (London 1993)
Guibernau, Montserrat and Rex, John, *The Ethnicity Reader. Nationalism, Multiculturalism and Migration* (Oxford 1997)
—, *Nationalisms. The Nation State in the Twentieth Century* (Cambridge 1996)
Hall, Patrick, 'Nationalism and Historicity' in *Nations and Nationalism*, 3, 1, 1997, pp 3-23
Halliday, Fred, 'The Siren of Nationalism' in Hartman, Chester and Vilanova, Pedro, *Paradigms Lost. The Post Cold War Era* (London 1992)
Hartman, C. and Vilanova, P. (eds), *Paradigms Lost. The Post Cold War Era* (London 1992)
Hastings, Adrian, *The Construction of Nationhood. Ethnicity, Religion and Nationalism* (Cambridge 1997)
Heater, Derek, *The Theory of Nationhood. A Platonic Symposium* (London 1998)
Hobsbawm, Eric J. and Ranger, Terence, *The Invention of Tradition* (Cambridge 1983)
—, *Nations and Nationalism Since 1780. Programme, Myth, Reality* (Cambridge1990)
Hooson, David (ed.), *Geography and National Identity* (Oxford 1994)
Hosking, Geoffrey and Schöpflin, George (eds), *Myths and Nationhood* (London 1997)
Hutchinson, John and Smith, Anthony, D. (eds), *Nationalism. A Reader* (Oxford 1994)

Ignatieff, Michael, 'Nationalism and Toleration' in Caplan, Richard and Feffer, John (eds), *Europe's New Nationalism. States and Minorities in Conflict* (Oxford 1996), pp 213-31
—, *Blood and Belonging. Journeys into the New Nationalism* (London 1993)
Jackson, Peter and Penrose, Jan (eds), *Constructions of Race, Place and Nation* (London 1993)
Jacobson, Jessica, 'Perceptions of Britishness' in *Nations and Nationalsim*, 3, 2, 1997, pp 181-99
Jenkins, B. and Sofos, S.A. (eds), *Nation and Identity in Contemporary Europe* (London 1996)
Jenkins, Richard, 'Nations and Nationalisms: Towards More Open Models' in *Nations and Nationalisms*, 1, 3, 1995, pp 369-90
Kellas, J.G., *The Politics of Nationalism and Ethnicity* (London 1991)
Knight, Franklin W., *The Caribbean. The Genesis of a Fragmented Nationalism* (New York 1978)
Leerssen, J.T. and Spiering, M. (eds), *National Identity – Symbol and Representation* (Amsterdam 1991)
Llobera, Josep R., *The God of Modernity. The Development of Nationalism in Western Europe* (Oxford 1994)
Lowenthal, David, 'Identity, Heritage and History' in Gills, John R. (ed.), *Commemorations. The Politics of National Identity* (Princeton 1994), pp 41-57
Lutz, Helma, Phoenix, Ann and Yuval-Davies, Nira (eds), *Nationalism, Racism and Gender in Europe* (London 1995)
Manzo, Kathryn A., *Creating Boundaries. The Politics of Race and Nation* (Boulder 1996)
Marx, Anthony W., 'Contested Citizenship: The Dynamics of Racial Identity and Social Movements' in *International Review of Social History*, 40, 3, 1995, pp 159-88
McClintock, Anne, Mufti, Aamir and Shohat, Ellie (eds), *Dangerous Liasons. Gender, Nation and Postcolonial Perspectives* (Minneapolis 1997)
McGrew, Anthony, 'A Global Society' in Hall, Stuart, Held, David and McGrew, Tony, *Modernity and Its Futures* (Cambridge 1993), pp 61-116
Miller, David, *On Nationality* (Oxford 1995)
Moore, Barrington, *The Social Origins of Democracy and Totalitarianism* (London 1967)
Moses, Wilson Jeremiah (ed.), *Classical Black Nationalism. From the American Revolution to Marcus Garvey* (New York 1996)
Mosse, George L., 'Racism and Nationalism' in *Nations and Nationalism*, 1, 2, 1995, pp 163-73
Nairn, Tom, *Faces of Nationalism. Janus Revisited* (London 1997)
—, *The Break-Up of Britain. Crisis and Neo-Nationalism* (London 1981, second edition)
Neuberger, Benyamin, 'National Self-determination: Dilemmas of a Concept' in *Nations and Nationalism*, 1, 3, 1995, pp 297-325
Paxman, Jeremy, *The Englis. A Portrait of a People* (London 1998)
Pearton, Maurice, 'Notions in Nationalism' in *Nations and Nationalism*, 2, 1, 1996, pp 1-15
Penrose, Jan, 'Essential Constructions? The Cultural Bases of Nationalist Movements' in *Nations and Nationalism*, 1, 3, 1995, pp 391-417
Robbins, Keith, *Great Britain: Identities, Institutions, and the Idea of Britishness* (London 1998)
Scheff, Thomas J., *Bloody Revenge. Emotions, Nationalism and War* (Boulder 1994)
Seton-Watson, Hugh, *Nations and States* (London 1977)
Shils, Edward, 'Nation, Nationality, Nationalism and Civil Society' in *Nations and Nationalism*, 1, 1, 1995, pp 93-118
Simons, Anna, 'Democratisation and Ethnic Conflict: The Kin Connection' in *Nations and Nationalism*, 3, 2, 1997, pp 273-89
Smith, Anthony D. and Gellner, Ernest, 'The Nation: Real or Imagined? The Warwick Debates on Nationalism' in *Nations and Nationalism*, 2, 3, 1996, pp 357-70
—, 'Memory and Modernity: Reflections on Ernest Gellner's Theory of Nationalism' in *Nations and Nationalism*, 2, 3, 1996, pp 371-88
—, *National Identity* (London 1991)
—, 'Gastronomy or Geology? The Role of Nationalism in the Reconstruction of Nations' in *Nations and Nationalism*, 1, 1, 1995, pp 3-23
Stewart, Kathleen, 'Nostalgia – A Polemic' in *Cultural Anthropology*, 3, 3, 1988, pp 227-41
Sugar, Peter F., 'Nationalism: The Victorious Ideology' in Sugar, Peter F., *Eastern European Nationalism in the Twentieth Century* (Washington 1995), pp 413-30
Tamir, Yael, *Liberal Nationalism* (Princeton 1993)
Tilly, Charles, 'Citizenship, Identity and Social History' in *International Review of Social History*, 40, 3, 1995, pp 1-19
Tomlinson, John, *Cultural Imperialism. A Critical Introduction* (London 1991)
Trumpener, Katie, *Bardic Nationalism. The Romantic Novel and the British Empire* (Princeton 1997)
Turner, Victor (ed.), *Celebration. Studies in Festivity and Ritual* (Washington 1982)

Van Horne, Winston A., *Global Convulsions. Race, Ethnicity and Nationalism at the End of the Twentieth Century* (New York 1997)

Viroli, Maurizo, *For Love of Country. An Essay on Patriotism and Nationalism* (Oxford 1995)

Volkan, Vamik, *Bloodlines. From Ethnic Pride to Ethnic Terrorism* (New York 1997)

Index

211